A JOURNAL

OF

THE FIRST VOYAGE

OF

VASCO DA GAMA,

1497-1499

A JOURNAL

OF

THE FIRST VOYAGE

OF

VASCO DA GAMA,

1497-1499

VASCO DA GAMA

TRANSLATED AND EDITED

BY

E. G. RAVENSTEIN

GYAN

Published by

GYAN

Gyan Publishing House
5, Ansari Road
Daryaganj, New Delhi-110002
Phone: 011-47034999, 9811692060
E-mail: books@gyanbooks.com

Distribution Network
gyanbooks.com
India, USA, Canada, UK, Australia

ISBN: 978-93-6208-328-9 (HB)
First Published, 1898

2nd Impression 2024

Printed at: Gyan Press, Delhi.

A JOURNAL OF THE FIRST VOYAGE OF VASCO DA GAMA, 1497-1499

Author: VASCO DA GAMA, Translator and Editor: E. G. RAVENSTEIN

A JOURNAL

OF

THE FIRST VOYAGE

OF

VASCO DA GAMA,

1497-1499.

(*From a Photograph by Sr. Camancho.*)

This Portrait, now in the Hall of Honours of the Lisbon Geographical Society, was presented by the Conde de Vidigueira to King D. Carlos.

A JOURNAL

OF

THE FIRST VOYAGE

OF

VASCO DA GAMA,

1497-1499.

Translated and Edited, with Notes, an Introduction and Appendices.

BY

E. G. RAVENSTEIN, F.R.G.S.,

CORRESPONDING MEMBER OF THE GEOGRAPHICAL SOCIETY OF LISBON.

LONDON:

PRINTED FOR THE HAKLUYT SOCIETY.

M.DCCC.XCVIII.

COUNCIL

OF

THE HAKLUYT SOCIETY.

CONTENTS.

APPENDICES.

LIST OF ILLUSTRATIONS.

Portraits.

Facsimiles.

Ships.

Other Illustrations.

LIST OF MAPS.

ERRATA.

P. 3, note 3. The wrong date is not August 18, but August 22, which ought to be October 22. See also p. 190, note 1.

P. 3, line 17. *Instead of* "lower mainsail", *read* "mainsail".

P. 4, note 2, to be read thus: "That is, towards Tristão da Cunha, Gama being at that time 400 miles to the N.N.W. of these islands".

P. 9, note 3. *Instead of* "Ant°", *read* "dent°" (dentro).

P. 15, note 1. *Instead of* "Rio do Infante", *read* "Rio de Infante".

P. 16, line 10. *Read* "when setting a bonnet we discovered the mast was sprung . . . and . . . secured it with lashings".

P. 22, line 8. *Instead of* "when putting the ship about", etc., *read* "in tacking towards the other ships, which were astern, Coelho", etc.

P. 23, note 4. *Add* "Aljofar, in Portuguese, means seed-pearls".

P. 73, line 17. *Instead of* "August 23", *read* "August 24".

P. 79, line 14. *Instead of* "Biaquotte", *read* "Biaquolle".

P. 80, note 1. For the identification of the Ilhas de S. Maria, see p. 200.

P. 92, line 13. *Add* "and left at once".

P. 148, line 20, and P. 175, line 60. The pilot was Pero Escolar, not Escovar. A Pero Escovar is mentioned by Barros (t. 1, part 1, p. 143) jointly with João de Santarem, as having made discoveries on the Gold Coast in 1471. He was a "cavalier" of the King's household. Another Pero Escovar went as pilot to the Congo in 1490. This latter may possibly have been our man.

P. 161, line 24. *Instead of* "D'Alberti", *read* "D'Albertis".

P. 167, line 17. *Instead of* "Rodriguez", *read* "Rodrigo".

P. 167, line 29. *Instead of* "Diogo de Vilhegas", *read* "Diogo Ortiz de Vilhegas".

INTRODUCTION.

THE discovery of an ocean route to India, in 1497-98, marks an epoch in the history of geographical exploration no less than in that of commerce. It confirmed the hypothesis of a circumambient ocean, first put forward by Hecataeus, but rejected by Ptolemy and his numerous followers; and, at the same time diverted into a new channel the profitable spice trade with the East which for ages had passed through Syria and Alexandria. In consequence of this diversion Venice lost her monopoly, and Lisbon became for a time the great spice-market of Europe.

But Portugal was a small country whose resources were hardly even equal to the task of waging the continuous wars with the Moors in which she had so unwisely been engaged for generations past. And when, in addition to her African forces, she was called upon to maintain great fleets in the distant East, in order to enforce her monopoly of the spice trade, at first in the face only of the Moors, and afterwards in that of powerful European rivals, her resources speedily came to an end, and she found herself exhausted and helpless. It may well be asked whether Portugal would not be happier now, and richer, too, had she never had the opportunity of dwelling upon these ancient

VASCO DA GAMA.
(*From a Contemporary Medallion in the Cloister of Belem.*)

glories; had the wealth of the Indies never been poured into her lap, only to breed corruption; and had her strength not been wasted in a struggle to which she was materially unequal, and which ended in exhaustion and ruin.

Portugal, however, notwithstanding the sad ending of her vast Eastern enterprises, is still justly proud of the achievements of her "great" Vasco da Gama, and boldly places him by the side of Magelhães and Christopher Columbus, as one of a noble triad which occupies the foremost rank among the great navigators of an Age of Great Discoveries.

Vasco da Gama was born, about 1460,[1] at Sines, of which coast-town his father, Estevão, was alcaide-mór. He was the youngest of three brothers. Genealogists trace back his pedigree to a valiant soldier, Alvaro Annes da Gama, who resided at Olivença in 1280, and greatly distinguished himself in the wars with the Moors. The Gamas could thus boast of gentle blood, though they neither belonged to the aristocracy of Portugal, nor were they possessed of much worldly wealth.

We know next to nothing of Vasco da Gama's youth. When King João, after the return of Bartholomeu Dias, decided to fit out an armada to complete the discovery of an ocean highway to India, he selected Vasco da Gama as its captain-major, and this choice of the King was confirmed by his successor, D. Manuel.[2] Such an appointment would not have been made had not Vasco da Gama already been known as a man of energy,

---

[1] He was thus eighteen years of age when Queen Isabella, in 1478, granted a safe-conduct to him and Fernão de Lemos, enabling them to pass through Castile on their way to Tangier (Navarrete, iii, p. 477). According to P. Antonio Carvalho da Costa's unsupported statement, Vasco da Gama was born in 1469.

[2] According to Castanheda, the appointment was at first offered to Paulo da Gama, Vasco's elder brother. He declined on account of ill-health, but offered to accompany his brother as captain of one of the vessels.

capacity and competent knowledge. We ought therefore not be surprised if Garcia de Resende, in his *Chronicle of D. João II* (c. 146), tells us that he was a man whom the King trusted, as he had already served in his fleets and in maritime affairs, and whom he had consequently charged, in 1492, with the task of seizing the French vessels lying in the ports of Algarve, in reprisal for the capture by a French pirate of a Portuguese caravel returning from S. Jorge da Mina with gold.

Castanheda (I, c. 2) speaks of Vasco as having done good service in the time of King João II, and as being experienced in the affairs of the sea. Mariz (*Dial.*, iv, c. 14; v, c. 1) calls him a young man (*mancebo*), high-spirited and indefatigable, who had such a thorough knowledge of navigation (*arte maritima*) that he would have been able to hold his own with the most experienced pilots of Europe. We know, moreover, from Barros and Goes that

---

[3] Vasco da Gama, after his return from India, married Catarina de Ataide. He proceeded a second time to India in 1502. When returning from Cananor he shaped a direct course across the Indian Ocean to Mozambique. After a long period of rest, King João III again sent him to India in 1524, but he died at Cochin on December 25th of the same year, at the age of sixty-five. His remains were taken to Portugal in 1538, and deposited at Vidigueira. Since 1880 they are supposed to have found their last resting-place in the church of Belem.

For an interesting estimate of the character of the great navigator, see Lord Stanley of Alderley's *The Three Voyages of Vasco da Gama* (Hakluyt Society), 1869. See also the Appendices of this volume for further information on the first voyage.

he landed at S. Helena Bay with his pilots in order to determine the latitude. These extracts show, at all events, that Vasco da Gama was not a mere landsman; nor is it likely that the command of an expedition, the one object of which was discovery, and not trade or war, would have been entrusted to such an one.

He was, moreover, well qualified for his post in other respects. His indomitable firmness made him shrink from no obstacle which opposed itself to the success of his expedition; and notwithstanding the unheard-of length of the voyage and the hardships endured, he retained the confidence of his men to the very last.

The question whether Da Gama can fairly be ranked with Columbus and Magelhães, has frequently been discussed.

The first place among these three undoubtedly belongs to Magelhães, the renegade Portuguese, who first guided a ship across the wide expanse of the Pacific. The second place is almost universally accorded to Columbus, whose unconscious discovery of a new world, fit to become the second home of the European races, was immensely more far-reaching in its consequences than the discovery of an ocean highway to India, now largely discarded in favour of the shorter route across the isthmus of Suez.

It is maintained, in support of the claims of Columbus, that he was the originator of the scheme the success of which covered him with everlasting glory, whilst Vasco da Gama simply obeyed the behests of his King, when he took the lead of an expedition which was to crown the efforts made by little Portugal for generations past.

There is much truth in this contention. The scheme of reaching the East by a westward course across the Atlantic had no doubt been entertained in Portugal in the reign of Affonso the African [1438-81]. Fernão Martinz, the Royal Chaplain, had discussed its prospects with Paolo Toscanelli, when in Italy, and had been instructed to apply for further particulars to the Florentine physician, in response to which he had received the famous letter of June 25th, 1474, and the chart which accompanied it. But practically nothing was done, except that an adventurer or two[1] were authorised to seek for the islands supposed to lie to the west of the Azores. Prince Henry the Navigator would perhaps have acted upon such a suggestion, had he been still alive, but the King's resources were devoted to Africa, or wasted in two disastrous wars with Spain.

Columbus, on the other hand, made the discarded scheme his own; he, too, applied to Toscanelli for counsel,[2] and found confirmation of that physician's

---

[1] Ruy Gonçalves da Camara in 1473, Fernão Telles in 1474.

[2] Toscanelli's letter to Columbus was written long after that addressed to Fernão Martinz, for the expression *ha dias* (perhaps a rendering of *pridem* or *haud diu*) does not mean "a few days ago", but "long ago." Columbus himself uses it in that sense when he writes from Jamaica that the "Emperor of Catayo asked

erroneous hypothesis as to the small breadth of the Atlantic by studying the *Imago Mundi* of Cardinal Pierre d'Ailly, and other writings. Nor did he rest until he found in Queen Isabella the Catholic a patron who enabled him to put his theories to the test of practical experience. It was his good fortune that Providence had placed the new world as a barrier between him and Marco Polo's Cipangu (Japan), which was his goal, or he might never have returned to claim the reward of his success.

On the accession of D. João II, in 1481, the discovery of Africa was resumed with renewed vigour, and the councillors of that King acted wisely when they advised him to decline the offers of Columbus,[1] for the resources of Portugal were quite unequal to pursuing at one and the same time a search for a western route and continuing the efforts for opening a practical route around the southern extremity of Africa. And thus it happened that Columbus "discovered a new world for Castile and Leon", and not for Portugal.

When, however, we come to consider the physical difficulties which had to be overcome by these great navigators in the accomplishment of their purpose, the greater credit must undoubtedly be awarded to Vasco da Gama. Columbus, trusting as implicitly to the chart and sailing directions

long ago (*ha dias*) for men of learning to instruct him in the faith of Christ." The request for missionaries had been made to the Pope in 1339 (Navarrete, *Colleccion*, 2nd ed., I, p. 457).

[1] Barros, *Dec. I*, l. 3, c. ii.

of Toscanelli as did Vasco da Gama to those of Dias, and, perhaps, of Pero de Covilhão, shaped a course westward of Gomera; and, having sailed in that direction for thirty-six days, and for a distance of 2,600 miles, made his first landfall at Guanahani, being favoured all the while by the prevailing easterly winds. The task which Vasco da Gama undertook was far more difficult of accomplishment. Instead of creeping along the coast, as had been done by his predecessors, he conceived the bold idea of shaping a course which would take him direct through the mid-Atlantic from the Cape Verde Islands to the Cape of Good Hope. The direct distance to be covered was 3,770 miles, but the physical obstacles presented by winds and currents could only be overcome by taking a circuitous course, and thus it happened that he spent ninety-three days at sea before he made his first landfall to the north of the bay of St. Helena. This first passage across the southern Atlantic is one of the great achievements recorded in the annals of maritime exploration.

Once beyond the Cape, Vasco had to struggle against the Agulhas current, which had baffled Bartholomeu Dias, and against the current of Mozambique; and it was only after he had secured a trustworthy pilot at Melinde that the difficulties of the outward voyage can be said to have been overcome.

In one other respect Vasco da Gama, or, perhaps, we ought to say his pilots, proved themselves the superiors of Columbus, namely, in the accuracy of the charts of their discoveries which they brought home to Portugal. Accepting the Cantino Chart[1] as a fair embodiment of the work done by this expedition, we find that the greatest error in latitude amounts to 1° 40′. The errors of Columbus were far more considerable. In three places of his Journal the latitude of the north coast of Cuba is stated to be 42° by actual observation; and that this is no clerical error, thrice repeated in three different places, seems to be proved by the evidence of the charts. On that of Juan de la Cosa, for instance, Cuba is made to extend to lat. 35° N. (instead of 23° 10′), and even on the rough sketch drawn by Bartolomeo Columbus after the return from the Fourth Voyage, Jamaica and Puerto Rico (Spagnola) are placed 6° too far to the north.[2]

Verily, the Portuguese of those days were superior as navigators to their Spanish rivals and the Italians.

Posterity is fortunate in possessing a very full abstract of the Journal which Columbus kept during

[1] It is quite possible that the draughtsman of the Cantino Chart placed St. Helena Bay incorrectly, and not as determined by Vasco da Gama. Canerio places this bay in lat. 32° 30′ S., which is only 10′ out of its true position.

[2] See Wieser, *Die Karte des Bartolomeo Columbo*, Innsbruck, 1893. Cuba is not shown on this chart, possibly because Bartolomeo would not do violence to his conscience by representing it as a part of Asia (as his brother believed it to be to the day of his death) after its insularity had been recognised.

his first voyage to the West Indies.[1] No such trustworthy record is available in the case of Vasco da Gama, whose original reports have disappeared. They were consulted, no doubt, by João de Barros and Damião de Goes; but these writers, much to our loss, dealt very briefly with all that refers to navigation. The only available account written by a member of the expedition is the *Roteiro* or Journal, a translation of which fills the bulk of this volume, and of which, later on, we shall speak at greater length. The only other contemporary accounts, which we also reproduce, are at second-hand, and are contained in the letters written by King Manuel and Girolamo Sernigi immediately after the return of Vasco da Gama's vessels from India.

Apart from these, our chief authorities regarding this voyage are still the *Decades* of João de Barros and the *Chronicle* of King Manuel, by Damião de Goes. Both these authors held official positions which gave them access to the records preserved in the India House. Castanheda relied almost wholly upon the *Roteiro*, but a few additional statements of interest may be found in his pages.

As to the *Lendas* of Gaspar Correa, we are unable to look upon his account of Vasco da Gama's first voyage as anything but a jumble of truth and

---

[1] *The Journal of Christopher Columbus*, by C. R. Markham (Hakluyt Society), 1893.

fiction,[1] notwithstanding that he claims to have made use of the diary of a priest, Figueiro, who is stated to have sailed in Vasco's fleet. Correa's long residence in India—from 1514 to the time of his death—must have proved an advantage when relating events which came under his personal observation, but it also precluded him from consulting the documents placed on record in the Archives of Lisbon. This much is certain: that whoever accepts Correa as his guide must reject the almost unanimous evidence of other writers of authority who have dealt with this important voyage.[2]

A few additional facts may be gleaned from Faria y Sousa's *Asia Portuguesa*, from Duarte Pacheco Pereira and Antonio Galvão; but in the main we are dependent upon the *Roteiro*, for recent searches[3] in the *Torre do Tombo* have yielded absolutely nothing, so far as we are aware, which throws additional light upon Da Gama's First Voyage, with which alone we are concerned.

---

[1] Thus Correa states correctly that the Cape was rounded in November, that is, in the height of summer, but introduces accessory details—perhaps taken from an account of some other voyage (Cabral's, for instance)—which could only have happened in mid-winter. (See p. 193).

[2] An excellent translation of Correa's account of *The Three Voyages of Vasco da Gama*, by Lord Stanley of Alderley, was published by the Hakluyt Society in 1869. It is accompanied by foot-notes, directing attention to those numerous instances in which Correa differs from other writers.

[3] Most of the documents discovered on these occasions were made known by Texeira de Aragão and Luciano Cordeiro, to whose published works frequent reference will be made.

And now we shall proceed to give an account of the *Roteiro.*

The Manuscript of the "Roteiro".

In giving an account of the manuscript of this Journal, we entrust ourselves to the guidance of Professors Kopke and Antonio da Costa Paiva, the two gentlemen who first published it.

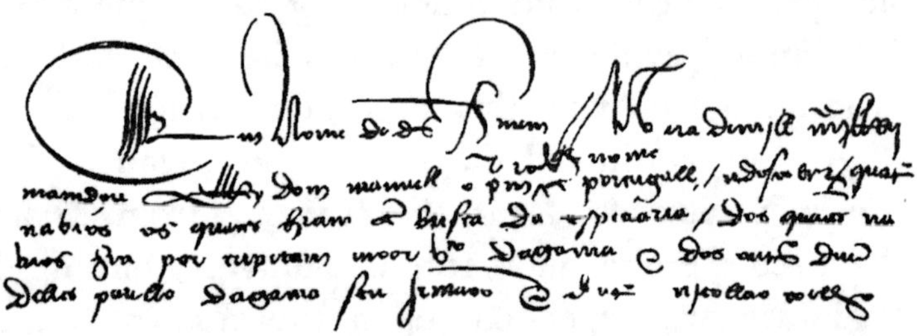

Signature of Fernam Lopes de Castanheda

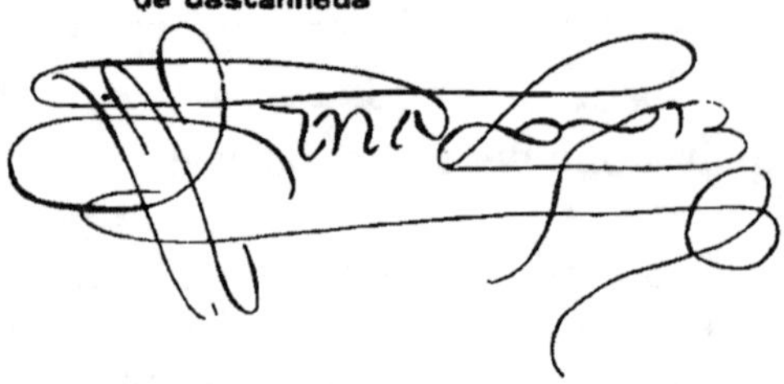

Water Mark

That is :—

"Em Nome de Ds Amem// Na era de mill iiij LR vij
mamdou Ellrey Dom manuell o primo desde nome em portugall/
a descobrir/ quat
navios/ os quaes hiam em busca da especiaria/ dos quaees na
vios hia por capitam moor Vco da Gama e dos outros duũ
delles Paullo da Gama seu jrmaoo e doutro njcollao Coelho".

The manuscript originally belonged to the famous Convent of Santa Cruz at Coimbra, whence it was transferred, together with other precious MSS., to the public library of Oporto.

It is not an autograph, for on fol. 64 (p. 77 of this translation), where the author has left a blank, the copyist, to guard against his being supposed to have been careless in his task, has added these words: "The author has omitted to tell us how these weapons were made". This copy, however, was taken in the beginning of the sixteenth century, as may be seen from the style of the writing as exhibited in the facsimile of the first paragraph of the work, shown on preceding page.

The MS. is in folio, and is rudely bound up in a sheet of parchment, torn out of some book of ecclesiastical offices. The ink is a little faded, but the writing is still perfectly legible. The paper is of ordinary strength, and of rather a dark tint; the manufacturer's water mark is shown in the above facsimile. Blank leaves of more modern make, and having a different water-mark, have been inserted at the front and back, and the first of these leaves contains the following inscription in a modern hand, which is still legible, although pains have been taken to erase it:—

"Pertinet ad usum fratris Theotonii de Sancto
G . . . . Canonici Regularis in Cenobio
Scte Crucis".

Immediately below this we read:—

"Dô Theotonio",

and near the bottom of the page, in a modern hand,

probably that of one of the librarians of the convent :—

"Descobrimento da India por D. Vasco
da Gamma".

Prof. Kopke suggests[1] that the copyist of this valuable MS. was the famous historian Fernão Lopes de Castanheda, who was Apparitor and Keeper of the Archives in the University of Coimbra, and was engaged there during twenty years, much to the injury of his health and private fortune, in collecting the materials for his *Historia do Descobrimento e Conquista da India.* In support of this assumption he publishes a signature (see the facsimile on page xxii) taken from a copy of the first book of Castanheda's history, published in 1551. But A. Herculano,[2] whilst admitting this signature to be genuine, points out that the cursive characters of the MS. are of a type exceedingly common during the first half of the sixteenth century, and that it would consequently not be safe to attribute it to any writer in particular. Until, therefore, further evidence is forthcoming, we cannot accept the Professor's theory that we are indebted for this copy to Castanheda; though, as we have already said, there can be no doubt that in writing his account of the First Voyage of Vasco da Gama he depended almost exclusively for his facts upon the anonymous author of this *Roteiro.*

---

[1] *Roteiro*, prim. ediçao, p. xix.
[2] *Roteiro*, seg. ediçao, p. xii.

The Author of the "Roteiro".

It is quite possible, as suggested by Prof. Kopke, that the title by which the *Roteiro* was known at the convent of Santa Cruz misled certain bibliographers into a belief that Vasco da Gama himself had written this account of his voyage.

Thus Nicoláo Antonio, in his *Bibliotheca Hispana Veta* (1672), lib. 10, c. 15, § 543, says:—

> "Vascus da Gama . . . . . dedit reversus Emanueli suo Regi populari Portugaliæ idiomate navigationis suae ad Indiam anno MCD XCVII relationem, quae lucem vidit."

The words "quae lucem vidit" need not, however, be understood as conveying the meaning that this narrative was actually printed and published, for the same author, in his *Bibliotheca Hispana Nova*, makes use of the same equivocal expression when describing another voyage to India, expressly stated by him to be still in MS.

Moreri, in his *Dictionnaire* (1732), quoting as his authority a *Bibliotheca Portuguesa* in MS., which he had from "a man of judgment and of vast erudition", states that Vasco da Gama is said to have published an account of his first voyage to India, but that no copy of it had up till then been discovered.

Similarly, Barbosa Machado, the author of the standard *Bibliotheca Lusitana* (t. iii, p. 775), 1752, accepting Nicoláo Antonio as his authority, says that Vasco da Gama "wrote an account of the voyage which he made to India in 1497".[1]

We are quite safe in assuming that no such a narrative has ever been published, although it is equally certain that Vasco da Gama furnished official reports of his proceedings, which were still available when João de Barros wrote his *Decades*, but are so no longer.

No one has yet succeeded in discovering the author of the *Roteiro*. Prof. Kopke attempts to arrive at the name by a process of elimination, and in doing so starts with several assumptions which we cannot accept. First of all he assumes that Castanheda must have known the writer of the MS. of which he made such excellent use in writing his history. But Castanheda only became acquainted with this MS. after 1530, when he took up his residence at Coimbra on his return from India, that is, more than thirty years after it had been written. Of course, the author might then have been still alive, notwithstanding the lapse of years; but had this been the case, and had Castanheda been personally acquainted with him, he would surely have obtained from him an account of the termination of the voyage, instead of abruptly breaking off in the same way as the *Roteiro* does, with the arrival of the fleet at the shoals of the

---

[1] Prof. Kopke (*Roteiro*, prim. ed., pp. ix-xiv) deals much more fully with this subject. We have been content to give the substance of his remarks.

Rio Grande (see p. 93), adding that he had been unable to ascertain the particulars of the further voyage of the captain-major, and only knew that Coelho arrived at Cascaes on July 10th, 1499.[1] It is probable, moreover, that if Castanheda had known the name of the author to whom he was so greatly indebted, he would have mentioned it in his book.

Prof. Kopke assumes further that the writer was a common sailor or soldier, and most probably the former: first, because he frequently makes use of the expression "nós outros" (we others) as if to draw a distinction between the officers of the ships and the class to which he himself belonged; and, secondly, because "the style of his narrative would seem to point to his humble condition". We can admit neither of these conclusions. The author by no means uses the expression "we others" in the restricted sense in which Prof. Kopke understands it. In proof of this we may refer to such sentences as are to be found at pp. 57 and 61:—"When the King beckoned to the captain he looked at us others"; "as to us others, we diverted ourselves"—the "others", in both these cases, including the thirteen men who attended Vasco da Gama to Calecut, and among whom were the three pursers, the captain-major's secretary, and others who may

[1] See livro I, c. xxvii, of the first edition (1551) of his *Historia*. In the edition of 1554 this passage is suppressed, but further particulars of the voyage are not given.

not have been "persons of distinction" but who nevertheless cannot be classed with "common soldiers or sailors". As to the literary style of the Journal, we may at once admit that its author cannot take rank with Barros, Castanheda or Correa, but this by no means proves him to have been an uncultured man, or of "humble condition." His spelling may not have been quite in accordance with the somewhat loose rules followed in the fifteenth century, but his narrative is straightforward and to the point, and shows that he was a man of judgment perfectly able to give an intelligent account of the many novel facts which came under his observation. If he looked upon the Hindus as fellow-Christians, he shared that opinion with the other members of the expedition, including its chief. It only needs a perusal of such a collection of letters, reports, and narratives as is to be found in *Alguns documentos do Archivo nacional* (Lisbon, 1892) to convince us that there were men holding high positions in those days whose literary abilities fell short of those which can be claimed on behalf of our author. Moreover, it is not likely that access to the information required to enable him to write a *Roteiro da Viagem* would have been given to a "common sailor or soldier", even if such a person had been bold enough to ask for it.

We shall now follow Prof. Kopke in his "process of elimination":—

1. The author, in the course of his narrative, mentions a number of persons by name, and these

we must eliminate forthwith. They are: Vasco and Paulo da Gama, Nicolau Coelho (p. 22), Pero d'Alenquer (p. 5), João de Coimbra (p. 30), Martin Affonso (pp. 12, 17), Sancho Mexia (p. 6), and Fernão Veloso (p. 7).

2. We know further that the author served on board the *S. Raphael*.[1] This disposes of Gonçalo Alvares and Diogo Dias[2] of the *S. Gabriel;* and of Gonçalo Nunes, Pero Escolar, and Alvaro de Braga, of the *Berrio.*

3. The author mentions certain things as having been done by persons whose names he does not give. The name of one of these is supplied by Castanheda and Barros. We thus learn from Barros that Fernão Martins was the sailor mentioned by the author (p. 23) as being able to speak the language of the Moors; and from Castanheda (I, p. 51) that he was one of the two men sent with a message to the King of Calecut (p. 50). The convict who was sent to Calecut on May 21st (p. 48) was João Nunez, according to Correa. The author states (p. 64, line 18, and p. 65, last line) that the captain-major sent three men along

---

[1] For a conclusive proof of this see p. 2. After the *S. Raphael* had been broken up, the author may have been transferred to Coelho's vessel, and have returned in her.

[2] This is the "secretary" (escrivão) of Vasco da Gama. Castanheda (I, p. 54) mentions also the comptroller (veador) of the captain-major, but we are inclined to think that this is a duplication of the same person, namely, Diogo Dias, the clerk or purser of the *S. Gabriel.*

the beach in search of the ships' boats. According to Castanheda (I, pp. 71 and 72), one of these men was Gonçalo Pires.

We may therefore strike out all these names from the list of possible authors.

4. Three members of the expedition are reported to have died during the voyage, namely, Pedro de Covilhão, the priest; Pedro de Faria de Figueredo, and his brother Francisco, all of them mentioned by Faria y Sousa alone.

5. Lastly, there are four convicts whose names are given by Correa, none of whom is likely to have been the author of the MS. The presence of some of these convicts is, moreover, very doubtful.

We have thus accounted for all the members of the expedition whose names are known, with the exception of eight.

Four of these—João de Sá, Alvaro Velho, João Palha and João de Setubal—are stated to have been among the thirteen who attended Vasco da Gama to Calecut (p. 51), and of these, João de Sá was clerk in the *S. Raphael*, the author's ship. He certainly might have been the author. Prof. Kopke thinks not, first, because of the author's supposed humble position; secondly, because João de Sá, if we may credit an anecdote recorded by Castanheda (I, p. 57),[1] had his doubts about the people of India being Christians, whilst the author unhesitatingly affirms them to be so. The only other person mentioned

[1] See p. 54, note 2, for this anecdote.

by Castanheda as having been connected with the expedition is Alvaro Velho, a soldier, who, according to Prof. Kopke, may "fairly be looked upon as the author of this Journal." He admits, however, that this conclusion is acceptable only on the assumption that Castanheda knew the author: a purely gratuitous assumption, in our opinion.

Castanheda only mentions six out of the thirteen who were present at Vasco da Gama's audience of the Zamorin. Correa mentions two others—João de Setubal and João Palha. Five remain thus to be accounted for; and, although these may have included servants and trumpeters, not likely to have troubled about keeping a journal, our author may have been among them. It will thus be seen that this process of elimination has led to no result, and that we cannot even tell whether the author's name occurs in any single account of this expedition. Comparing his "Journal" with the contents of Sernigi's first letter, it almost seems as if he had been the person from whom the Florentine derived the bulk of his information. In that case his name may perhaps turn up some day in the Italian archives. If our choice were limited to Alvaro Velho and João de Sá, we should feel inclined to decide in favour of the latter.

Correa mentions three other persons as having been with Vasco da Gama: namely, João Figueiro, whose diary he claims to have used, and who cannot therefore have been the author of a "Journal" the contents of which are so widely different; André

Gonçalves and João d'Amoxeira. Camões adds a fourth name, that of Leonardo Ribeyra. This exhausts the muster-roll, as far as the names are known to us.

The Portuguese Editions of the "Roteiro".[1]

The *Roteiro* was printed for the first time in 1838. The editors, Diogo Kopke and Dr. Antonio da Costa Paiva, both teachers at the *Academia Polytechnica* of Oporto, furnished it with an introduction, in which they give an account of the manuscript and discuss its authorship, add sixty-nine notes, explanatory of the text, and append King Manuel's letters patent of January 10th, 1502 (see p. 230). The illustrations include a map, the facsimile of a page of the MS., a portrait, and an illustrated title-page of poor design. The book was published by subscription. Three hundred and ninety-two copies were subscribed for, including two hundred and thirty-seven by residents in Oporto, among whom British wine-merchants figure prominently. Only five copies went abroad, and three of these were subscribed for by Captain Washington, R.N., the Royal Geographical Society, and the Geographical Society of Paris.

A second edition appeared at Lisbon in 1861.

---

[1] *Roteiro da Viagem que em descobrimento da India pelo Cabo da Boa Esperança fez Dom Vasco da Gama em* 1497. Porto, 1838. 8vo, pp. xxviii, 184.

Its editors, A. Herculano, the famous historian, and Baron do Castello de Paiva, claim to have "got rid of those imperfections in the text, as also in the notes of the first edition,[1] which must be attributed to the inexperience of the editors, and to their eagerness to bring before the public so precious an historical document". Their emendations, however, are not of a kind to justify this somewhat brutal reference to the work done by their predecessors. They consist, in the main, of a modernisation of the spelling, the introduction of a few "philological" notes of no particular interest, and a short preface in which Correa's *Lendas da India* are spoken of in terms of eulogy. These *Lendas* the editors consider to be "far superior in substance (*quanto á substancia*) to the *Decades* of João de Barros, and to the exuberant but evidently honest narrative of Castanheda." After praising Correa "for depicting in firm contours and vivid colours" the human passions brought into play by close companionship within the narrow limits of a ship, they admit that as to "facts" "he is often vague, forgetful, or ambiguous". They conclude by saying that the author of the *Roteiro* and the chronicle-writers mutually complement each other, and jointly acquaint us with all the details of one of the great events in the history of modern nations.[2]

---

[1] *Roteiro da Viagem de Vasco da Gama em* MCCCCXCVII. Segunda edição. Lisboa (Imprensa Nacional), 1861. 8vo, pp. xliv, 182.

[2] Compare p. xvii, and numerous references to Correa throughout this volume.

The French Translations of the "Roteiro".

Two have been published. The first of these, by M. Ferdinand Denis, will be found in the third volume of Charton's *Voyageurs Anciens et Modernes*, Paris, 1855. It is based upon the first Portuguese edition, and ends with the arrival of the two vessels at the Rio Grande. The notes by Professor Kopke are embodied in those of the translator, who has added an introduction, giving a short but excellent biography of Vasco da Gama, and a bibliography. The map of the original is retained, and there are twenty illustrations, including two portraits of Vasco da Gama, the one stated to be from Count Farrobo's painting, as published in the *Panorama*, the other from a Paris MS. of Barretto de Rezende.[1]

For the second French translation[2] we are indebted to M. Arthur Morelet. It is from the second Portuguese edition, and not a word of either text or notes has been omitted. The translator has confined himself to supplying a short introduction. The map is retained, but a free rendering of Count Farrobo's painting[3] has been substituted for the poor portrait of Vasco da Gama in the original, and the portrait of King Manuel has been omitted as being "flat, without relief and vigour, and

[1] Reproduced on p. 150.

[2] *Journal du Voyage de Vasco da Gama en* MCCCCXCVII, *traduit du Portugais par Arthur Morelet*, Lyon, 1864.

[3] Reproduced by us, p. 171.

wanting even in that unaffected simplicity which marks the works of that period."[1]

The English Translation.

In 1869 the Hakluyt Society published Lord Stanley of Alderley's translation of the *Three Voyages of Vasco da Gama*, from the *Lendas* of Gaspar Correa, with numerous foot-notes indicating those instances in which Correa differs from Barros, Goes, Castanheda and other historians, as well as from the poetical version of this voyage presented in the *Lusiadas* of Camões.

It was intended at the same time to bring out an English version of the *Roteiro*, but no definite arrangements were made, and thus the matter was left in abeyance until the present Editor revived the idea, and suggested that the volume proposed might prove acceptable as an interesting though humble contribution to the literature of the Fourth Centenary of Vasco da Gama's arrival in India, which Portugal is about to celebrate.

The translation of the *Roteiro* itself is literal and complete. The notes of the Portuguese editors have, however, been abridged, and only the substance of what they say in their introductions has been retained.

On the other hand, the Editor has added translations of the letters of King Manuel and Sernigi, and of three Portuguese accounts of the voyage. He has,

[1] For a copy of this contemned portrait, see p. 109.

moreover, added Appendices, among which the one dealing with early maps will, he hopes, prove of some interest.

In conclusion, the Editor fulfils an agreeable duty in acknowledging the kindly help and advice extended to him by a number of gentlemen. To Capt. E. J. de Carvalho e Vasconcellos and Senhor José Bastos, of Lisbon, he is indebted for the fine portraits which ornament this edition; to Prof. Gallois for a tracing of the unpublished portion of Canerio's chart; to Dr. M. C. Caputo for a photograph of the African portion of the Cantino chart; to Prof. Biagi for a copy of Sernigi's letter in the *Biblioteca Riccardiana;* to Sir J. Kirk for several illustrations and important notes; to the late Rt. Rev. Dr. J. M. Speechley, and the Rev. J. J. Jaus, of the Basel Missionary Society, for notes on Calecut; and for help in minor matters to Dr. Garnett, of the British Museum; Baron Hulot, Secretary of the Paris Geographical Society; M. Marcel, of the *Bibliothèque Nationale;* Prof. Dalla Vedova, of Rome; Prof. Berchet, of Venice; and Capt. B. B. da Silva, of Lisbon.

His special thanks are due to three members of the Hakluyt Society, namely, Sir Clements Markham, the President; Admiral Albert H. Markham, who acted as the Editor's nautical adviser; and Mr. William Foster, the Secretary, whose careful reading of the proofs kept this volume free from many a blunder.

LONDON, *March*, 1898.

A JOURNAL

OF THE FIRST

VOYAGE OF VASCO DA GAMA

IN 1497-99.

[*Words and Dates not in the MS. have been placed within square brackets.*]

IN the name of God. Amen!

In the year 1497 King Dom Manuel, the first of that name in Portugal, despatched four vessels to make discoveries and go in search of spices. Vasco da Gama was the captain-major of these vessels; Paulo da Gama, his brother, commanded one of them, and Nicolau Coelho another.[1]

[*Lisbon to the Cape Verde Islands.*]

We left Restello[2] on Saturday, July 8, 1497. May God our Lord permit us to accomplish this voyage in his service. Amen!

---

[1] These vessels, as appears in the course of the Journal, were the *S. Gabriel* (flag-ship), the *S. Raphael* (Paulo da Gama), the *Berrio* (Nicolau Coelho), and a store-ship (Gonçalo Nunes). The author served on board the *S. Raphael*. See Introduction.

[2] In the suburb of Restello, four miles below the Arsenal of Lisbon,

On the following Saturday [July 15] we sighted the Canaries, and in the night passed to the lee of Lançarote. During the following night, at break of day [July 16] we made the Terra Alta, where we fished for a couple of hours, and in the evening, at dusk, we were off the Rio do Ouro.[1]

The fog[2] during the night grew so dense that Paulo da Gama lost sight of the captain-major, and when day broke [July 17] we saw neither him nor the other vessels. We therefore made sail for the Cape Verde islands, as we had been instructed to do in case of becoming separated.

On the following Saturday, [July 22], at break of day, we sighted the Ilha do Sal,[3] and an hour afterwards discovered three vessels, which turned out to be the store-ship, and the vessels commanded by Nicolau Coelho and Bartholameu Diz [Dias], the last of whom sailed in our company as far as the Mine.[4] They, too, had lost sight of

---

stood a chapel or *ermida*, which had been built by Henry the Navigator for the use of mariners. In this chapel Vasco da Gama and his companions spent the night previous to their departure in prayer. After his victorious return, D. Manuel founded on its site the magnificent monastery of Our Lady of Bethlehem or Belem.

[1] The forbidding line of low cliffs, extending for 35 miles from Leven Head to Elbow Point, in lat. 24° N., was known to the Portuguese of the time as *terra alta* (see D. Pacheco Pereira, *Esmeraldo de Situ Orbis*, p. 40). The Rio do Ouro or River of Gold is a basin, extending about 20 miles inland and four miles wide at its mouth. No river flows into it. The real "River of Gold" is the Senegal or the Upper Niger.

[2] Castanheda attributes the separation of the vessels to the fog and a storm.

[3] At the southern extremity of Ilha do Sal, in lat. 16° 31′ N., is the Porto de Santa Maria.

[4] S. Jorge da Mina, the famous fort built on the Gold Coast in 1482, by Diogo d'Azambuja, one of whose captains had been the very Bartholomew Dias who five years afterwards doubled the Cape, and who now returned to the *Mine*, having been made its captain, in recognition of his great services. (See L. Cordeira, *Diogo d'Azambuja*, Lisbon, 1890, and Barros, edition of 1778, to. I, part 1, p. 271.)

the captain-major. Having joined company we pursued our route, but the wind fell, and we were becalmed until Wednesday [July 26]. At ten o'clock on that day we sighted the captain-major, about five leagues ahead of us, and having got speech with him in the evening we gave expression to our joy by many times firing off our bombards[1] and sounding the trumpets.

The day after this, a Thursday [July 27], we arrived at the island of Samtiago [São Thiago],[2] and joyfully anchored in the bay of Santa Maria, where we took on board meat, water and wood, and did the much-needed repairs to our yards.

[*Across the Southern Atlantic.*]

On Thursday, August 3, we left in an easterly direction. On August 18,[3] when about 200 leagues from Samtiaguo, going south, the captain-major's main yard broke, and we lay to under foresail and lower mainsail for two days and a night. On the 22nd of the same month, when going

---

[1] Bombardas, originally catapults, subsequently any piece of ordnance from which stone balls were thrown. In the north of Europe the term was restricted to mortars. Gama, however, carried breech-loading guns, with movable *cameras* or chambers. (See Stanley's *Vasco da Gama*, p. 226, *note* and *Introduction.*)

[2] São Thiago, the largest of the Cape Verde Islands. The Porto da Praia, within which lies the Island of Santa Maria (14° 50′ N.), is no doubt the bay referred to in the text.

[3] This date, August 18th, is obviously wrong. Deducting the delay of two days, Vasco da Gama spent 95 days on his passage from São Thiago to the Bay of St. Helena, the distance being about 1,170 leagues (4,290 miles), his daily progress amounted to 12 leagues or 45 miles. If the dates in the text were correct, he would have made 12½ leagues daily up to August 18th, and between that date and the 22nd (allowing for the delay) at least 300 leagues (1,010 miles), which is quite impossible. It is evident that the second date is wrong, and instead of "the same month", we ought perhaps to read "October". In that case the daily progress, up to October 22nd, would have averaged 10 leagues (34 miles). Thence, to St. Helena Bay, a distance

S. by W., we saw many birds resembling herons.[1] On the approach of night they flew vigorously to the S.S.E., as if making for the land.[2] On the same day, being then quite 800 leagues out at sea [*i.e.*, reckoning from S. Thiago], we saw a whale.

On Friday, October 27, the eve of St. Simon and Jude, we saw many whales, as also quoquas[3] and seals.[4]

On Wednesday, November 1, the day of All Saints, we perceived many indications of the neighbourhood of land, including gulf-weed,[5] which grows along the coast.

---

of 370 leagues accomplished in 16 days, the daily progress would have averaged nearly 23 leagues (78 miles). Of course these are merely rough approximations, as the course taken by Vasco da Gama and the incidents of this memorable passage are not known to us. We may mention that modern sailing vessels going from S. Thiago by way of Sierra Leone and Ascension to the Cape, a distance of 5,410 miles, occupy on an average 49½ days on the passage, making thus 110 miles daily (58 in crossing from Sierra Leone to Ascension). A ship going direct (3,770 miles) has performed the passage in 41 days, thus averaging 92 daily. (See Admiral Fitzroy's "Passage Tables" in the *Meteorological Papers* published by the Admiralty in 1858.)

[1] The MS. has *Garçôees*, a word not to be found in the dictionary, but evidently an augmentative of *garça*, a heron. Pimental, in his *Arte de Navegar*, mentions large birds with dark wings and white bodies as being met with a hundred leagues to the west of the Cape of Good Hope, which are known as *Gaivotões*.—KOPKE.

The Gaivota, or gull, however, in no respect resembles a heron.

[2] That is, towards Africa, Gama being at that time considerably to the north of Walvisch Bay.

[3] Kopke supposes that we should read *phoca* instead of *quoqua*, but this is not very likely, as *lobo marinho* is employed throughout the *Rutter* to describe the *phocæ* or seals. Among the animals which these early navigators must have met with, but which are not mentioned, are porpoises (*peixe de porco*) and dolphins (*doiradas* or gilt-heads).

[4] *Lobo marinho*, sea-wolf, a term vaguely applied to all species of seals, as also to the sea-elephant, has been translated throughout as *seal.*

[5] *Golfão*, *i.e.*, Zostera nana, which is met with along the coast of South-Western Africa.

On Saturday, the 4th of the same month, a couple of hours before break of day, we had soundings in 110 fathoms,[1] and at nine o'clock we sighted the land.[2] We then drew near to each other, and having put on our gala clothes, we saluted the captain-major by firing our bombards, and dressed the ships with flags and standards. In the course of the day we tacked so as to come close to the land, but as we failed to identify it,[3] we again stood out to sea.

[*The Bay of St. Helena.*]

On Tuesday [November 7] we returned to the land, which we found to be low, with a broad bay opening into it. The captain-major sent Pero d'Alenquer[4] in a boat to take soundings and to search for good anchoring ground. The bay was found to be very clean, and to afford shelter against all winds except those from the N.W. It extended east and west, and we named it Santa Helena.

On Wednesday [November 8] we cast anchor in this bay, and we remained there eight days, cleaning the ships, mending the sails, and taking in wood.

The river Samtiagua [S. Thiago] enters the bay four

---

[1] A Portuguese fathom, or *braça*, is equal to 5.76 feet 10 inches.

[2] This was considerably to the north of St. Helena Bay, which was only reached three days later.

[3] A reference, no doubt, to Pero d'Alenquer, Vasco da Gama's pilot, who had been with B. Dias during his memorable voyage round the Cape, as had probably others of this armada.

[4] Castanheda and Goes state that Nicolau Coelho was sent to take the soundings. It is, however, much more probable that this duty was intrusted to Pero d'Alenquer, who had already doubled the Cape with Bartholomew Dias, and had touched at several points in its vicinity.—KOPKE.

I cannot see how his having been with Dias can have conferred any very special qualification for taking soundings in a bay which Pero d'Alenquer had never seen before. On subsequent occasions Coelho seems to have been employed repeatedly upon this duty.

leagues to the S.E. of the anchorage. It comes from the interior (sertão), is about a stone's throw across at the mouth, and from two to three fathoms in depth at all states of the tide.[1]

The inhabitants of this country are tawny-coloured.[2] Their food is confined to the flesh of seals, whales and gazelles, and the roots of herbs. They are dressed in skins, and wear sheaths over their virile members.[3] They are armed with poles of olive wood to which a horn, browned in the fire, is attached.[4] Their numerous dogs resemble those of Portugal, and bark like them. The birds of the country, likewise, are the same as in Portugal, and include cormorants, gulls, turtle doves, crested larks, and many others. The climate is healthy and temperate, and produces good herbage.

On the day after we had cast anchor, that is to say on Thursday [November 9], we landed with the captain-major, and made captive one of the natives, who was small of stature like Sancho Mexia. This man had been gathering honey in the sandy waste, for in this country the bees deposit their honey at the foot of the mounds around the

---

[1] Now called Berg River.—KOPKE.

[2] *Baço*, a vague term, meaning also brown or blackish.

[3] Castanheda, in his first edition (1551), adopted this statement, but subsequently suppressed it. D. Jeronymo Osorio, Bishop of Silves, in *De rebus Emanuelsis*, has "pudènta ligneis vaginis includunt .—KOPKE.

The use of such a sheath is universal among the Bantu tribes of Southern Africa, but seems now to be more honoured in the breach than the observance among the Hottentots, here spoken of. John of Empoli, who went to India with Afonso de Albuquerque (*Ramusio*, i), observed such a sheath made of leather with the hair on, among the Hottentots of the Bay of S. Blas. Leguat (Hakluyt Society's edition, 1891, p. 288) found it still in use in 1698.

[4] The shafts of their assegais are made of assegai- or lance-wood (*Curtisea faginda*), and not of olive-wood, and even in John of Empoli's time had iron blades. Their spears for spearing fish, on the other hand, are tipped with the straight horn of the gemsbuck.

bushes. He was taken on board the captain-major's ship, and being placed at table he ate of all we ate. On the following day the captain-major had him well dressed and sent ashore.[1]

On the following day [November 10] fourteen or fifteen natives came to where our ships lay. The captain-major landed and showed them a variety of merchandise, with the view of finding out whether such things were to be found in their country. This merchandise included cinnamon, cloves, seed-pearls, gold, and many other things, but it was evident that they had no knowledge whatever of such articles, and they were consequently given round bells and tin rings. This happened on Friday, and the like took place on Saturday.

On Sunday [November 12] about forty or fifty natives made their appearance, and having dined, we landed, and in exchange for the çeitils[2] with which we came provided, we obtained shells, which they wore as ornaments in their ears, and which looked as if they had been plated, and fox-tails attached to a handle, with which they fanned their faces. I also acquired for one çeitil one of the sheaths which they wore over their members, and this seemed to show that they valued copper very highly; indeed, they wore small beads of that metal in their ears.

On that day Fernão Velloso, who was with the captain-major, expressed a great desire to be permitted to accompany the natives to their houses, so that he might find out how they lived and what they ate. The captain-major yielded to his importunities, and allowed him to accompany them, and when we returned to the captain-major's vessel to sup, he went away with the negroes. Soon after they

---

[1] We learn from Barros that Vasco da Gama landed for the purpose of observing the latitude. The captive was handed over to two ship's boys, one of whom was a negro, with orders to treat him well.

[2] *Çeitil*, a copper coin, worth about one-third of a farthing.

had left us they caught a seal, and when they came to the foot of a hill in a barren place they roasted it, and gave some of it to Fernão Velloso, as also some of the roots which they eat. After this meal they expressed a desire that he should not accompany them any further, but return to the vessels. When Fernão Velloso came abreast of the vessels he began to shout, the negroes keeping in the bush.

We were still at supper; but when his shouts were heard the captain-major rose at once, and so did we others, and we entered a sailing boat. The negroes then began running along the beach, and they came as quickly up with Fernão Velloso[1] as we did, and when we endeavoured to get him into the boat they threw their assegais, and wounded the captain-major and three or four others. All this happened because we looked upon these people as men of little spirit, quite incapable of violence, and had therefore landed without first arming ourselves. We then returned to the ships.

[*Rounding the Cape*].

At daybreak of Thursday the 16th of November, having careened our ships and taken in wood, we set sail. At that time we did not know how far we might be abaft the Cape

---

[1] We gather from Barros and Goes that Fernão Velloso was granted the desired permission at the intercession of Paulo da Gama. When Vasco da Gama returned to his vessel, Coelho and some of the crew were left behind, collecting wood and lobsters. Paulo amused himself by harpooning a whale, which nearly cost him dearly, for the whale dived, and would have capsized the boat had not the water been shallow. In the afternoon, when Coelho and his people were returning to the vessels, Velloso was observed to run down a hill. Vasco da Gama, ever observant, saw this from his ship, and at once ordered Coelho back, entering himself a boat to join him. Some delay or misunderstanding occurred, the "negroes" threw stones and discharged arrows, and several men were wounded, including the captain-major and Gonçalo Alvarez. For further particulars see Stanley's *Vasco da Gama*, p. 46.

of Good Hope. Pero d'Alenquer thought the distance about thirty leagues,[1] but he was not certain, for on his return voyage [when with B. Dias] he had left the Cape in the morning and had gone past this bay with the wind astern, whilst on the outward voyage he had kept at sea, and was therefore unable to identify the locality where we now were. We therefore stood out towards the S.S.W. and late on Saturday [November 18] we beheld the Cape. On that same day we again stood out to sea, returning to the land in the course of the night. On Sunday morning, November 19, we once more made for the Cape, but were again unable to round it, for the wind blew from the S.S.W., whilst the Cape juts out towards the S.W. We then again stood out to sea, returning to the land on Monday night. At last, on Wednesday [November 22], at noon, having the wind astern, we succeeded in doubling the Cape, and then ran along the coast.[2]

To the south of this Cape of Good Hope, and close to it, a vast bay, six leagues broad at its mouth, enters about six leagues into the land.[3]

[*The Bay of São Braz*].[4]

Late on Saturday, November 25, the day of St. Catherine's, we entered the bay (angra) of Sam Brás,

---

[1] The distance is 33 leagues.

[2] Castanheda says that the Cape was doubled on "Wednesday, November 20", but Wednesday was the 22nd. Barros says "Tuesday, 20th", but Tuesday was the 21st. Compare Stanley's *Vasco da Gama*, p. 48.

[3] The actual dimensions of False Bay are about 5 by 5 leagues. The bay is called "Golfo Antº delle Serre" on the map of Henricus Martellus Germanus, 1489, which illustrates the voyage of B. Dias (Add. MS. 15760, Brit. Mus.).

[4] This is without the shadow of a doubt Mossel Bay (see plan on map II). It is also most probably the Bahia de los Vaqueiros of B. Dias, who certainly was here [see below]. Barros refers to it as

where we remained for thirteen days, for there we broke up our store-ship and transferred her contents to the other vessels.[1]

On Friday [December 1], whilst still in the bay of Sam Brás, about ninety men resembling those we had met at St. Helena Bay made their appearance. Some of them walked along the beach, whilst others remained upon the hills. All, or most of us, were at the time in the captain-major's vessel. As soon as we saw them we launched and armed the boats, and started for the land. When close to the shore the captain-major threw them little round bells, which they picked up. They even ventured to approach us, and took some of these bells from the captain-major's hand. This surprised us greatly, for when Bartholomeu Dias[2] was here the natives fled without taking any of the objects which he offered them. Nay, on one occasion, when Dias was taking in water, close to the beach, they sought to prevent him, and when they pelted him with stones, from a hill, he killed one of them with the arrow of a cross-bow. It appeared to us that they did not fly on this occasion, because they had heard from the people at the bay of St. Helena (only sixty leagues distant by sea)[3] that there was no harm in us, and that we even gave away things which were ours.

The captain-major did not land at this spot, because there was much bush, but proceeded to an open part of the beach, when he made signs to the negroes to approach. This they did. The captain-major and the other cap-

---

being *now* called S. Braz. Its original name had thus been abandoned in favour of that bestowed by Vasco da Gama.

[1] The thirteen days are counted from November 25 to December 7, both these days being counted. According to Castanheda (I, p. 12), the store-ship was burnt.

[2] See note 4, p. 9.

[3] The distance by sea is over 90 leagues, that by land 64. "By sea" is probably a slip of the pen.

tains then landed, being attended by armed men, some of whom carried cross-bows. He then made the negroes understand, by signs, that they were to disperse, and to approach him only singly or in couples. To those who approached he gave small bells and red caps, in return for which they presented him with ivory bracelets, such as they wore on their arms, for it appears that elephants are plentiful in this country. We actually found some of their droppings near the watering place where they had gone to drink.

On Saturday [December 2] about two hundred negroes came, both young and old. They brought with them about a dozen oxen and cows and four or five sheep. As soon as we saw them we went ashore. They forthwith began to play on four or five flutes,[1] some producing high notes and others low ones, thus making a pretty harmony for negroes who are not expected to be musicians ; and they danced in the style of negroes. The captain-major then ordered the trumpets to be sounded, and we, in the boats, danced, and the captain-major did so likewise when he rejoined us. This festivity ended, we landed where we had landed before, and bought a black ox for three bracelets. This ox we dined off on Sunday. We found him very fat, and his meat as toothsome as the beef of Portugal.

On Sunday [December 3] many visitors came, and brought with them their women and little boys, the women remaining on the top of a hill near the sea. They had with them many oxen and cows. Having collected in two spots on the beach, they played and danced as they had done on Saturday. It is the custom of this people for the young men to remain in the bush with their weapons. The [older] men came to converse with us. They carried a

---

[1] The "gora" is the great musical instrument of the Hottentots. It s not a flute or reed-pipe.

short stick in the hand, attached to which was a fox's tail, with which they fan the face. Whilst conversing with them, by signs, we observed the young men crouching in the bush, holding their weapons in their hands. The captain-major then ordered Martin Affonso, who had formerly been in Manicongo [Congo] to advance, and to buy an ox, for which purpose he was supplied with bracelets. The natives, having accepted the bracelets, took him by the hand, and, pointing to the watering place, asked him why we took away their water, and simultaneously drove their cattle into the bush. When the captain-major observed this he ordered us to gather together, and called upon Martin Affonso to retreat, for he suspected some treachery. Having drawn together we proceeded [in our boats] to the place where we had been at first. The negroes followed us. The captain-major then ordered us to land, armed with lances, assegais, and strung cross-bows, and wearing our breast-plates, for he wanted to show that we had the means of doing them an injury, although we had no desire to employ them. When they observed this they ran away. The captain-major, anxious that none should be killed by mischance, ordered the boats to draw together; but to prove that we were able, although unwilling to hurt them, he ordered two bombards to be fired from the poop of the long boat. They were by that time all seated close to the bush, not far from the beach, but the first discharge caused them to retreat so precipitately that in their flight they dropped the skins with which they were covered and their weapons. When they were in the bush two of them turned back to pick up the articles which had been dropped. They then continued their flight to the top of a hill, driving their cattle before them.

The oxen of this country are as large as those of Alemtejo, wonderfully fat and very tame. They are geldings, and hornless. Upon the fattest among them the negroes place a packsaddle made of reeds, as is done in Castille, and upon this saddle they place a kind of litter made of sticks, upon which they ride. If they wish to sell an ox they pass a stick through his nostrils, and thus lead him.

There is an island in this bay, three bowshots from the land, where there are many seals.[1] Some of these are as big as bears, very formidable, with large tusks. These attack man, and no spear, whatever the force with which it is thrown, can wound them. There are others much smaller and others quite small. And whilst the big ones roar like lions, the little ones cry like goats. One day, when we approached this island for our amusement, we counted, among large and small ones, three thousand, and we fired among them with our bombards from the sea. On the same island there are birds as big as ducks, but they cannot fly, because they have no feathers on their wings. These birds, of whom we killed as many as we chose, are called Fotylicayos, and they bray like asses.[2]

Whilst taking in water in this bay of Sam Brás, on a Wednesday, we erected a cross and a pillar.[3] The cross was made out of a mizzen-mast, and very high. On the following Thursday [December 7], when about to set sail, we saw about ten or twelve negroes, who demolished both the cross and the pillar before we had left.

---

[1] This island is still known as "Seal" Island, although its former visitors no longer make their appearance. The islet lies about half a mile from the land, is only 250 ft. in length and 15 ft. high.

[2] Usually called *Sotilicaires* by Portuguese writers. They are clearly Cape Penguins.—KOPKE (abridged).

[3] The word used by the author is "padrão", that is, a stone pillar bearing the arms of Portugal and an inscription, such as King John first ordered to be set up by his explorers. None of the "pillars" set up by Vasco da Gama has been recovered, for the "pillar" near Malindi is clearly of later date (see p. 90).

[*São Braz to Natal.*]

Having taken on board all we stood in need of we took our departure, but as the wind failed us we anchored the same day, having proceeded only two leagues.

On Friday morning, the day of the Immaculate Concepcion [December 8], we again set sail. On Tuesday [December 12], the eve of Santa Lucia, we encountered a great storm, and ran before a stern-wind with the foresail much lowered. On that day we lost sight of Nicolau Coelho, but at sunset we saw him from the top four or five leagues astern, and it seemed as if he saw us too. We exhibited signal lights and lay to. By the end of the first watch he had come up with us, not because he had seen us during the day, but because the wind, being scant, he could not help coming in our waters.

On the morning of Friday [December 15] we saw the land near the Ilhéos chãos (Flat Islands). These are five leagues beyond the Ilhéo da Cruz (Cross Island). From the Bay of Sam Brás to Cross Island is a distance of sixty leagues, and as much from the Cape of Good Hope to the Bay of Sam Brás. From the Flat Islands to the last pillar erected by Bartholomeu Dias is five leagues, and from this pillar to the Rio do Infante is fifteen leagues.[1]

On Saturday [December 16] we passed the last pillar,

---

[1] This paragraph is of the greatest importance with reference to the voyage of B. Dias, for Pero d'Alenquer, one of his companions, is the real authority for these statements. The usual statement that this pillar was erected on the Ilha da Cruz must henceforth be rejected, as had already been done in 1575, when M. de Mesquita Perestrello made a survey of this coast (see his Report in Pimental's *Roteiro da Navegação da India Oriental*).

The distances given by the author are remarkably correct. From the Cape of Good Hope to Mossel Bay (São Braz) is 60 leagues, as and as we ran along the coast we observed two men running along the beach in a direction contrary to that which we followed. The country about here is very charming and well wooded; we saw much cattle, and the further we advanced the more did the character of the country improve, and the trees increase in size.

During the following night we lay to. We were then already beyond the last discovery made by Bartholomeu Dias.[1] On the next day [December 17], till vespers, we sailed along the coast before a stern-wind, when the wind springing round to the east we stood out to sea. And thus we kept making tacks until sunset on Tuesday [December 19], when the wind again veered to the west. We then lay to during the night, in order that we might on the following day examine the coast and find out where we were.

In the morning [December 20] we made straight for the land, and at ten o'clock found ourselves once more at the Ilhéo da Cruz (Cross Island), that is sixty leagues abaft our dead reckoning! This was due to the currents, which are very strong here.[2]

---

stated by him. Thence to Santa Cruz is 56 leagues; from Santa Cruz to the Rio do Infante is 21 leagues.

Santa Cruz is the largest of a group of islands in the western part of Algoa Bay. It is 4 cables in length, rises to a height of 195 ft., and is nearly all bare rock. *There are no springs.* The *Ilhéos chãos* are readily identified with a cluster of low rocky islets about 7 leagues to the east. The Cape Padrone of the charts marks the site of the last pillar erected by Dias, and 5 leagues beyond it rises "Ship Rock," in the locality where Perestrello claims to have discovered the *Penedo das Fontes* of Barros and other writers. Perestrello had, no doubt, in his possession original documents (now lost) which enabled him to identify the localities named by the early explorers. His substantial agreement with the author of this *Roteiro* is most satisfactory.

[1] That is the Rio do Infante, now known as the Great Fish river.

[2] The Agulhas current hereabouts runs at the rate of 1 to 4 knots an hour to the westward.

That very day we again went forward by the route we had already attempted, and being favoured during three or four days by a strong stern-wind, we were able to overcome the currents which we had feared might frustrate our plans. Henceforth it pleased God in His mercy to allow us to make headway! We were not again driven back. May it please Him that it be thus alway!

[*Natal.*]

By Christmas Day, the 25th of December, we had discovered seventy leagues of coast [beyond Dias' furthest]. On that day, after dinner, when setting a studding-sail, we discovered that the mast had sprung a couple of yards below the top, and that the crack opened and shut. We patched it up with backstays, hoping to be able to repair it thoroughly as soon as we should reach a sheltered port.

On Thursday [December 28] we anchored near the coast, and took much fish.[1] At sunset we again set sail and pursued our route. At that place the mooring-rope snapped and we lost an anchor.

We now went so far out to sea, without touching any port, that drinking-water began to fail us, and our food had to be cooked with salt water. Our daily ration of water was reduced to a quartilho.[2] It thus became necessary to seek a port.

[*Terra da boa Gente and Rio do Cobre.*]

On Thursday, January 11th [1498][3] we discovered a small river and anchored near the coast. On the following day we went close in shore in our boats, and saw a crowd

---

[1] On Canerio's map there is a Ponta da Pescaria, to the north of Port Natal.

[2] Equivalent to three-fourths of a pint.

[3] The MS. says January 10th, but Thursday was the 11th.

of negroes, both men and women. They were tall people, and a chief ("Senhor") was among them. The captain-major ordered Martin Affonso, who had been a long time in Manicongo, and another man, to land. They were received hospitably. The captain-major in consequence sent the chief a jacket, a pair of red pantaloons, a Moorish cap and a bracelet. The chief said that we were welcome to anything in his country of which we stood in need: at least this is how Martin Affonso understood him. That night, Martin Affonso and his companion accompanied the chief to his village, whilst we returned to the ships. On the road the chief donned the garments which had been presented to him, and to those who came forth to meet him he said with much apparent satisfaction, "Look, what has been given to me!" The people upon this clapped hands as a sign of courtesy, and this they did three or four times until he arrived at the village. Having paraded the whole of the place, thus dressed up, the chief retired to his house, and ordered his two guests to be lodged in a compound, where they were given porridge of millet, which abounds in that country, and a fowl, just like those of Portugal. All the night through, numbers of men and women came to have a look at them. In the morning the chief visited them, and asked them to go back to the ships. He ordered two men to accompany them, and gave them fowls as a present for the captain-major, telling them at the same time that he would show the things that had been given him to a great chief, who appears to be the king of that country. When our men reached the landing place where our boats awaited them, they were attended by quite two hundred men, who had come to see them.

This country seemed to us to be densely peopled. There are many chiefs,[1] and the number of women seems to be

[1] Hence called "Terra dos Fumos", or, more correctly, "Mfumos"

greater than that of the men, for among those who came to to see us there were forty women to every twenty men. The houses are built of straw. The arms of the people include long bows and arrows and spears with iron blades. Copper seems to be plentiful, for the people wore [ornaments] of it on their legs and arms and in their twisted hair. Tin, likewise, is found in the country, for it is to be seen on the hilts of their daggers, the sheaths of which are made of ivory. Linen cloth is highly prized by the people, who were always willing to give large quantities of copper in exchange for shirts. They have large calabashes in which they carry sea-water inland, where they pour it into pits, to obtain the salt [by evaporation].

We stayed five days at this place, taking in water, which our visitors conveyed to our boats. Our stay was not, however, sufficiently prolonged to enable us to take in as much water as we really needed, for the wind favoured a prosecution of our voyage.

We were at anchor here, near the coast, exposed to the swell of the sea. We called the country *Terra da Boa Gente* (land of good people), and the river *Rio do Cobre* (copper river).[1]

---

the "land of petty chiefs". Dr. Hamy's chart of 1502 has the name; Canerio has a "terra thrimias", an exceptionally unrecognisable corruption of it; whilst on Ribero's map (1529) we find the name, although in a slightly corrupted form (humos). The appellation has nothing to do with either "smoke" (fumo), or "moisture" (humor).

[1] Barros (*Dec. I.*, l. 4, c. 4) tells us that Vasco da Gama entered the Rio dos Reis, by others called Rio do Cobre, on Twelfth Night (January 6). Goes, on the other hand, confirms the author of the *Roteiro*, and there cannot be a doubt that Barros is mistaken. The Rio dos Reis is, indeed, one of the rivers which enters the bay subsequently called after Lourenço Marques, but discovered, either in 1501 by Sancho de Toar, one of the captains of Cabral's fleet, or in the following year by Antonio de Campo.

Dr. Hamy's Chart has "R. do reys", Canerio's "G. de lom raios" (evidently a corrupt rendering of "Golfo dos or delos Reis", which

[*Rio dos Bons Signaes.*][1]

On Monday [January 22] we discovered a low coast thickly wooded with tall trees. Continuing our course we perceived the broad mouth of a river. As it was necessary to find out where we were, we cast anchor. On Thursday [January 25], at night, we entered. The *Berrio* was already there, having entered the night before—that is eight days before the énd of January [*i.e.*, January 24.][2]

The country is low and marshy, and covered with tall

---

thus seems to have been the earliest name bestowed upon what is now known as Delagoa Bay). The "agoada de bon passa" of Dr. Hamy's Chart, and the "Rio d'aguada" of Canerio, between this bay and Cabo das Correntes, is clearly the locality referred to by the author. Ribero (1529) has a "Rio de la laguna," a "*rio de los reyes*", and further east, an "aguada de buena paz". M. de Mesquita Perestrello (1575) places the "Aguada da boa Paz" 15 leagues to the east of "Rio do Ouro" (the Limpopo), and 43 leagues to the west of Cabo das Correntes. This position corresponds to that of the Zavora River of Admiralty Chart No. 648, in 34° 25′ E. It was here that Vasco da Gama cast anchor. The reference to the "swell of the sea' quite precludes the notion that he entered the well-sheltered Delagoa Bay.

M. Kopke (in a note, *Roteiro*, p. 147) would place the "Aguada da Boa Gente" between the Lagoa River and the Limpopo (Inhambane), in 32° 23′ E., and says that this locality is still generally known as "Aguada da Boa Paz", but I can find no confirmation of this. Moreover, if this be the "Aguada", where, on this barren coast, are we to look for the "Rio do Cobre"? (Compare Stanley's *Vasco da Gama*, p. 66). See Map III.

[1] João dos Santos (*Ethiopia Oriental*, l. 2, c. 20) already identified this river with the Kiliman River. Dr. Hamy's Chart calls it "Rio de bon Signals", an evident corruption. Barros and Goes both call it "Rio dos Bons Signals", whilst Correa refers to it as Rio da Misericordia, the river of Mercy (see Stanley's *Vasco da Gama*, p. 11). Comp. Map III.

[2] A very involved sentence! Gama arrived off the bar of the Kiliman on January 24, cast anchor, and sent the smallest of his vessels, the *Berrio*, within, to take soundings. On the day after, the 25th, he crossed the bar with the two other vessels.

trees yielding an abundance of various fruits, which the inhabitants eat.

These people are black and well made. They go naked, merely wearing a piece of cotton stuff around their loins, that worn by the women being larger than that worn by the men. The young women are good-looking. Their lips are pierced in three places, and they wear in them bits of twisted tin. These people took much delight in us. They brought us in their *almadias*[1] what they had, whilst we went into their village to procure water.

When we had been two or three days at this place two gentlemen (senhores) of the country came to see us. They were very haughty, and valued nothing which we gave them. One of them wore a *touca*,[2] with a fringe embroidered in silk, and the other a cap of green satin. A young man in their company—so we understood from their signs—had come from a distant country, and had already seen big ships like ours. These tokens (signaes) gladdened our hearts, for it appeared as if we were really approaching the bourne of our desires. These gentlemen had some huts built on the river bank, close to the ships, in which they stayed seven days, sending daily to the ships, offering to barter cloths which bore a mark of red ochre. And when they were tired of being there, they left in their *almadias* for the upper river.

As to ourselves, we spent thirty-two days[3] in the river taking in water, careening the ships,[4] and repairing the mast of the *Raphael*. Many of our men fell ill here, their feet

---

[1] *Almadia*, a "dug-out", properly El Maziyah, ferry-boat (Burton's *Camoens*, iv, p. 577.)

[2] Burton (*Commentary*, p. 408), points out that the "touca" is not a turban, but a kind of cap. Its shape, however, was not that of the "toque" of our milliners.

[3] From January 24 to February 24, both days included, is thirty-two days.

[4] Barros says they were beached for that purpose.

and hands swelling, and their gums growing over their teeth, so that they could not eat.[1]

We erected here a pillar which we called the pillar of St. Raphael,[2] because it had been brought in the ship bearing that name. The river we called Rio dos Bons Signaes (River of good signs or tokens).

[*To Moçambique.*]

On Saturday [February 24] we left this place and gained the open sea. During the night we stood N.E., so as to keep away from the land, which was very pleasing to look upon. On Sunday [February 25] we still stood N.E., and at vesper time discovered three small islands, out in the open, of which two were covered with tall trees, while the third and smallest was barren. The distance from one island to the other was four leagues.[3]

On the following day we pursued our route, and did so during six days, lying to at night.[4]

---

[1] This disease was evidently scurvy, so fatal to our early navigators. Castanheda (I. c. 4) tells us that in this time of trouble Paulo da Gama visited the sick night and day, condoled with them, and freely distributed the medicines which he had brought for his own use.

[2] The Padrão de São Raphael is distinctly marked and named on Dr. Hamy's and Canerio's Charts. No trace of it has ever been discovered.

[3] These are the "Insule primeras" (*i.e.*, Ilhas primeiras) of Dr. Hamy's and Canerio's Charts. They are five in number, and form a chain less than 5 leagues in length. The three southern islands (Silva, do Fogo, and Crown) form a separate group, and are bare, whilst the two northern islands (Casuarina and Epidendron) have trees. Gama, apparently, missed the two southernmost islands.

[4] These six days are reckoned from February 24 to March 1.

Correa (Stanley's *Vasco da Gama*, pp. 76-84) says that on the voyage from the river of Mercy to Moçambique, Davane, a Moor, was taken out of a zambuk. Barros and Goes know nothing of this incident. Later on (p. 128) we are told that this Davane agreed to accompany the Portuguese as broker, and that he was finally dis-

On Thursday, the 1st of March, we sighted islands and the mainland, but as it was late we again stood out to sea, and lay to till morning. We then approached the land, of which I shall speak in what follows.

[*Moçambique.*][1]

On Friday morning [March 2] Nicolau Coelho, when attempting to enter the bay, mistook the channel and came upon a bank. When putting about ship, towards the other ships which followed in his wake, Coelho perceived some sailing boats approaching from a village on this island, in order to welcome the captain-major and his brother. As for ourselves we continued in the direction of our proposed anchorage, these boats following us all the while, and making signs for us to stop. When we had cast anchor in the roadstead of the island from which these boats had come, there approached seven or eight of them, including *almadias*, the people in them playing upon *anafils*.[2] They invited us to proceed further into the bay, offering to take us into port if we desired it. Those among them who boarded our ships ate and drank what we did, and went their way when they were satisfied.[3]

The captain thought that we should enter this bay in order that we might find out what sort of people we had to deal with; that Nicolau Coelho should go first in his vessel, to take soundings at the entrance, and that, if found practicable, we should follow him. As Coelho prepared to

---

charged at Cananor with good testimonials (p. 235). He was nicknamed "tayyib", which in Arabic means "good" (p. 132). See Appendix E.

[1] See plan on Map III. See also Stanley's *Vasco da Gama*, p. 80.

[2] Arabic, el Nafir, a sort of straight Moorish trumpet or tuba.

[3] They took their visitors for "Turks", or at all events for Mohammedans. All this changed after their true character had been discovered.

enter he struck the point of the island and broke his helm, but he immediately disengaged himself and regained deep water. I was with him at the time. When we were again in deep water we struck our sails and cast anchor at a distance of two bowshots from the village.[1]

The people of this country are of a ruddy complexion[2] and well made. They are Mohammedans, and their language is the same as that of the Moors.[3] Their dresses are of fine linen or cotton stuffs, with variously coloured stripes, and of rich and elaborate workmanship. They all wear *toucas* with borders of silk embroidered in gold. They are merchants, and have transactions with white Moors, four of whose vessels were at the time in port, laden with gold, silver, cloves, pepper, ginger, and silver rings, as also with quantities of pearls, jewels,[4] and rubies, all of which articles are used by the people of this country. We understood them to say that all these things, with the exception of the gold, were brought thither by these Moors; that further on, where we were going to, they abounded, and that precious stones, pearls and spices were so plentiful that there was no need to purchase them as they could be collected in baskets. All this we learned through a sailor the captain-major had with him, and who, having formerly been a prisoner among the Moors, understood their language.[5]

These Moors, moreover, told us that along the route which we were about to follow we should meet with numerous

---

[1] It appears from this that Vasco da Gama entered the port immediately on his arrival, and took up a position close to the town.

[2] "Ruivo", red, in the original. Castanheda, who made use of this Journal, substitutes baço, tawny, which is equally inapplicable.

[3] That is, Arabic. The "Moors" of the author are, in fact, either pure Arabs (white Moors) or Swahilis speaking Arabic.

[4] "Aljofar", cf. Arabic jauhar, johar, a jewel or precious stone (Burton).

[5] Barros says that Fernão Martins was their interpreter.

shoals; that there were many cities along the coast, and also an island, one half the population of which consisted of Moors and the other half of Christians,[1] who were at war with each other. This island was said to be very wealthy.

We were told, morever, that Prester John[2] resided not far from this place; that he held many cities along the coast, and that the inhabitants of those cities were great merchants and owned big ships. The residence of Prester John was said to be far in the interior, and could be reached only on the back of camels. These Moors had also brought hither two Christian captives from India.[3] This information, and many other things which we heard, rendered us so happy that we cried with joy, and prayed God to grant us health, so that we might behold what we so much desired.

In this place and island of Moncobiquy [Moçambique]

---

[1] The notions about the Christianity of India prevailing at that time in Portugal (and among the earlier navigators) will be referred to elsewhere. We may add that Vasco da Gama was instructed to find out a mighty sovereign, known as Prester John, said to be a Christian, but the situation of whose states was very uncertain.—KOPKE.

[2] On Prester John, see Zarncke (*Abhd. K. Sächs. G. der Wiss.*, 1876 and 1879), and G. Uzielli (*Boll. della Soc. Africana d'Italia*, 1892, viii). Vasco da Gama had no doubt received special instructions to inquire for that Christian potentate. At one time he was looked for inland from Benin, but the information received from Pero de Covilhão, whom King John had despatched overland to India, in 1487, no less than that furnished by Lucas Marcos, an Abyssinian priest, who came to Lisbon soon after Covilhão's departure, confirmed the Portuguese in the belief that the "Prester John" they were in quest of was the Emperor of Ethiopia, whose capital at that time was in Shoa. (See Covilhão's narrative, as given by *Alvarez*, Hakluyt Soc., 1881.)

[3] Barros calls them Abyssinians from the country of Prester John, and says that when they saw the image of the saint which formed the figure-head of the St. Gabriel, they knelt down and worshipped. The Abyssinian Christians, whatever their shortcomings, do not worship images, as is the practice of the Roman Church. These captives, therefore, must have been Indians, as stated by our author.

there resided a chief [senhor] who had the title of Sultan, and was like a vice-roy.[1] He often came aboard our ships attended by some of his people. The captain-major gave him many good things to eat, and made him a present of hats, *marlotas*,[2] corals and many other articles. He was, however, so proud that he treated all we gave him with contempt, and asked for scarlet cloth, of which we had none. We gave him, however, of all the things we had.

One day the captain-major invited him to a repast, when there was an abundance of figs and comfits, and begged him for two pilots to go with us. He at once granted this request, subject to our coming to terms with them. The captain-major gave each of them thirty mitkals[3] in gold and two *marlotas*, on condition that from the day on which they received this payment one of them should always remain on board if the other desired to go on land. With these terms they were well satisfied.

On Saturday, March 10, we set sail and anchored one league out at sea, close to an island,[4] where mass was said on Sunday, when those who wished to do so confessed and joined in the communion.

One of our pilots lived on the island, and when we had anchored we armed two boats to go in search of him. The captain-major went in one boat and Nicolau Coelho in the other. They were met by five or six boats (barcas) coming from the island, and crowded with people armed

---

[1] Barros calls this sheikh Zacoeja (Shah Khwajah ?).

[2] Marlota, a short dress of silk or wool worn in Persia and India. (Moura, *Vestig. da lingua Arab.*, sub "marlota.")

[3] A Mozambique matikal (miskal) weighs 4.41346 grammes (Antonio Nunes, *O livro dos Pesos*, 1554, p. 50, published at Lisbon, 1868), and its value in standard gold would consequently be about 12*s.*; elsewhere (p. 64) he makes this coin the equivalent of 467 reis, or about 11*s.* 4*d.* (*see* Index, under *Cruzado*).

[4] The island of S. Jorge.

with bows and long arrows and bucklers,[1] who gave them to understand by signs that they were to return to the town. When the captain saw this he secured the pilot whom he had taken with him, and ordered the bombards to fire upon the boats. Paulo da Gama, who had remained with the ships, so as to be prepared to render succour in case of need, no sooner heard the reports of the bombards than he started in the *Berrio*. The Moors, who were already flying, fled still faster, and gained the land before the *Berrio* was able to come up with them. We then returned to our anchorage.

The vessels of this country are of good size and decked. There are no nails, and the planks are held together by cords,[2] as are also those of their boats (barcos). The sails are made of palm-matting.[3] Their mariners have Genoese needles,[4] by which they steer, quadrants, and navigating charts.

---

[1] Tavolochinha, in the original, is an obsolete word, which from its etymology seems to refer to a defensive armour presenting a broad surface (tavola). Castanheda, in relating this incident, substitutes *escudo*—shield—whilst Goes and Osorio speak of *adargas* or *parmae*, that is, bucklers.—KOPKE.

[2] Tamiça, lit. "spatry-cord", popularly known as coir-rope. These "sewn boats" were already in use when the *Periplus of the Erythrean Sea* was written, and the town of Rhapta (from ῥάπτειν, *to sew*) derived its name from them. (See McCrindle, *The Commerce and Navigation of the Erythrean Sea*, p. 71).

[3] "Mats were the wings wherewith they lightly flew,
From certain palm-fronds wove by cunning hand."
Camoens, Canto I, st. 46.—Burton's Translation.

[4] The "Genoese needle" is, of course, the mariner's compass.—According to the "Mohit" of Admiral Sidi Ali ben Hosein (1554), published by Dr. Bittner and Dr. Tomascheck (Vienna, 1897), the pilots of the Indian Ocean determined relative latitudes by observing the altitudes of certain stars. The result was expressed, not in degrees as was done by the scientific astronomers of the day, but in *isbas* or

The palms of this country yield a fruit as large as a melon, of which the kernel is eaten.[1] It has a nutty flavour. There also grow in abundance melons and cucumbers, which were brought to us for barter.

On the day in which Nicolau Coelho entered the port, the Lord of the place came on board with a numerous suite. He was received well, and Coelho presented him with a red hood, in return for which the Lord handed him a black rosary, which he made use of when saying his prayers, to be held as a pledge. He then begged Nicolau Coelho for the use of his boat, to take him ashore. This was granted. And after he had landed he invited those

---

"fingers", each equivalent to 1° 42′ 50″. The instrument which they used consisted of three staffs. Two of these were moveable on a hinge, and were directed respectively upon the horizon, and the star the altitude of which it was desired to determine. A third staff (or an octant) was fixed at the end of the horizon-staff, and upon it the angle observed could be read off. Vasco da Gama brought one of these instruments with him to Portugal, but the astronomer of Cabral's expedition, who had been instructed to test its qualities, reported unfavourably (*Alguns documentos*, 1892, p. 122). Yet the results obtained by means of this instrument by the pilots of the Indian Ocean were very satisfactory, and the charts prepared by these very practical men were far more correct than the abortions produced by "scientific" Arab geographers. Parallels (at intervals of one-eighth of an *isba*) and meridians were marked upon these charts, and they were superior in this respect to the Portulani of the Mediterranean pilots. The meridians were probably drawn at intervals of *zams*, which were equal to one-eighth *isba*, or three hours' sail, or nearly thirteen of our sea-miles. It is quite possible, as suggested by Dr. Bittner, that these pilots also invented the cross-staff, for *balhestilho*, the name by which this instrument became known in Portugal, is more likely to be derived from the Arabic *al-balista* (altitude), than from the Latin *ballista*. Compare also Barros (*Dec. I*, liv. 4, c. 6), where an allusion is made to the instrument employed by the pilot who joined Vasco da Gama at Malindi. Barros says that the instrument consisted of three *taboas* or plates.

[1] This fruit is the coco-nut.

who had accompanied him to his house, where he gave them to eat. He then dismissed them, giving them a jar of bruised dates made into a preserve with cloves and cumin, as a present for Nicolau Coelho. Subsequently he sent many things to the captain-major. All this happened at the time when he took us for Turks or for Moors from some foreign land, for in case we came from Turkey he begged to be shown the bows of our country and our books of the Law. But when they learnt that we were Christians they arranged to seize and kill us by treachery. The pilot, whom we took with us, subsequently revealed to us all they intended to do, if they were able.

[*False Start and Return to Moçambique.*]

On Sunday [March 11] we celebrated mass beneath a tall tree on the island [of S. Jorge]. We returned on board and at once set sail, taking with us many fowls, goats and pigeons, which had been given us in exchange for small glass-beads.

On Tuesday [March 13] we saw high mountains rising on the other side of a cape. The coast near the cape was sparsely covered with trees, resembling elms. We were at that time over twenty leagues from our starting-place, and there we remained becalmed during Tuesday and Wednesday. During the following night we stood off shore with a light easterly wind, and in the morning [March 15] found ourselves four leagues abaft Moçambique, but we went again forward on that day until the evening, when we anchored once more close to the island [of S. Jorge] on which mass had been celebrated the preceding Sunday, and there we remained eight days waiting for a favourable wind.

During our stay here the King of Moçambique sent word that he wanted to make peace with us and to be our friend.

His ambassador was a white Moor and sharif,[1] that is priest, and at the same time a great drunkard.

Whilst at this place a Moor with his little son came on board one of our ships, and asked to be allowed to accompany us, as he was from near Mecca, and had come to Moçambique as pilot of a vessel from that country.

As the weather did not favour us it became necessary once more to enter the port of Moçambique, in order to procure the water of which we stood in need, for the watering place is on the mainland. This water is drunk by the inhabitants of the island, for all the water they have there is brackish.[2]

On Thursday [March 22] we entered the port, and when it grew dark we lowered our boats. At midnight the captain-major and Nicolau Coelho, accompanied by some of us, started in search of water. We took with us the Moorish pilot, whose object appeared to be to make his escape, rather than to guide us to a watering-place. As a matter of fact he either would not or could not find a watering-place, although we continued our search until morning. We then withdrew to our ships.

In the evening [March 23] we returned to the main land, attended by the same pilot. On approaching the watering-place we saw about twenty men on the beach. They were armed with assegais, and forbade our approach. The captain-major upon this ordered three bombards to be fired upon them, so that we might land. Having effected our landing, these men fled into the bush, and we

[1] The sharifs ("nobles") are the descendants of the Prophet, and although not "priests", they enjoy a certain religious rank. Strictly speaking, this title can be claimed only by the head of the family which descends from the Prophet in a direct line. All others can only claim the title of *Saiyid*, Lord. The "white" Moors are, of course, true Arabs.

[2] There are Government tanks now on the island, which are filled by the prisoners of Fort St. Sebastian.

took as much water as we wanted. When the sun was about to set we discovered that a negro belonging to João de Coimbra had effected his escape.

On Sunday morning, the 24th of March, being the eve of Lady Day, a Moor came abreast our ships, and [sneeringly] told us that if we wanted water we might go in search of it, giving us to understand that we should meet with something which would make us turn back. The captain-major no sooner heard this [threat] than he resolved to go, in order to show that we were able to do them harm if we desired it. We forthwith armed our boats, placing bombards in their poops, and started for the village [town]. The Moors had constructed palisades by lashing planks together, so that those behind them could not be seen. They were at the time walking along the beach, armed with assegais, swords,[1] bows, and slings, with which they hurled stones at us. But our bombards soon made it so hot for them that they fled behind their palisades; but this turned out to their injury rather than their profit. During the three hours that we were occupied in this manner [bombarding the town] we saw two men killed, one on the beach and the other behind the palisades. When we were weary of this work we retired to our ships to dine. They at once began to fly, carrying their chattels in *almadias* to a village on the mainland.

After dinner we started in our boats, in the hope of being able to make a few prisoners, whom we might exchange for the two Indian Christians whom they held captive and the negro who had deserted. With this object in view we chased an *almadia*, which belonged to the sharif and was laden with his chattels, and another in

---

[1] *Agonia*, Arabic *El Jumbiyah*, a crooked poniard, worn in the waist-belt.

which were four negroes.[1] The latter was captured by Paulo da Gama, whilst the one laden with chattels was abandoned by the crew as soon as they reached the land. We took still another *almadia* which had likewise been abandoned. The negroes we took on board our ships. In the *almadias* we found fine cotton-stuffs, baskets made of palm-fronds, a glazed jar containing butter, glass phials with scented water, books of the Law, a box containing skeins of cotton, a cotton net, and many small baskets filled with millet. All these things, with the exception of the books, which were kept back to be shown to the king, were given by the captain-major to the sailors who were with him and with the other captains.

On Sunday [March 25] we took in water, and on Monday we proceeded in our armed boats to the village, when the inhabitants spoke to us from their houses, they daring no longer to venture on the beach. Having discharged a few bombards at them we rejoined our ships.

On Tuesday [March 27] we left the town and anchored close to the islets of São Jorge,[2] where we remained for three days, in the hope that God would grant us a favourable wind.

[*Moçambique to Mombaça*].

On Thursday, the 29th of March, we left these islets of S. Jorge, and as the wind was light, we only covered twenty-eight leagues up to the morning of Saturday, the 31st of the month.[3]

In the morning of that day we were once more abreast

---

[1] Barros calls these captives "Moors", and the author himself does the same at a later stage of his Journal (see note, p. 37).

[2] That is S. Jorge, and the small islet of S. Thiago, 1¾ miles to the south.

[3] The text has 30th, but Saturday was the 31st.

of the land of the Moors, from which powerful currents had previously carried us.[1]

On Sunday, April 1, we came to some islands close to the mainland. The first of these we called *Ilha do Açoutado* ("Island of the flogged-one"), because of the flogging inflicted upon our Moorish pilot, who had lied to the captain on Saturday night, by stating that these islands were the mainland. Native craft take their course between these islands and the mainland, where the water is four fathoms deep, but we kept outside of them. These islands are numerous, and we were unable to distinguish one from the other; they are inhabited.

On Monday [April 2] we sighted other islands five leagues off the shore.[2]

On Wednesday, the 4th of April, we made sail to the N.W., and before noon we sighted an extensive country, and two islands close to it, surrounded with shoals. And when we were near enough for the pilots to recognise these islands, they told us that we had left three leagues behind us an island[3] inhabited by Christians. We manœuvred all day in the hope of fetching this island, but in vain, for the wind was too strong for us. After this we thought it best to bear away for a city called Mombaça, reported to be four days ahead of us.

The above island was one of those which we had come

---

1 These were the Kerimba islands, the southernmost of which is Kiziwa, 12° 35′ S. The mainland being generally low, will rarely be seen when coasting outside the reefs (*Africa Pilot*, Part III, p. 254).

2 These were the islands off Cabo Delgado, called Ilhas das Cabecas (Cabras ?) on Dr. Hamy's and Canerio's maps. None of these, however, is more than nine miles from the mainland.

3 This island was Quiloa (Kilwa), whose king, at that time, was the most powerful along the coast, Sofala, the Zambezi, Angoshe and Mozambique being subject to him (*Duarto Barbosa*, p. 10).—KOPKE.

When Vasco da Gama attempted to put back he had probably reached Ras Tikwiri, 8° 50′ S.

to discover, for our pilots said that it was inhabited by Christians.

When we bore away for the north it was already late, and the wind was high. At nightfall we perceived a large island, which remained to the north of us.[1] Our pilot told us that there were two towns on this island, one of Christians and the other of Moors.

That night we stood out to sea, and in the morning [April 5] we no longer saw the land. We then steered to the N.W., and in the evening we again beheld the land. During the following night we bore away to the N. by W., and during the morning-watch we changed our course to the N.N.W. Sailing thus before a favourable wind, the *S. Raphael*, two hours before break of day [April 6], ran aground on a shoal, about two leagues from the land. Immediately the *Raphael* touched bottom, the vessels following her were warned by shouts, and these were no sooner heard than they cast anchor about the distance of a gunshot from the stranded vessel, and lowered their boats. When the tide fell the *Raphael* lay high and dry. With the help of the boats many anchors were laid out, and when the tide rose again, in the course of the day, the vessel floated and there was much rejoicing.

On the mainland, facing these shoals, there rises a lofty range of mountains, beautiful of aspect. These mountains we called *Serras de São Raphael*, and we gave the same name to the shoals.[2]

---

[1] Mafia.—KOPKE.

[2] On the homeward voyage, in January 1499, the *S. Raphael* was burnt at these shoals, which are described as lying off the town of Tamugata (Mtangata), and this enables us to fix upon the locality with much certainty. There still is a roadstead or bay called Mtangata, which "the long roll of the Indian Ocean renders a place of trembling to the coast trader" (Burton, *Journal Royal Geographical Society*, 1858, p. 200). A "town" of this name exists no longer, but Burton describes

Whilst the vessel was high and dry, two *Almadias* approached us. One was laden with fine oranges, better than those of Portugal. Two of the Moors remained on board, and accompanied us next day to Mombaça.

On Saturday morning, the 7th of the month, and eve of Palm Sunday, we ran along the coast and saw some islands at a distance of fifteen leagues from the mainland, and about six leagues in extent. They supply the vessels of the country with masts. All are inhabited by Moors.[1]

[*Mombaça*].

On Saturday [April 7] we cast anchor off Mombaça, but did not enter the port. No sooner had we been perceived than a *zavra*[2] manned by Moors came out to us: in front of the city there lay numerous vessels all dressed in flags.[3] And we, anxious not to be outdone, also dressed

---

the ruins of what was once an extensive city near the village of Tongoni.

There are no "mountains" close to the coast corresponding to the "Serras de S. Raphael", but the mountains of Usambara, rising 20 to 25 miles inland to an altitude of 3,500 ft., are visible in clear weather for a distance of 62 miles.

Sir John Kirk writes to me: "The baixas de S. Raphael are undoubtedly the coral reefs of Mtangata; and the Usambara mountains, with their valleys, steep precipices, and lofty summits would especially at that season of the year, be plainly seen from the ships. There can be no doubt as to this point, as these are the only mountains that approach the coast and form so marked an object from the sea when the air is clear. They are then visible from the town of Zanzibar."

1 This was Pemba, which, owing to its deep bays, appeared to consist of a number of islands. Its distance from the mainland is only 30 miles (9 leagues), its length 37 miles. The trees of that island still supply masts for native vessels (Note by Sir J. Kirk).

2 Zavra or zabra, a dhow, which is a small open vessel, sharp at the stern, with a square sail of matting.

3 The Swahili "dress" their vessels at the feast that follows the Ramadan month (Sir J. Kirk), but Ramadan, of the year of the Hejra

our ships, and we actually surpassed their show, for we wanted in nothing but men, even the few whom we had being very ill. We anchored here with much pleasure, for we confidently hoped that on the following day we might go on land and hear mass jointly with the Christians reported to live there under their own *alcaide*[1] in a quarter separate from that of the Moors.

The pilots who had come with us told us there resided both Moors and Christians in this city; that these latter lived apart under their own lords, and that on our arrival they would receive us with much honour and take us to

Native Craft in the Harbour of Mombasa.
(*From a photograph by the late Capt. Foot, R.N.*)

their houses. But they said this for a purpose of their own, for it was not true. At midnight there approached us a *zavra* with about a hundred men, all armed with cutlasses (tarçados) and bucklers. When they came to the vessel of the captain-major they attempted to board her, armed as they were, but this was not permitted, only four or five of the most distinguished men among them being allowed

---

903, *began* on April 23, 1498, and the Bairam therefore lasted from May 22-24. These dates are according to the Old Style.

[1] *Alcaide*, from the Arabic *Alkadi*, the Judge.

on board. They remained about a couple of hours, and it seemed to us that they paid us this visit merely to find out whether they might not capture one or the other of our vessels.

On Palm Sunday [April 8] the King of Mombaça sent the captain-major a sheep and large quantities of oranges, lemons and sugar-cane, together with a ring, as a pledge of safety, letting him know that in case of his entering the port he would be supplied with all he stood in need of. This present was conveyed to us by two men, almost white, who said they were Christians, which appeared to be the fact. The captain-major sent the king a string of coral-beads as a return present, and let him know that he purposed entering the port on the following day. On the same day the captain-major's vessel was visited by four Moors of distinction.

Two men were sent by the captain-major to the king, still further to confirm these peaceful assurances. When these landed they were followed by a crowd as far as the gates of the palace. Before reaching the king they passed through four doors, each guarded by a doorkeeper with a drawn cutlass. The king received them hospitably, and ordered that they should be shown over the city. They stopped on their way at the house of two Christian merchants, who showed them a paper (carta), an object of their adoration, on which was a sketch ot the Holy Ghost.[1] When they had seen all, the king sent them back with samples of cloves, pepper and corn,[2] with which articles he would allow us to load our ships.

---

[1] Burton (*Camoens*, iv, p. 241) suggests that this picture of the Holy Ghost may have been a figure of Kapot-eshwar, the Hindu pigeon-god and goddess, an incarnation of Shiva and his wife, the third person of the Hindu Triad.

[2] Trigo tremez, corn that ripens in three months. This, according to a note furnished by Sir John Kirk, would be sorghum (the

On Tuesday [April 10], when weighing anchor to enter the port, the captain-major's vessel would not pay off, and struck the vessel which followed astern. We therefore again cast anchor. When the Moors who were in our ship saw that we did not go on, they scrambled into a *zavra* attached to our stern ; whilst the two pilots whom we had brought from Moçambique jumped into the water, and were picked up by the men in the *zavra*. At night the captain-major "questioned" two Moors [from Moçambique][1] whom we had on board, by dropping boiling oil upon their skin, so that they might confess any treachery intended against us. They said that orders had been given to capture us as soon as we entered the port, and thus to avenge what we had done at Moçambique. And when this torture was being applied a second time, one of the Moors, although his hands were tied, threw himself into the sea, whilst the other did so during the morning watch.

About midnight two *almadias*, with many men in them, approached. The *almadias* stood off whilst the men entered the water, some swimming in the direction of the *Berrio*, others in that of the *Raphael*. Those who swam to the *Berrio* began to cut the cable. The men on watch thought at first that they were tunny fish, but when they perceived their mistake they shouted to the other vessels. The other swimmers had already got hold of the rigging of the mizzen-mast. Seeing themselves discovered, they silently slipped down and fled. These and other wicked

"matama" of the Swahili), which is sent in shiploads to Arabia and the Persian Gulf.

[1] These two "Moors" were undoubtedly two of the four men whom Paulo da Gama had captured at Moçambique, but whom the author previously described as "Negroes". Of the two pilots who escaped, one had been given them by the Sultan of Moçambique, the other must have been the old Moor who came on board voluntarily, unless one of the men taken by Paulo was a pilot. (See note 1, p. 31).

tricks were practised upon us by these dogs, but our Lord did not allow them to succeed, because they were unbelievers.

Mombaça is a large city seated upon an eminence washed by the sea. Its port is entered daily by numerous vessels. At its entrance stands a pillar, and by the sea a low-lying fortress.[1] Those who had gone on

A Tower at Mombasa.
(*From a photograph by Sir John Kirk.*)

shore told us that in the town they had seen many men in irons; and it seemed to us that these must be Christians,

[1] Barros (*Dec. I*, liv. 8, c. 7) says erroneously that this fort was built *after* Vasco da Gama's visit. When the vessel of Sancho de Toar, of the armada of Pedro Alvarez Cabral, was lost near Mombaça, the Moors succeeded in fishing up seven or eight of her guns. These they placed in this fort, in the vain hope of being thus enabled to resist the attack of D. Francisco d'Almeida in 1505.—KOPKE.

as the Christians in that country are at war with the Moors.

The Christian merchants in the town are only temporary residents, and are held in much subjection, they not being allowed to do anything except by the order of the Moorish King.

It pleased God in his mercy that on arriving at this city all our sick recovered their health, for the climate ("air") of this place is very good.

After the malice and treachery planned by these dogs had been discovered, we still remained on Wednesday and Thursday [April 11 and 12].[1]

[*Mombaça to Malindi.*]

We left in the morning [April 13], the wind being light, and anchored about eight leagues from Mombaça, close to the shore. At break of day [April 14] we saw two boats (*barcas*) about three leagues to the leeward, in the open sea, and at once gave chase, with the intention of capturing them, for we wanted to secure a pilot who would guide us to where we wanted to go. At vesper-time we came up with one of them, and captured it, the other escaping towards the land. In the one we took we found seventeen men, besides gold, silver, and an abundance of maize and other provisions; as also a young woman, who was the wife of an old Moor of distinction, who was a passenger. When we came up with the boat they all threw themselves into the water, but we picked them up from our boats.

That same day [April 14] at sunset, we cast anchor off a

---

[1] Castanheda (*I*, c. 10, p. 35) says they waited two days in the hope of being able to secure a pilot to take them to Calecut. On crossing the bar they were unable to heave up one of the anchors. The Moors subsequently fished it up and placed it near the royal palace, where D. Francisco d'Almeida found it when he took the town in 1505.

place called Milinde (Malindi),[1] which is thirty leagues from Mombaça. The following places are between Mombaça and Milinde, viz., Benapa, Toça and Nuguoquioniete.[2]

[*Malindi.*][3]

On Easter Sunday [April 15] the Moors whom we had taken in the boat told us that there were at this city of Melinde four vessels belonging to Christians from India,[4] and that if it pleased us to take them there, they would provide us, instead of them, Christian pilots and all we stood in need of, including water, wood and other things. The captain-major much desired to have pilots from the country, and having discussed the matter with his Moorish prisoners, he cast anchor off the town, at a distance of about half a league from the mainland. The inhabitants of the town did not venture to come aboard our ships, for they had already learnt that we had captured a vessel and made her occupants prisoners.

On Monday morning [April 16] the captain-major had

---

[1] The author spells Milinde, Milynde, Milingue.

[2] Sir J. Kirk suggests to me that these places are Mtwapa, Takaungu and Kilifi, distorted into Benapa, Toca-nuguo and Quioniete. "Kioni" is the native name of the village usually called Kilifi.

[3] The ruins of the ancient town of Malindi lie to the south of the modern village of that name, and are of great extent. They include the remains of a town wall. Persian and Arabic inscriptions have been discovered, but, with the exception of Vasco da Gama's pillar, no traces of occupation by the Portuguese. Malindi Road, or Port Melinda of the Admiralty chart, lies about three miles to the south of the town, but Vasco da Gama anchored off the town, and not in this sheltered road. The anchorage is less than half a mile from the town in four fathoms and a half. Comp. Lord Stanley's *Vasco da Gama*, p. 109.

[4] Barros speaks of these Christians as Banyans, while Goes and Castanheda say that these vessels belonged to merchants from Cranganor, in Malabar,

the old Moor taken to a sandbank in front of the town, where he was picked up by an *almadia*.[1] The Moor explained to the king the wishes of the captain-major, and how much he desired to make peace with him. After dinner the Moor came back in a *zavra*, accompanied by one of the king's cavaliers and a sharif: he also brought three sheep. These messengers told the captain-general that the king would rejoice to make peace with him, and to enter into friendly relations; that he would willingly grant to the captain-major all his country afforded, whether pilots or anything else. The captain-major upon this sent word that he proposed to enter the port on the following day, and forwarded by the king's messengers a present consisting of a *balandrau*,[2] two strings of coral, three wash-hand basins, a hat, little bells and two pieces of *lambel*.[3]

Consequently, on Tuesday [April 17] we approached nearer to the town. The king sent the captain-major six sheep, besides quantities of cloves, cumin, ginger, nutmeg and pepper, as also a message, telling him that if he desired to have an interview with him he (the king) would come out in his *zavra*, when the captain-major could meet him in a boat.

On Wednesday [April 18], after dinner, when the king came up close to the ships in a *zavra*, the captain-major at once entered one of his boats, which had been well furnished, and many friendly words were exchanged when they lay side by side. The king having invited the captain-major to come to his house to rest, after which he

---

[1] Correa (p. 113) says that the Moor sent with this message was the Davane already referred to, and (p. 115) distinguishes him from the Moor who was captured on April 14th.

[2] *Balandrau*, a surtout worn by the Brothers of Mercy in Portugal.

[3] *Lambel*, a striped cotton stuff which had a large sale at the beginning of the African trade.—HERCULANO.

(the king) would visit him on board his ship, the captain-major said that he was not permitted by his master to go on land, and if he were to do so a bad report would be given of him. The king wanted to know what would be said of himself by his people if he were to visit the ships, and what account could he render them? He then asked for the name of our king, which was written down for him, and said that on our return he would send an ambassador with us, or a letter.

When both had said all they desired, the captain-major sent for the Moors whom he had taken prisoner, and surrendered them all. This gave much satisfaction to the king, who said that he valued this act more highly than if he had been presented with a town. And the king, much pleased, made the circuit of our ships, the bombards of which fired a salute. About three hours were spent in this way. When the king went away he left in the ship one of his sons and a sharif, and took two of us away with him, to whom he desired to show his palace. He, moreover, told the captain that as he would not go ashore he would himself return on the following day to the beach, and would order his horsemen to go through some exercises.

The king wore a robe (royal cloak) of damask trimmed with green satin, and a rich *touca*. He was seated on two cushioned chairs of bronze, beneath a round sunshade of crimson satin attached to a pole. An old man, who attended him as page, carried a short sword in a silver sheath. There were many players on *anafils*, and two trumpets of ivory,[1] richly carved, and of the size of a man,

---

[1] I am indebted for a photograph of one of these trumpets to Sir John Kirk, who states that the Royal Trumpet, or *Siwa*, was peculiar to the cities ruled by the descendants of the Persians of Shiraz, who settled on this coast in the eleventh and twelfth centuries. They were of ivory, or copper and wood, and consisted of three pieces. The

which were blown from a hole in the side, and made sweet harmony with the *anafils*.

A Siwa Blower.
(From a photograph by Sir John Kirk.)

---

ivory or copper was sometimes most elaborately carved, and bore Arabic texts.

On Thursday [April 19] the captain-major and Nicolau Coelho rowed along the front of the town, bombards having been placed in the poops of their long-boats. Many people were along the shore, and among them two horsemen, who appeared to take much delight in a sham-fight. The king was carried in a palanquin from the stone steps of his palace to the side of the captain-major's boats. He again begged the captain to come ashore, as he had a helpless father who wanted to see him, and that he and his sons would go on board the ships as hostages. The captain, however, excused himself.[1]

We found here four vessels belonging to Indian Christians. When they came for the first time on board Paulo da Gama's ship, the captain-major being there at the time, they were shown an altar-piece representing Our Lady at the foot of the cross, with Jesus Christ in her arms and the apostles around her. When the Indians saw this picture

[1] We learn from this passage that the "king" referred to by the author was in reality the king's son, who acted as regent. He may be supposed to be the Sheikh Wagerage (Wajeraj), who in 1515 wrote a letter to D. Manuel, in which he begged for permission to send annually *one* vessel to Goa and to Mozambique. He very humbly (or sarcastically?) addresses the king as the "fountain of the commerce of all cities and kingdoms, the most equitable of sovereigns, and the enricher of all people"; when, indeed, the Portuguese had crippled the trade of Malindi, which had received them with open arms. Another letter addressed to King Manuel was written by "Ali, King of Melinde", in 1520. Was this "king" the son of Wajeraj, or of the "prince who visited Vasco da Gama on board his vessel"? F. João de Sousa, who publishes these letters (*Documentos Arabicos*, Lisbon, 1790, pp. 67, 123), with a few comments, only obscures the point, unless indeed Wajeraj the Sheikh and Ali the Prince be one and the same person.

Cabral met a Sheikh Omar, a brother of the King of Malindi, who was present at Malindi when Vasco da Gama touched at that place; as also a Sheikh Foteima, an uncle of the king (Barros, *Dec. I*, liv. 5, c. 3).

On the ungenerous treatment dealt to the King of Malindi, see D. F. d'Almeida's letter of 1507 (Stanley's *Vasco da Gama*, p. 125).

they prostrated themselves, and as long as we were there they came to say their prayers in front of it, bringing offerings of cloves, pepper, and other things.[1]

These Indians are tawny men; they wear but little clothing and have long beards and long hair, which they braid. They told us that they ate no beef. Their language differs from that of the Arabs, but some of them know a little of it, as they hold much intercourse with them.

On the day on which the captain-major went up to the town in the boats, these Christian Indians fired off many bombards from their vessels, and when they saw him pass they raised their hands and shouted lustily *Christ! Christ!*[2]

That same night they asked the king's permission to give us a night-fête. And when night came they fired off many bombards, sent up rockets, and raised loud shouts.

These Indians warned the captain-major against going on shore, and told him not to trust to their "fanfares", as they neither came from their hearts nor from their good will.

On the following Sunday, the 22nd of April, the king's *zavra* brought on board one of his confidential servants, and as two days had passed without any visitors, the captain-major had this man seized, and sent word to the king that he required the pilots whom he had promised. The king, when he received this message, sent a Christian pilot,[3] and the captain-major allowed the gentleman, whom he had retained in his vessel, to go away.

---

[1] Of course they looked upon these Romish images and pictures as outlandish representations of their own gods or idols.

[2] Burton (*Camoens*, IV, p. 420) suggests that they cried *Krishna*, the name of the eighth Incarnation of Vishnu, the second person of the Hindu Trinity, and the most popular of Indian gods. Sir J. Kirk knows of no word resembling "Krist" likely to have been called out by these Indians.

[3] This pilot was a native of Gujarat, whom Goes (c. 38), Barros

We were much pleased with the Christian pilot whom the king had sent us. We learnt from him that the island of which we heard at Moçambique as being inhabited by Christians was in reality an island subject to this same King of Moçambique; that half of it belonged to the Moors and the other half to the Christians; that many pearls were to be found there, and that it was called Quyluee.[1] This is the island the Moorish pilots wanted to take us to, and we also wished to go there, for we believed that what they said was true.

The town of Malindi lies in a bay and extends along the shore. It may be likened to Alcouchette.[2] Its houses are lofty and well white-washed, and have many windows; on the landside are palm-groves, and all around it maize and vegetables are being cultivated.

We remained in front of this town during nine days,[3] and all this time we had fêtes, sham-fights, and musical performances ("fanfares").

[*Across the Gulf—the Arabian Sea.*]

We left Malindi on Tuesday, the 24th of the month [of April] for a city called Qualecut [Calecut], with the pilot whom the king had given us. The coast there runs north and south, and the land encloses a huge bay with a strait.

(*Dec. I*, liv. 4, c. 6), and Faria y Sousa call Malema Cana, or Canaqua. Malema is a corruption of Mallim, master or teacher, whilst Canaqua (Kanaka), is the name of his caste. It is also used for sailing master.

[1] The island in question is Kilwa. The information furnished by this Malindi pilot is scarcely more correct than that previously obtained from the Moors (see note 3, p. 32).

[2] Alcochete, a town on the left bank of the estuary of the Tagus, above Lisbon.

[3] From April 15 to 23 is nine days.

In this bay,[1] we were told, were to be found many large cities of Christians and Moors, including one called Quambay [Cambay], as also six-hundred known islands, and within it the Red Sea and the "house" [Kaabah] of Mecca.

On the following Sunday [April 29] we once more saw the North Star, which we had not seen for a long time.

On Friday, the 18th of May,[2] after having seen no land for twenty-three days,[3] we sighted lofty mountains, and having all this time sailed before the wind we could not have made less than 600 leagues. The land, when first sighted,[4] was at a distance of eight leagues, and our lead reached bottom at forty-five fathoms. That same night we took a course to the S.S.W., so as to get away from the coast. On the following day [May 19] we again approached the land, but owing to the heavy rain and a thunderstorm,[5] which prevailed whilst we were sailing along the coast, our pilot was unable to identify the exact locality. On Sunday [May 20] we found ourselves close to some mountains,[6] and when we were near enough for the pilot to recognise

---

[1] The "Bay" is the Arabian Sea, which the "Strait" of Bab el Mandeb joins to the Red Sea. Cambay (Khambhat), in Gujarat, when the Portuguese first came to India, was one of the most flourishing marts of commerce. The silting up of the Gulf accounts, in a large measure, for its commercial decline since then.

[2] The MS. says 17th, but Friday was the 18th.

[3] From April 24 to May 18, both days inclusive, is twenty-five days; the African coast was within sight for several days.

[4] Mount Eli (Dely) was probably the land first sighted, a conspicuous hill forming a promontory about 16 miles to the north of Cananor, and named thus from the Cardamoms which are largely exported from this part of Malabar, and are called Ela in Sanscrit (Yule's *Marco Polo*, ii, p. 321).

[5] The rains in Malabar begin about April or May, and continue until September or October. They are synchronous with the S.W. monsoon, and are heaviest in June, July, and August. The annual rainfall exceeds 150 inches!

[6] Cotta Point, or Cape Kadalur, the "Monte Formosa", of the Portuguese, 15 miles N.N.W. of Calecut.

them he told us that they were above Calecut, and that this was the country we desired to go to.

[*Calecut.*]

[*Arrival.*] That night [May 20] we anchored two leagues from the city of Calecut, and we did so because our pilot mistook *Capua*,[1] a town at that place, for Calecut. Still further[2] there is another town called *Pandarani*.[3] We anchored about a league and a half from the shore. After we were at anchor, four boats (*almadias*) approached us from the land, who asked of what nation we were. We told them, and they then pointed out Calecut to us.

On the following day [May 21] these same boats came again alongside, when the captain-major sent one of the convicts[4] to Calecut, and those with whom he went took him to two Moors from Tunis, who could speak Castilian and Genoese.[5] The first greeting that he received was in these words: "May the Devil take thee! What brought you hither?" They asked what he sought so far away from home, and he told them that we came in search of Christians and of spices. They said: "Why does not the

---

[1] Castanheda and Barros call this place Capocate. It was seven miles N.N.W. of Calecut, at the mouth of the Elatur River.

[2] The MS. says "abaixo", below, with reference no doubt to the latitude, which is less than that of Calecut.

[3] Pandaramy (Pandarani) is Batuta's Fandarain. Barros calls it Pandarane. It is identical with Pantharini Kollam, the northern Kollam or Quillan, and boasts one of the nine original mosques built on the Malabar coast by Malik Ibn Dinar. It is 14 miles N.N.W. of Calecut. The author of the MS. elsewhere spells Pandaramy and Pandarin.

[4] According to Correa (Stanley's *Vasco da Gama*, p. 159), his name was João Nunez. See Appendix E.

[5] One of the "Moors" is frequently referred to as "Monçaide". See Appendix E.

King of Castile, the King of France, or the Signoria of Venice send hither?" He said that the King of Portugal would not consent to their doing so, and they said he did the right thing. After this conversation they took him to their lodgings and gave him wheaten bread and honey. When he had eaten he returned to the ships, accompanied by one of the Moors, who was no sooner on board, than he said these words: "A lucky venture, a lucky venture! Plenty of rubies, plenty of emeralds! You owe great thanks to God, for having brought you to a country holding such riches!" We were greatly astonished to hear his talk, for we never expected to hear our language spoken so far away from Portugal.[1]

[*A description of Calecut.*] The city of Calecut is inhabited by Christians. They are of a tawny complexion. Some of them have big beards and long hair, whilst others clip their hair short or shave the head, merely allowing a tuft to remain on the crown as a sign that they are Christians. They also wear moustaches. They pierce the ears and wear much gold in them. They go naked down to the waist, covering their lower extremities with very fine cotton stuffs. But it is only the most respectable who do this, for the others manage as best they are able.[2]

The women of this country, as a rule, are ugly and of small stature. They wear many jewels of gold round the neck, numerous bracelets on their arms, and rings set with

---

[1] Castanheda (I, c. 15) retails the conversation which this Moor is supposed to have had with Gama on board ship, and says that the captain-major was much pleased with his offers of service.

[2] The visitors thus became at once acquainted with the various castes constituting the population of Calecut, including the *Nairs*, or fighting caste of Malabar, who eat meat (which shows a servile origin), but wear the thread of the Dwija (twice-born), rank next to the Brahmans, and practise polyandry; and the turbulent *Moplah*, who are descendants of Arab fathers and native women. These latter are the "native" Moors.

precious stones on their toes. All these people are well-disposed and apparently of mild temper. At first sight they seem covetous and ignorant.

[*A messenger sent to the King*]. When we arrived at Calecut the king was fifteen leagues away.[1] The captain-major sent two men[2] to him with a message, informing him that an ambassador had arrived from the King of Portugal with letters, and that if he desired it he would take them to where the king then was.

The king presented the bearers of this message with much fine cloth. He sent word to the captain bidding him welcome, saying that he was about to proceed to Qualecut (Calecut). As a matter of fact he started at once with a large retinue.

[*At Anchor at Pandarani*, May 27]. A pilot accompanied our two men, with orders to take us to a place called Pandarani, below the place [Capua] where we anchored at first. At this time we were actually in front of the city of Calecut. We were told that the anchorage at the place to which we were to go was good, whilst at the place we were then it was bad, with a stony bottom, which was quite true;[3] and, moreover, that it was customary for the ships which came to this country to anchor there for the sake of safety. We ourselves did not feel comfortable, and the captain-major had no sooner received this royal message than he ordered the sails to be set, and we departed. We did not, however, anchor as near the shore as the king's pilot desired.

---

1 Goes (I, c. 39) and Castanheda (I, c. 15) say that he was at Panane, a coast town, 28 miles to the south of Calecut.

2 One of these messengers was Fernão Martins. They were accompanied by Monçaide (Castanheda, I, c. 15).

3 Off Calecut there are banks and reefs which may endanger the safety of a ship, but the anchorage in the roadstead within them is perfectly safe.

When we were at anchor, a message arrived informing the captain-major that the king was already in the city. At the same time the king sent a *bale*,[1] with other men of distinction, to Pandarani, to conduct the captain-major to where the king awaited him. This *bale* is like an *alcaide*, and is always attended by two hundred men armed with swords and bucklers. As it was late when this message arrived, the captain-major deferred going.

[*Gama goes to Calecut.*] On the following morning, which was Monday, May 28th, the captain-major set out to speak to the king, and took with him thirteen men, of whom I was one.[2] We put on our best attire, placed bombards in our boats, and took with us trumpets and many flags. On landing, the captain-major was received by the *alcaide*, with whom were many men, armed and unarmed. The reception was friendly, as if the people were pleased to see us, though at first appearances looked threatening, for they carried naked swords in their hands. A palanquin was provided for the captain-major, such as is used by men of distinction in that country, as also by some of the merchants, who pay something to the king for this privilege. The captain-major entered the palanquin, which was carried by six men by turns. Attended by all

---

[1] *Bale* in the Arabic Wali, governor. *Alcaide*, in Portuguese, has this same meaning. Barros and Castanheda give this official the title of "Catual" (Kot-wal, governor of a fort, in Hindustani). He was the civil intendant of the Rajah and head of the police. Correa calls him *gosil*, or *guozil* (pron. Wozil), a corruption, probably, of the Arabic *wazir*, minister.

[2] Among the thirteen men were Diogo Dias, João de Sá, Gonçalo Pirez, Alvaro Velho, Alvaro de Braga, João de Setubal, João de Palha, and six others, whose names are not recorded. Paulo da Gama and Coelho were left in charge of the vessels, with orders to sail at once for Portugal should any disaster happen to their chief. Coelho was, moreover, ordered to await his chief's return in the boats. See Appendix E.

these people we took the road of Qualecut, and came first to another town, called Capua. The captain-major was there deposited at the house of a man of rank, whilst we others were provided with food, consisting of rice, with much butter, and excellent boiled fish. The captain-major did not wish to eat, and when we had done so, we embarked on a river close by, which flows between the sea and the mainlaind, close to the coast.[1] The two boats in which we embarked were lashed together,[2] so that we were not separated. There were numerous other boats, all crowded with people. As to those who were on the banks I say nothing; their number was infinite, and they had all come to see us. We went up that river for about a league, and saw many large ships drawn up high and dry on its banks, for there is no port here.

When we disembarked, the captain-major once more entered his palanquin. The road was crowded with a countless multitude anxious to see us. Even the women came out of their houses with children in their arms and followed us.

[*A Christian Church.*][3] When we arrived [at Calecut] they took us to a large church, and this is what we saw:—

The body of the church is as large as a monastery, all built of hewn stone and covered with tiles. At the main entrance rises a pillar of bronze as high as a mast, on the top of which was perched a bird, apparently a cock. In

---

[1] This river is the Elatur. See Map IV.

[2] Burton (*Goa*, p. 191) says that even now the usual ferry-boat consists of a platform of planks lashed to two canoes and usually railed round.

[3] This "church" was, of course, a pagoda or temple. The high pillar in front of it is used for suspending the flag which indicates the commencement of the Temple festival. It is of wood, but usually covered with copper or silver. The cock, which surmounts it, is the symbol of the War-god Subraumainar. The smaller pillar supports the coco-oil lamps during the festival.—Rev. J. J. Jaus.

addition to this, there was another pillar as high as a man, and very stout. In the centre of the body of the church rose a chapel,[1] all built of hewn stone, with a bronze door sufficiently wide for a man to pass, and stone steps leading up to it. Within this sanctuary stood a small image which

Krishna nursed by Devaki.

they said represented Our Lady.[2] Along the walls, by

[1] Corucheo, which literally means spire or minaret; but further on the author calls this sanctuary a chapel, capella. Goes (c. 40) calls it a "round" chapel.

[2] Goes (c. 40) says that the four priests alone entered this sanctuary, and, pointing to the image, said "Maria, Maria", upon which the natives prostrated themselves, whilst the Portuguese knelt, in adoration of the Virgin. Burton suggests that this was an image of Gauri, the "White Goddess", whilst Charton (III, p. 246) suggests Maha Maja and her son Shakya. Our illustration is taken from E. Moor, *The*

the main entrance, hung seven small bells.[1] In this church the captain-major said his prayers, and we with him.[2]

We did not go within the chapel, for it is the custom that only certain servants of the church, called *quafees*,[3] should enter. These *quafees* wore some threads passing over the left shoulder and under the right arm, in the same manner as our deacons wear the stole. They threw holy water over us, and gave us some white earth,[4] which the Christians of this country are in the habit of putting on their foreheads, breasts, around the neck, and on the forearms. They threw holy water upon the captain-

---

Hindu Pantheon, new edition by Rev. W. O. Simpson (Madras, 1864) Plate xxxv. It represents Krishna and his mother Devaki. When Kansa (Devaki's brother) heard of his birth, he ordered all newly-born infants to be slain. The trays with animals and fruit are supposed to symbolise Krishna's power over the animal and vegetable kingdoms. On the low table are placed food, poison, and amrita, symbolising life, death, and immortality, as also a small triangular die denoting trinity in unity.

The Rev. J. Jacob Jaus, of the Baṣel Mission at Calicut, informs me that there is a local deity called Māṛi, or Māriaṃma, much dreaded as the goddess of small-pox, and highly venerated. Amma, in Malayalam, means mother.

[1] These bells are struck by the Brahmans when they enter the temple, but must not be touched by people of inferior castes.

[2] It is just possible that some of the Portuguese doubted whether these Hindu Gods and images represented the saints of their own churches. Castanheda (i, p. 57) says that when João de Sá knelt down by the side of Vasco da Gama, he said: "If these be devils, I worship the true God"; at which his chief smiled. But however this may be, it is equally true that the reports furnished by the heads of the expedition described these Hindus as Christians, and that the king believed them to be so (see Appendix A.).

[3] The "quafees" are, of course, Brahman priests. The Rev. J. J. Jaus suggests *kāz* (Arabic), meaning "judge".

[4] The "white earth" is a mixture of dust, cow-dung, sacrificial ashes, sandal wood, etc., cemented in rice-water (see Belnos, *The Sundya or Daily Prayer of the Brahmans*, Lond., 1851).

major and gave him some of the earth, which he gave in charge of someone, giving them to understand that he would put it on later.

Many other saints were painted on the walls of the church, wearing crowns. They were painted variously, with teeth protruding an inch from the mouth, and four or five arms.

Below this church there was a large masonry tank, similar to many others which we had seen along the road.

[*Progress through the Town.*] After we had left that place, and had arrived at the entrance to the city [of Calecut] we were shown another church, where we saw things like those described above. Here the crowd grew so dense that progress along the street became next to impossible, and for this reason they put the captain into a house, and us with him.

The king sent a brother of the *bale*, who was a lord of this country, to accompany the captain, and he was attended by men beating drums, blowing *anafils* and bagpipes, and firing off matchlocks. In conducting the captain they showed us much respect, more than is shown in Spain to a king. The number of people was countless, for in addition to those who surrounded us, and among whom there were two thousand armed men, they crowded the roofs and houses.

[*The King's Palace.*][1] The further we advanced in the direction of the king's palace, the more did they increase in number. And when we arrived there, men of much distinction and great lords came out to meet the captain, and joined those who were already in attendance upon him. It was then an hour before sunset. When we reached the palace we passed through a gate into a courtyard of great

---

[1] For a description of this palace, see *Travels of Pietro della Valle* (Hakluyt Society, 1892), pp. 367-377.

size, and before we arrived at where the king was, we passed four doors, through which we had to force our way, giving many blows to the people. When, at last, we reached the door where the king was, there came forth from it a little old man, who holds a position resembling that of a bishop, and whose advice the king acts upon in all affairs of the church. This man embraced the captain when he entered the door. Several men were wounded at this door,[1] and we only got in by the use of much force.

[*A Royal Audience, May 28.*][2] The king was in a small court, reclining upon a couch covered with a cloth of green velvet, above which was a good mattress, and upon this again a sheet of cotton stuff, very white and fine, more so than any linen. The cushions were after the same fashion. In his left hand the king held a very large golden cup [spittoon], having a capacity of half an almude [8 pints]. At its mouth this cup was two palmas [16 inches] wide, and apparently it was massive. Into this cup the king threw the husks of a certain herb which is chewed by the people of this country because of its soothing effects, and which they call *atambor*.[3] On the right side of the king stood a basin of gold, so large that a man might just encircle it with his arms: this contained the herbs. There were likewise many silver jugs. The canopy above the couch was all gilt.

---

[1] Goes says that knives were used.

[2] For Correa's elaborate but quite untrustworthy narrative of this audience, see Stanley's *Vasco da Gama*, pp. 193-6.

[3] Atambor, a corruption of the Arabic *tambur*, the betel-nut. It is the fruit of Areca Catechu, and is universally chewed throughout India, the Indian Archipelago and Southern China. Its juice discolours the teeth, but is said to make the breath sweet, and to be conducive to health. "Erva" (herb) is quite inapplicable to this fruit. Usually it is cut up into four slices, which are wrapped up in a leaf of Betel-pepper (Piper Betle), and chewed with an admixture of lime and catechu.

The captain, on entering, saluted in the manner of the country : by putting the hands together, then raising them towards Heaven, as is done by Christians when addressing God, and immediately afterwards opening them and shutting the fists quickly. The king beckoned to the captain with his right hand to come nearer, but the captain did not approach him, for it is the custom of the country for no man to approach the king except only the servant who hands him the herbs, and when anyone addresses the king he holds his hand before the mouth, and remains at a distance. When the king beckoned to the captain he looked at us others, and ordered us to be seated on a stone bench near him, where he could see us. He ordered that water for our hands should be given us, as also some fruit, one kind of which resembled a melon, except that its outside was rough and the inside sweet, whilst another kind of fruit resembled a fig, and tasted very nice.[1] There were men who prepared these fruits for us; and the king looked at us eating, and smiled; and talked to the servant who stood near him supplying him with the herbs referred to.

Then, throwing his eyes on the captain, who sat facing him, he invited him to address himself to the courtiers present, saying they were men of much distinction, that he could tell them whatever he desired to say, and they would repeat it to him (the king). The captain-major replied that he was the ambassador of the King of Portugal, and the bearer of a message which he could only deliver to him personally. The king said this was good, and immediately asked him to be conducted to a chamber. When the captain-major had entered, the king, too, rose and joined him, whilst we remained where we were.[2] All

[1] These fruits were the Jack (*Artocarpus integrifolia*) and bananas.

[2] According to Goes (c. 41), Gama was attended by his interpreter, Fernão Martins, whilst the king was attended by the head Brahman,

this happened about sunset. An old man who was in the court took away the couch as soon as the king rose, but allowed the plate to remain. The king, when he joined the captain, threw himself upon another couch, covered with various stuffs embroidered in gold, and asked the captain what he wanted.

And the captain told him he was the ambassador of a King of Portugal, who was Lord of many countries and the possessor of great wealth of every description, exceeding that of any king of these parts; that for a period of sixty years his ancestors had annually sent out vessels to make discoveries in the direction of India, as they knew that there were Christian kings there like themselves. This, he said, was the reason which induced them to order this country to be discovered, not because they sought for gold or silver, for of this they had such abundance that they needed not what was to be found in this country. He further stated that the captains sent out travelled for a year or two, until their provisions were exhausted, and then returned to Portugal, without having succeeded in making the desired discovery. There reigned a king now whose name was Dom Manuel, who had ordered him to build three vessels, of which he had been appointed captain-major, and who had ordered him not to return to Portugal until he should have discovered this King of the Christians, on pain of having his head cut off. That two letters[1] had been

---

his betle carrier, and his factor (veador da fazenda), who, he said, were persons in his confidence.

[1] These are, of course, the letters referred to by Barros and other historians, which were given to Gama when he left Portugal. Correa's story, that Vasco and his brother Paulo concocted the letters whilst off Calecut, and forged the king's signature, is therefore quite incredible. Nor is Gama made to say in the "Roteiro" that he had been sent with a fleet of fifty ships, and that the voyage took two years (Stanley's *Vasco da Gama*, pp. 168, 173). The "grand" Vasco has many sins to answer for, and we ought not, without good proof, to fasten upon him

intrusted to him to be presented in case he succeeded in discovering him, and that he would do so on the ensuing day; and, finally, he had been instructed to say by word of mouth that he [the King of Portugal] desired to be his friend and brother.

In reply to this the king said that he was welcome; that, on his part, he held him as a friend and brother, and would send ambassadors with him to Portugal. This latter had been asked as a favour, the captain pretending that he would not dare to present himself before his king and master unless he was able to present, at the same time, some men of this country.

These and many other things passed between the two in this chamber, and as it was already late in the night, the king asked the captain with whom he desired to lodge, with Christians or with Moors? And the captain replied, neither with Christians nor with Moors, and begged as a favour that he be given a lodging by himself. The king said he would order it thus, upon which the captain took leave of the king and came to where we were, that is, to a veranda lit up by a huge candlestick. By that time four hours of the night had already gone.[1]

[*A Night's Lodging.*] We then all went forth with the captain in search of our lodgings, and a countless crowd with us. And the rain poured down so heavily that the streets ran with water. The captain went on the back of six men [in a palanquin], and the time occupied in passing through the city was so long that the captain at last grew tired, and complained to the king's factor, a Moor of distinction, who attended him to the lodgings. The Moor then took him to his own house,[2] and we were admitted

---

the charge of forgery. As to truthfulness, that seems not to have been a strong point with the diplomatists of that age.

[1] That is, it was about 10 P.M.

[2] This was done to afford shelter until the rain should have ceased.

to a court within it, where there was a veranda roofed in with tiles. Many carpets had been spread, and there were two large candlesticks like those at the Royal palace. At the top of each of these were great iron lamps, fed with oil or butter, and each lamp had four wicks, which gave much light. These lamps they use instead of torches.

This same Moor then had a horse brought for the captain to take him to his lodgings, but it was without a saddle, and the captain refused to mount it.[1] We then started for our lodgings, and when we arrived we found there some of our men [who had come from the ships] with the captain's bed, and with numerous other things which the captain had brought as presents for the king.[2]

[*Presents for the King.*] On Tuesday [May 29] the captain got ready the following things to be sent to the king, viz., twelve pieces of *lambel*,[3] four scarlet hoods, six hats, four strings of coral, a case containing six wash-hand basins, a case of sugar, two casks of oil, and two of honey. And as it is the custom not to send anything to the king without the knowledge of the Moor, his factor, and of the *bale*, the captain informed them of his intention. They came, and when they saw the present they laughed at it, saying that it was not a thing to offer to a king, that the poorest merchant from Mecca, or any other part of India, gave more, and that if he wanted to make a present it should be in gold, as the king would not accept such things. When the captain heard this he grew sad, and said that he had brought no gold, that, moreover, he was no merchant, but an ambassador; that he gave of that which he had, which

---

[1] It is still the practice in Calecut to ride horses without a saddle, and no slight seems therefore to have been intended.

[2] According to G. Correa's not very credible narrative, the captain slept at the factory, which had been established previously to the audience of which an account has just been given.

[3] *Lambel*, striped cloth, see p. 41, note 3.

was his own [private gift] and not the king's;[1] that if the King of Portugal ordered him to return he would intrust him with far richer presents; and that if King Çamolim[2] would not accept these things he would send them back to the ships. Upon this they declared that they would not forward his presents, nor consent to his forwarding them himself. When they had gone there came certain Moorish merchants, and they all depreciated the present which the captain desired to be sent to the king.

When the captain saw that they were determined not to forward his present, he said, that as they would not allow him to send his present to the palace he would go to speak to the king, and would then return to the ships. They approved of this, and told him that if he would wait a short time they would return and accompany him to the palace. And the captain waited all day, but they never came back. The captain was very wroth at being among so phlegmatic and unreliable a people, and intended, at first, to go to the palace without them. On further consideration, however, he thought it best to wait until the following day. As to us others, we diverted ourselves, singing and dancing to the sound of trumpets, and enjoyed ourselves much.

[*A Second Audience, May* 30.] On Wednesday morning the Moors returned, and took the captain to the palace, and us others with him. The palace was crowded with armed men. Our captain was kept waiting with his conductors for fully four long hours, outside a door, which was only

---

1 As a matter of fact, Vasco da Gama was very poorly provided with suitable merchandise, as may be seen from the king's letter printed in the Appendix.

2 Barros writes Çamorij; Correa, Samori and Çamorin, and others Zamorin. It is a title; according to some a corrupt reading of Tamuri Rajah, Tamuri being the name of the most exalted family of the Nair caste, whilst others derive it from "Samudriya Rajah", that is, "King of the Coast" (see G. P. Badger's *Varthema*, pp. lxii and 137).

opened when the king sent word to admit him, attended by two men only, whom he might select. The captain said that he desired to have Fernão Martins with him, who could interpret, and his secretary.[1] It seemed to him, as it did to us, that this separation portended no good.

When he had entered, the king said that he had expected him on Tuesday. The captain said that the long road had tired him, and that for this reason he had not come to see him. The king then said that he had told him that he came from a very rich kingdom, and yet had brought him nothing; that he had also told him that he was the bearer of a letter, which had not yet been delivered. To this the captain rejoined that he had brought nothing, because the object of his voyage was merely to make discoveries, but that when other ships came he would then see what they brought him; as to the letter, it was true that he had brought one, and would deliver it immediately.

The king then asked what it was he had come to discover: stones or men? If he came to discover men, as he said, why had he brought nothing? Moreover, he had been told that he carried with him the golden image of a Santa Maria. The captain said that the Santa Maria was not of gold, and that even if she were he would not part with her, as she had guided him across the ocean, and would guide him back to his own country. The king then asked for the letter. The captain said that he begged as a favour, that as the Moors wished him ill and might misinterpret him, a Christian able to speak Arabic should be sent for. The king said this was well, and at once sent for a young man, of small stature, whose name was Quaram. The captain then said that he had two letters, one written in

[1] Whom others call his "veador", that is butler or comptroller of the household.

his own language and the other in that of the Moors; that he was able to read the former, and knew that it contained nothing but what would prove acceptable; but that as to the other he was unable to read it, and it might be good, or contain something that was erroneous. As the Christian was unable to *read* Moorish, four Moors took the letter and read it between them, after which they translated it to the king, who was well satisfied with its contents.

The king then asked what kind of merchandise was to be found in his country. The captain said there was much corn, cloth, iron, bronze, and many other things. The king asked whether he had any merchandise with him. The captain replied that he had a little of each sort, as samples, and that if permitted to return to the ships he would order it to be landed, and that meantime four or five men would remain at the lodgings assigned them. The king said no! He might take all his people with him, securely moor his ships, land his merchandise, and sell it to the best advantage. Having taken leave of the king the captain returned to his lodgings, and we with him. As it was already late no attempt was made to depart that night.

[*Return to Pandarani, May* 31.] On Thursday morning a horse without a saddle was brought to the captain, who declined to mount it, asking that a horse of the country, that is a palanquin, might be provided, as he could not ride a horse without a saddle. He was then taken to the house of a wealthy merchant of the name of Guzerate,[1] who ordered a palanquin to be got ready. On its arrival the captain started at once for Pandarani, where our ships were, many people following him. We others, not being able to keep up with him, were left behind. Trudging thus along we were overtaken by the *bale*, who passed on to join the captain. We lost our way, and wandered far inland, but

[1] That is, a man of Guzerat.

the *bale* sent a man after us, who put us on the right road. When we reached Pandarani we found the captain inside a rest-house, of which there were many along the road, so that travellers and wayfarers might find protection against the rain.

[*Detention at Pandarani, May* 31 *to June* 2.] The *bale* and many others were with the captain. On our arrival the captain asked the *bale* for an *almadia*, so that we might go to our ships; but the *bale* and the others said that it was already late—in fact, the sun had set—and that he should go next day. The captain said that unless he provided an *almadia* he would return to the king, who had given orders to take him back to the ships, whilst they tried to detain him—a very bad thing, as he was a Christian like themselves. When they saw the dark looks of the captain they said he was at liberty to depart at once, and that they would give him thirty *almadias* if he needed them. They then took us along the beach, and as it seemed to the captain that they harboured some evil design, he sent three men in advance, with orders that in case they found the ship's boats and his brother, to tell him to conceal himself. They went, and finding nothing, turned back; but as we had been taken in another direction we did not meet.

They then took us to the house of a Moor—for it was already far in the night—and when we got there they told us that they would go in search of the three men who had not yet returned. When they were gone, the captain ordered fowls and rice to be purchased, and we ate, notwithstanding our fatigue, having been all day on our legs.

Those who had gone [in search of the three men] only returned in the morning, and the captain said that after all they seemed well disposed towards us, and had acted with the best intentions when they objected to our departure the day before. On the other hand we suspected them on account of what had happened at Calecut, and looked upon them as ill-disposed.

When they returned [June 1] the captain again asked for boats to take him to his ships. They then began to whisper among themselves, and said that we should have them if we would order our vessels to come nearer the shore. The captain said that if he ordered his vessels to approach his brother would think that he was being held a prisoner, and that he gave this order on compulsion, and would hoist the sails and return to Portugal. They said that if we refused to order the ships to come nearer we should not be permitted to embark. The captain said that King Çamolin had sent him back to his ships, and that as they would not let him go, as ordered by the king, he should return to the king, who was a Christian like himself. If the king would not let him go, and wanted him to remain in his country, he would do so with much pleasure. They agreed that he should be permitted to go, but afforded him no opportunity for doing so, for they immediately closed all the doors, and many armed men entered to guard us, none of us being allowed to go outside without being accompanied by several of these guards.

They then asked us to give up our sails and rudders. The captain declared that he would give up none of these things: King Çamolin having unconditionally ordered him to return to his ships, they might do with him whatever they liked, but he would give up nothing.

The captain and we others felt very down-hearted, though outwardly we pretended not to notice what they did. The captain said that as they refused him permission to go back, they would at least allow his men to do so, as at the place they were in they would die of hunger. But they said that we must remain where we were, and that if we died of hunger we must bear it, as they cared nothing for that. Whilst thus detained, one of the men whom we had missed the night before turned up. He told the captain that Nicolau Coelho had been awaiting him with the boats since last night. When the captain heard this he sent a man away secretly to Nicolau Coelho, because of the guards by whom we were surrounded, with orders to go back to the ships and place them in a secure place. Nicolau Coelho, on receipt of this message, departed forthwith But our guards having information of what was going on, at once launched a large number of *almadias* and pursued him for a short distance. When they found that they could not overtake him they returned to the captain, whom they asked to write a letter to his brother, requesting him to bring the ships nearer to the land and further within the port [roadstead]. The captain said he was quite willing, but that his brother would not do this ; and that even if he consented those who were with him, not being willing to die, would not do so. But they asked how this could be, as they knew well that any order he gave would be obeyed.

The captain did not wish the ships to come within the port, for it seemed to him—as it did to us—that once inside they could easily be captured, after which they would first kill him, and then us others, as we were already in their power.

We passed all that day most anxiously. At night more people surrounded us than ever before, and we were no longer allowed to walk in the compound, within which we were, but confined within a small tiled court, with a multitude of people around us. We quite expected that on the following day we should be separated, or that some harm would befall us, for we noticed that our gaolers were much annoyed with us. This, however, did not prevent our making a good supper off the things found in the village. Throughout that night we were guarded by over a hundred men, all armed with swords, two-edged battle-axes,[1] shields, and bows and arrows. Whilst some of these slept, others kept guard, each taking his turn of duty throughout the night.

On the following day, Saturday, June 2, in the morning, these gentlemen [*i.e.*, the *bale* and others] came back, and this time they "wore better faces." They told the captain that as he had informed the king that he intended to land his merchandise, he should now give orders to have this done, as it was the custom of the country that every ship on its arrival should at once land the merchandise it brought, as also the crews, and that the vendors should not return on board until the whole of it had been sold. The captain consented, and said he would write to his brother to see to its being done. They said this was well, and that immediately after the arrival of the merchandise he would be permitted to return to his ship. The captain at once wrote to his brother to send him certain things, and he did so at once. On their receipt the captain was allowed to go on board, two men remaining behind with the things that had been landed.[2]

At this we rejoiced greatly, and rendered thanks to God for having extricated us from the hands of people who had no more sense than beasts, for we knew well that once the captain was on board those who had been landed would have nothing to fear. When the captain reached his ship he ordered that no more merchandise should be sent.

[*The Portuguese Merchandise at Pandarani, June* 2-23.]

Five days afterwards [on June 7] the captain sent word to the king that, although he had sent him straight back to

---

[1] "Bisarma" in the original. Herculano accepts the definition of Spelmann (*v.* Ducange, *sub* bisarma).

[2] These men were Diogo Dias, as factor, and Alvaro de Braga as his assistant (Castanheda, I, 74.)

his ships, certain of his people had detained him a night and a day on the road ; that he had landed his merchandise as he had been ordered, but that the Moors only came to depreciate it ; and that for these reasons he looked forward to what he (the king) would order ; that he placed no value upon this merchandise, but that he and his ships were at his service. The king at once sent word saying that those who acted thus were bad Christians, and that he would punish them. He, at the same time, sent seven or eight merchants to inspect the merchandise, and to become purchasers if they felt inclined. He also sent a man of quality to remain with the factor already there, and authorised them to kill any Moor who might go there, without fear of punishment.

The merchants whom the king had sent remained about eight days, but instead of buying they depreciated the merchandise. The Moors no longer visited the house where the merchandise was, but they bore us no good-will, and when one of us landed they spat on the ground, saying: "Portugal, Portugal." Indeed from the very first they had sought means to take and kill us.

When the captain found that the merchandise found no buyers at that place, he applied to the king for permission to forward it to Calecut. The king at once ordered the *bale* to get a sufficient number of men who were to carry the whole on their backs to Calecut, this to be done at his expense, as nothing belonging to the King of Portugal was to be burthened with expenses whilst in his country. But all this was done because it was intended to do us some ill-turn, for it had been reported to the king that we were thieves and went about to steal. Nevertheless, he did all this in the manner shown.

[*The Merchandise removed to Calecut, June* 24.]

On Sunday, the 24th of June, being the day of St. John the Baptist, the merchandise left for Calecut. The captain then ordered that all our people should visit that town by turns, and in the following manner:—Each ship was to send a man ashore, on whose return another should be sent. In this way all would have their turn, and would be able to make such purchases as they desired. These men were made welcome by the Christians along the road, who showed much pleasure when one of them entered a house, to eat or to sleep, and they gave them freely of all they had. At the same time many men came on board our ships to sell us fish in exchange for bread, and they were made welcome by us. Many of them were accompanied by their sons and little children, and the captain ordered that they should be fed. All this was done for the sake of establishing relations of peace and amity, and to induce them to speak well of us and not evil. So great was the number of these visitors that sometimes it was night before we could get rid of them; and this was due to the dense population of the country and the scarcity of food. It even happened that when some of our men were engaged in mending a sail, and took biscuits with them to eat, that old and young fell upon them, took the biscuits out of their hands, and left them nothing to eat.

In this manner all on board ship went on land by twos and threes, taking with them bracelets, clothes, new shirts, and other articles, which they desired to sell. We did not, however, effect these sales at the prices hoped for when we arrived at Moncobiquy [Moçambique], for a very fine shirt which in Portugal fetches 300 reis, was worth here only two fanôes,[1] which is equivalent only to 30 reis, for

[1] The fanão of Calecut (according to Nunes, *O Livro dos Pesos*, 1554) is worth 25$\frac{5}{9}$ reis, or 7.45d. Three hundred reis of the coinage of 1485 were of the value of 7s. 7d., taking the gold cruzado at 9s. 8d.

30 reis in this country is a big sum. And just as we sold shirts cheaply so we sold other things, in order to take some things away from this country, if only for samples. Those who visited the city bought there cloves, cinnamon, and precious stones ; and having bought what they desired they came back to the ships, without any one speaking to them.

When the captain found the people of the country so well disposed, he left a factor with the merchandise, together with a clerk and some other men.

[*Diogo Dias Carries a Message to the King, August 13.*]

When the time arrived for our departure the captain-major sent a present to the king, consisting of amber, corals, and many other things. At the same time he ordered the king to be informed that he desired to leave for Portugal, and that if the king would send some people with him to the King of Portugal, he would leave behind him a factor, a clerk and some other men, in charge of the merchandise. In return for the present he begged on behalf of his lord [the King of Portugal] for a bahar[1] of cinnamon, a bahar of cloves, as also samples of such other spices as he thought proper, saying that the factor would pay for them, if he desired it.

Four days were allowed to pass after the dispatch of this message before speech could be had with the king. And when the bearer of it entered the place where the king was, he (the king) looked at him with a "bad face," and asked what he wanted. The bearer then delivered his message, as explained above, and then referred to the present which had been sent. The king said that what he brought ought to have been sent to his factor, and that he did not want to look at it. He then desired the captain to be informed that as he wished to depart he should pay him 600

[1] The bahar at Calecut is equivalent to 208.16 kilogrammes (Nunes, *O Livro dos Pesos.*)

xerafins,[1] and that then he might go: this was the custom of the country and of those who came to it. Diogo Dias, who was the bearer of the message, said he would return with this reply to the captain. But when he left [the palace] certain men followed him, and when he arrived at the house in Calecut where the merchandise was deposited, they put a number of men inside with him to watch that none of it was sent away. At the same time proclamation was made throughout the town prohibiting all boats from approaching our ships.

When they [the Portuguese] saw that they were prisoners, they sent a young negro who was with them along the coast to seek for some one to take him to the ships, and to give information that they had been made prisoners by order of the king. The negro went to the outskirts of the town, where there lived some fishermen, one of whom took him on board, on payment of three fanões. This the fisherman ventured to do because it was dark, and they could not be seen from the city; and when he had put his passenger on board he at once departed. This happened on Monday, the 13th August, 1498.

This news made us sad; not only because we saw some of our men in the hands of our enemies, but also because it interfered with our departure. We also felt grieved that a Christian king, to whom we had given of ours, should do us such an ill turn. At the same time we did not hold him as culpable as he seemed to be, for we were well aware that the Moors of the place, who were merchants from Mecca and elsewhere, and who knew us, could ill digest us. They had told the king that we were thieves, and that if once we navigated to his country, no more ships from Mecca, nor from Quambaye [Cam-

---

[1] The xerafin at Calecut is worth about 7s. 5d.; the sum demanded therefore amounted to £223.

bay], nor from Imgros,[1] nor from any other part, would visit him. They added that he would derive no profit from this [trade with Portugal] as we had nothing to give, but would rather take away, and that thus his country would be ruined. They, moreover, offered rich bribes to the king to capture and kill us, so that we should not return to Portugal.

All this the captain learnt from a Moor of the country,[2] who revealed all that was intended to be done, warning the captains, and more especially the captain-major, against going on shore. In addition to what we learnt through the Moor, we were told by two Christians that if the captains went ashore their heads would be cut off, as this was the way the king dealt with those who came to his country without giving him gold.

Such then was the state of affairs. On the next day [August 14] no boats came out to the ships. On the day after that [August 15] there came an *almadia*, with four young men, who brought precious stones for sale; but it appeared to us that they came rather by order of the Moors, in order to see what we should do to them, than for the purpose of selling stones. The captain, however, made them welcome, and wrote a letter to his people on shore, which they took away with them. When the people saw that no harm befell them, there came daily many merchants, and others who were not merchants, from curiosity, and all were made welcome by us and given to eat.

On the following Sunday [August 19] about twenty-five men came. Among them were six persons of quality, and the captain perceived that through these we might recover the men who were detained as prisoners on land. He there-

---

[1] Can this be Ormuz?

[2] This Moor was Monçaide; elsewhere more accurately referred to as "a Moor of Tunis". See Appendix E.

fore laid hands upon them, and upon a dozen of the others, being eighteen[1] in all. The rest he ordered to be landed in one of his boats, and gave them a letter to be delivered to the king's Moorish factor, in which he declared that if he would restore the men who were being kept prisoners he would liberate those whom he had taken. When it became known that we had taken these men, a crowd proceeded to the house where our merchandise was kept, and conducted our men to the house of the factor, without doing them any harm.

On Thursday, the 23rd,[2] of the same month, we made sail, saying we were going to Portugal, but hoped to be back soon, and that then they would know whether we were thieves. We anchored about four leagues to the leeward of Calecut, and we did this because of the head-wind.

On the next day [August 23] we returned towards the land, but not being able to weather certain shoals in front of Calecut, we again stood off and anchored within sight of the city.

On Saturday [August 25] we again stood off and anchored so far out at sea that we could scarcely see the land. On Sunday [August 26] whilst at anchor, waiting for a breeze, a boat which had been on the look-out for us approached, and informed us that Diogo Dias was in the king's house, and that if we liberated those whom we detained, he should be brought on board. The captain, however, was of opinion that he had been killed, and that they said this in order to detain us until they had completed their armaments, or until ships of Mecca able to capture us had arrived. He therefore bade them retire,

---

[1] The author says nineteen; but it appears from what precedes that there were only eighteen in all. See Appendix E.

[2] The author says Wednesday, but that day was the 22nd.

threatening otherwise to fire his bombards upon them, and not to return without bringing him [Dias] and his men, or at least a letter from them. He added that unless this were done quickly he intended to take off the heads of his captives. A breeze then sprang up, and we sailed along the coast until we anchored.

[*The King sends for Diogo Dias.*]

When the king heard that we had sailed for Portugal, and that he was thus no longer able to carry his point, he thought of undoing the evil he had done. He sent for Diogo Dias, whom he received with marked kindness, and not in the way he did when he was the bearer of [Vasco's] present. He asked why the captain had carried off these men. Diogo Dias said it was because the king would not allow him and his to return to the ships, and detained them as prisoners in the city. The king said he had done well. He then asked whether his factor had asked for anything,[1] giving us to understand that he was ignorant of the matter, and that the factor alone was responsible for this extortion. Turning to his factor, he asked whether he was unaware that quite recently he had killed another factor because he had levied tribute upon some merchants that had come to this country? The king then said: "Go you back to the ships, you and the others who are with you; tell the captain to send me back the men he took; that the pillar, which I understood him to say he desires to be erected on the land shall be taken away by those who bring you back, and put up; and, moreover, that you will remain here with the merchandise." At the same time he forwarded a letter to the captain, which had been written for him by Diogo Dias with an iron pen upon a palm-leaf, as is the custom

[1] A reference to the 600 xerafins.

of the country, and which was intended for the King of Portugal. The tenor[1] of this letter was as follows:—

"Vasco da Gama, a gentleman of your household, came to my country, whereat I was pleased. My country is rich in cinnamon, cloves, ginger, pepper, and precious stones. That which I ask of you in exchange is gold, silver, corals and scarlet cloth."

[*Off Calecut, August* 27-30.] On Monday, the 27th of this month, in the morning, whilst we were at anchor, seven boats with many people in them brought Diogo Dias and the other [Portuguese] who were with him. Not daring to put him on board, they placed him in the captain's long boat, which was still attached to the stern. They had not brought the merchandise, for they believed that Diogo Dias would return with them. But once the captain had them back on board, he would not allow them to return to the land. The pillar[2] he gave to those in the boat, as the king had given orders for it to be set up. He also gave up, in exchange, the six most distinguished among his prisoners, keeping six others, whom he promised to surrender if on the morrow the merchandise were restored to him.

On Tuesday [August 28], in the morning, whilst at anchor, a Moor of Tunis,[3] who spoke our language, took refuge on board one of our ships, saying, that all he had had been taken from him, that worse might happen, and that this was his usual luck. The people of the country, he said, charged him with being a Christian, who had come to Calecut by order of the King of Portugal; for this

---

1 The "tenor", not the literal phraseology; and hence the absence of the complimentary verbiage so usual with Orientals must not be interpreted as an intentional insult to the King of Portugal.

2 This pillar was dedicated to S. Gabriel. There exists apparently no record of its having actually been set up by the king, as promised.

3 This "Moor of Tunis", according to Castanheda (I, c. 24, p. 8), was Bontaibe (Monçaide), concerning whom see Appendix E.

reason he preferred going away with us, rather than remain in a country where any day he might be killed.

At ten o'clock seven boats with many people in them approached us. Three of them carried on their benches the striped cloth which we had left on land, and we were given to understand that this was all the merchandise which belonged to us.[1] These three came to within a certain distance of the ships, whilst the other four kept away. We were told that if we sent them their men in one of our boats they would give our merchandise in exchange for them. However, we saw through their cunning, and the captain-major told them to go away, saying that he cared nought for the merchandise, but wanted to take these men to Portugal.[2] He warned them at the same time to be careful, as he hoped shortly to be back in Calecut, when they would know whether we were thieves, as had been told them by the Moors.

On Wednesday, the 29th [of August], the captain-major and the other captains agreed that, inasmuch that we had discovered the country we had come in search of, as also spices and precious stones, and it appeared impossible to establish cordial relations with the people, it would be as well to take our departure. And it was resolved that we should take with us the men whom we detained, as, on our return to Calecut, they might be useful to us in establishing friendly relations. We therefore set sail and left for Portugal, greatly rejoicing at our good fortune in having made so great a discovery.

On Thursday [August 30], at noon, being becalmed

---

[1] As a matter of fact, it was only a portion of what had been landed, and Cabral was instructed to demand payment from the Samorin for what had not been returned (*Alguns documentos*, p. 98).

[2] Five of these men of Calecut were actually taken to Lisbon. They were restored to their country by Cabral (see *Alguns documentos*, p. 97).

about a league below [that is, north of] Calecut, about seventy boats approached us.[1] They were crowded with people wearing a kind of cuirass made of red cloth, folded. Their weapons for the body, the arms and the head were these[2] . . . . When these boats came within the range of our bombards, the captain-major ordered us to fire upon them. They followed us for about an hour and a half, when there arose a thunderstorm which carried us out to sea; and when they saw they could no longer do us harm they turned back, whilst we pursued our route.

[*Calecut and its Commerce.*]

From this country of Calecut, or Alta India,[3] come the spices which are consumed in the East and the West, in Portugal, as in all other countries of the world, as also precious stones of every description. The following spices are to be found in this city of Calecut, being its own produce: much ginger and pepper and cinnamon, although the last is not of so fine a quality as that brought from an island called Çillan [Ceylon],[4] which is eight days journey from Calecut. Calecut is the staple for all this cinnamon. Cloves are brought to this city from an island called Melequa [Malacca].[5] The Mecca vessels carry these spices

---

[1] Castanheda calls these "barcas", *tones.* The "tone" is a rowing boat, the planks of which are "sewn" together.

[2] A note by the copyist says:—"The author has omitted to tell us how these weapons were made."

[3] The country of Prester John (Abyssinia) was known as "Lower India."

[4] Ceylon cinnamon still enjoys this pre-eminence, its cultivation in other parts of the world not having hitherto been attended with success. The "cinnamon", or cassia, found in Malabar is of very inferior quality.

[5] The Moluccas, and more especially Amboina, are the true home of the clove, the cultivation of which is now carried on widely in different parts of the world.

from there to a city in Mecca[1] called Judeâ [Jidda], and from the said island to Judeâ is a voyage of fifty days sailing before the wind, for the vessels of this country cannot tack. At Judeâ they discharge their cargoes, paying customs duties to the Grand Sultan.[2] The merchandise is then transshipped to smaller vessels, which carry it through the Red Sea to a place close to Santa Catarina of Mount Sinai, called Tuuz,[3] where customs dues are paid once more. From that place the merchants carry the spices on the back of camels, which they hire at the rate of 4 cruzados each, to Quayro [Cairo], a journey occupying ten days. At Quayro duties are paid again. On this road to Cairo they are frequently robbed by thieves, who live in that country, such as the Bedouins and others.

At Cairo the spices are embarked on the river Nile, which rises in Prester John's country in Lower India, and descending that river for two days they reach a place called Roxette [Rosetta], where duties have to be paid once more. There they are placed on camels, and are conveyed in one day to a city called Alexandria, which is a sea-port. This city is visited by the galleys of Venice and Genoa, in search of these spices, which yield the Grand Sultan a revenue of 600,000 cruzados[4] in customs duties, out of which he pays to a king called Cidadym[5] an annual

---

[1] Should be Arabia.

[2] The "Grand Sultan" is, of course, the Circassian Mamluk Sultan of Egypt.

[3] Prof. Kopke rashly identifies this place with Suez, but M. F. Denis points out that it must be Tor.

[4] The cruzado was a Portuguese gold coin worth about 9s. 8d.; 600,000 cruzados amounted thus to £290,000.

[5] This Cidadym (called Cadadin in the *Commentaries of Afonso Dalbuquerque*, Hakluyt Society, 1875, i, p. 202) can be identified with Sultan Muhammed ben Azhar ed-din ben Ali ben Abu Bekr ben Sa'd ed din, of Harar, who ruled 1487-1520 (see Paulitschke, *Harar*, p. 506).

subsidy of 100,000 cruzados for making war upon Prester John. The title of Grand Sultan is bought for money, and does not pass from father to son.

[THE VOYAGE HOME.]

I now again speak of our voyage home.

Going thus along the coast we kept tacking, with the aid of the land and sea breezes, for the wind was feeble. When becalmed in the day we lay to.

On Monday, September 10, the captain-major landed one of the men whom we had taken, and who had lost an eye, with a letter to the Çamolin, written in Moorish [Arabic] by one of the Moors who came with us.[1] The country where we landed this Moor was called Compia,[2] and its king, Biaquotte, was at war with the King of Calecut.

On the following day [September 11], whilst becalmed, boats approached the ships, and the boatmen, who offered fish for sale, came on board without exhibiting any fear.

---

[1] Castanheda (I, c. 25, p. 84) says that Monçaide wrote this letter, in which Vasco da Gama apologised for having carried off the Malabaris; explained that he had done so in order that they might bear witness to the discoveries he had made; and said that he would have left a factor behind him if he had not been afraid that the Moors would kill him. He expressed a hope that ultimately friendly relations would be established to their mutual advantage. Goes (c. 43), who also gives a version of this letter, says the king was much pleased with it, and read it to his wives and the relatives of the kidnapped men.

[2] Burton (*Camoens*) identifies Compia with Cananor, which, on the partition of the dominions of Cherman Perumal was included in the kingdom of the Chirrakal Rajahs. From João de Sousa (*Documentos Arabicos*, p. 80) we learn that the king with whom Vasco da Gama made a treaty in 1502 was called Cotelery. Correa (Stanley's *Vasco da Gama*, p. 224) gives a circumstantial account of Vasco da Gama's transactions with the king of Cananor during this first voyage. Neither Goes nor Barros knows anything about these events.

[*Santa Maria Islands.*][1]

On Saturday, the 15th of said month, we found ourselves near some islets, about two leagues from the land. We there launched a boat and put up a pillar on one of these islets, which we called Santa Maria, the king having ordered three pillars (padrãos), to be named S. Raphael, S. Gabriel, and Santa Maria. We had thus succeeded in erecting these three, *scilicet*, the first, that of S. Raphael, on the Rio dos bons signaes; the second, that of S. Gabriel, at Calecut; and this, the last, named Santa Maria.

Here again many boats came to us with fish, and the captain made the boatmen happy by presenting them with shirts. He asked them whether they would be glad if he placed a pillar upon the island. They said that they would be very glad indeed, for its erection would confirm the fact that we were Christians like themselves. The pillar was consequently erected in much amity.

[*Anjediva, September* 20 *to October* 5.][2]

That same night, with a land breeze, we made sail and pursued our route. On the following Thursday, the 20th of the month,[3] we came to a hilly country, very beautiful and salubrious, close to which there were six small islands.

---

[1] These are the Netrani or Pigeon Islands (Ilhas dos Pombos), in lat. 14° 1′ N., the largest being about half a mile in length, and rising to a height of 300 feet.

[2] The Anjediva or "Five Islands" lie close to the coast in 14° 45′ N., and about 40 miles to the south of Goa. The largest of these is not quite a mile in length. It rises boldly from the sea, but a beach on its northern side affords facilities for landing. D. Francisco de Almeida built a fort there in 1505, but it was demolished seven months afterwards. The existing fortifications were erected by order of Francisco de Tavora, Conde d'Alvar, in 1682. (See A. Lopez Mendes, *A India Portugueza*, ii, 1886, p. 209, with map.)

[3] The author says 19th, but Thursday was the 20th.

There we anchored, near the land, and launched a boat to take in water and wood to last us during our voyage across the Gulf, which we hoped to accomplish, if the wind favoured us. On landing we met a young man, who pointed out to us a spring of excellent water rising between two hills on the bank of a river. The captain-major gave this man a cap, and asked whether he was a Moor or a Christian. The man said that he was a Christian, and when told that we too were Christians he was much pleased.

On the following day [September 21] an *almadia* came to us with four men, who brought gourds and cucumbers. The captain-major asked whether cinnamon, ginger, or any other spices were to be found in this country. They said there was plenty of cinnamon, but no other kind of spice. The captain at once sent two men with them to the mainland to bring him a sample, and they were taken to a wood where a large number of trees yielding cinnamon were growing, and they cut off two big branches, with their foliage. When we went in our boats to fetch water we met these two men with their cinnamon branches, and they were accompanied by about twenty others, who brought the captain fowls, cow-milk and gourds. They asked the captain to send these two men along with them, as there was much dry cinnamon not far off, which they would show them, and of which they would bring samples.[1]

Having taken in water we returned to the ships, and these men promised to come on the ensuing day to bring a present of cows, pigs and fowls.

Early on the next morning [September 22] we observed two vessels close to the land, about two leagues off, but took no further notice of them. We cut wood whilst waiting

---

[1] These branches and leaves were carried to Portugal, as we learn from the king's letter (see Appendix A), but they had most certainly not been taken from true cinnamon trees, for only an inferior cassia is found in that part of India.

for the tide to enable us to enter the river to take in water, and being thus engaged it struck the captain that these vessels were larger than he had thought at first. He therefore ordered us into the boats, as soon as we had eaten, and sent us to find out whether these vessels belonged to Moors or Christians. After his return on board, the captain-major ordered a mariner to go aloft and look out for vessels, and this man reported that out in the open sea and at a distance of about six leagues he saw eight vessels becalmed. The captain, when he heard this, at once gave orders to sink these vessels. They, as soon as they felt the breeze, put the helm hard a-lee, and when they were abreast of us, at a distance of a couple of leagues, and we thought they might discover us, we made for them. When they saw us coming they bore away for the land. One of them being disabled, owing to her helm breaking, the men in her made their escape in the boat, which they dragged astern, and reached the land in safety. We, who were nearest to that vessel, at once boarded her, but found nothing in her except provisions, coco-nuts, four jars of palm-sugar, and arms, all the rest being sand used as ballast. The seven other vessels grounded, and we fired upon them from our boats.

On the following morning [September 23], whilst at anchor, seven men in a boat visited us, and they told us that these vessels had come from Calecut in search of us, and that if they had succeeded in taking us we should have been killed.[1]

On the following morning, having left this place, we anchored at a distance of two bombard-shots from the

---

[1] Barros and Goes say that the leader of these vessels was a pirate named Timoja, whose head-quarters were at Onor. He subsequently rendered valuable services to the Portuguese. (See Stanley's *Vasco da Gama*, p. 244.)

place at which we had been at first, and close to an island, where we had been told that water would be found.[1] The captain-major at once sent Nicolau Coelho in an armed boat in search for this watering place. He came there upon the ruins of a large stone church which had been destroyed by the Moors, with the exception of a chapel which had been roofed with straw. This, at least, was told us by the natives of the country, who prayed there to three black stones which stood in the middle of the chapel.[2] Beside this church we discovered a tank of the same workmanship as the church itself—that is, built of hewn stone—from which we took as much water as we needed. Another tank, of large size and four fathoms deep, occupied the highest part of the island. On the beach, in front of the church, we careened the *Berrio* and the ship of the captain-major. The *Raphael* was not drawn up on the beach, on account of difficulties which will be referred to further on.

Being one day in the *Berrio*, which was drawn up on the beach, there approached two large boats, or *fustas*,[3] crowded with people. They rowed to the sound of drums and bagpipes, and displayed flags at the masthead. Five other boats remained on the coast for their protection. As they came nearer we asked the people whom we had with us who they were. They told us not to allow them to come on board, as they were robbers who would seize us if they could. The people of this country, they said, carried arms and boarded vessels as if they came as friends, and having succeeded, and feeling strong enough, they laid hands upon them. For this reason they were fired upon from the *Raphael* and the captain-major's ship, as soon as they

[1] This island was the largest of the Anjediva.

[2] Three lingams, emblems of the generative power?

[3] The *fusta* is a galley or undecked rowing boat, with one mast. For an illustration see Linschoten's *Itinerarium ofte Schip-vaert*, etc.

came within range of our bombards. They began to shout "Tambaram,"[1] which meant that they were Christians, for the Christians of India call God "Tambaram." When they found that we took no notice of this, they fled towards the land. Nicolau Coelho pursued them for a short distance, when he was recalled by a signal flag on the ship of the captain-major.

On the following day, whilst the captain and many of our people were on land, careening the *Berrio*, there arrived two small boats with a dozen well-dressed men in them, who brought a bundle of sugar-cane as a present for the captain-major. After they had landed they asked permission to see the ships. The captain thought they were spies, and grew angry. Just then two other boats, with as many people, made their appearance, but those who had come first, seeing that the captain was not favourably disposed towards them, warned these new-comers not to land, but to turn back. They, too, re-embarked at once, and went away.

Whilst the ship of the captain-major was being careened there arrived a man,[2] about forty years of age, who spoke Venetian well. He was dressed in linen, wore a fine *touca* on his head, and a sword in his belt. He had no sooner landed than he embraced the captain-major and the captains, and said that he was a Christian from the west, who had come to this country in early youth; that he was now in the service of a Moorish lord,[3] who could muster 40,000 horsemen; that he, too, had become a Moor, although at heart still a Christian. He said that, being one day at his master's house, news was brought that men had

[1] Tambaram, in Malayalam, has merely the meaning of lord or master.

[2] This man subsequently became known as Gaspar da Gama. See Appendix E.

[3] The Sabayo or Governor of Goa.

arrived at Calecut, whose speech none could understand, and who were wholly clad; that when he heard this he said that these strangers must be Franks, for this is the name by which we [Europeans] are known in these parts. He then begged permission of his master to be allowed to visit us, saying that a refusal would cause him to die of sorrow. His master thereupon had told him to go and tell us that we might have anything in his country which suited us, including ships and provisions, and that if we desired to remain permanently it would give him much pleasure. When the captain had cordially thanked him for these offers, which appeared to him to have been made in good faith, our visitor asked as a favour that a cheese be given him, which he desired to take to one of his companions who had remained on the mainland, as a token that all had gone well. The captain ordered a cheese and two soft loaves to be given to him. He remained on the island, talking so much and about so many things, that at times he contradicted himself.

Paulo da Gama, in the meanwhile, had sought the Christians who had come with this visitor, and asked who he was. They said he was a pirate (*armador*), who had come to attack us, and that his ships, with many people in them, had remained on the coast. Knowing this much, and conjecturing the rest, we seized him, took him to the vessel drawn up on the beach, and there began to thrash him, in order to make him confess whether he was really a pirate, or what was the object with which he had come to us. He then told us that he was well aware that the whole country was ill-disposed towards us, and that numbers of armed men were around, hidden within the creeks, but that they would not for the present venture to attack us, as they were expecting some forty vessels which were being armed to pursue us. He added that he did not know when they would be ready to attack us. As to himself he said nothing except what he had said at first. Afterwards he was "questioned"[1] three or four times, and although he did not definitely say so, we understood from his gestures that he had come to see the ships, so that he might know what sort of people we were, and how we were armed.

At this island we remained twelve days, eating much fish, which was brought for sale from the mainland, as also many pumpkins and cucumbers. They also brought us boat-loads of green cinnamon-wood with the leaves still on. When our ships had been careened, and we had taken in as much water as we needed, and had broken up the vessel which we had captured, we took our departure. This happened on Friday, October 5.[2]

Before the vessel referred to was broken up, its captain offered us 1000 fanões for it, but the captain-major said that it was not for sale, and as it belonged to an enemy he preferred to burn it.

When we were about two hundred leagues out at sea, the Moor whom we had taken with us declared that the time for dissembling was now past. It was true that he had heard at the house of his master that we had lost ourselves along the coast, and were unable to find our way home; that for this reason many vessels had been despatched to capture us; and that his master had sent him to find out what we were doing and to entice us to his country, for if a privateer had taken us he would not have received a share of the booty, whilst if we had landed within his territory we should have been completely in

---

[1] The original MS. uses the verb "perguntar", that is, to question; but Barros says that he was tortured, and this would account for his attempting to make himself understood by "gestures", when previously he had spoken very fluently, and had been understood.

[2] September 24 to October 5 is twelve days, both days inclusive.

his power, and being valiant men, he could have employed us in his wars with the neighbouring kings. This reckoning, however, was made without the host.

[*The Voyage across the Arabian Sea.*]

Owing to frequent calms and foul winds it took us three months less three days to cross this gulf,[1] and all our people again suffered from their gums, which grew over their teeth, so that they could not eat. Their legs also swelled, and other parts of the body, and these swellings spread until the sufferer died, without exhibiting symptoms of any other disease. Thirty of our men died in this manner—an equal number having died previously—and those able to navigate each ship were only seven or eight, and even these were not as well as they ought to have been. I assure you that if this state of affairs had continued for another fortnight, there would have been no men at all to navigate the ships. We had come to such a pass that all bonds of discipline had gone. Whilst suffering this affliction we addressed vows and petitions to the saints on behalf of our ships. The captains had held council, and they had agreed that if a favourable wind enabled us we would return to India whence we had come.

But it pleased God in his mercy to send us a wind which, in the course of six days, carried us within sight of land, and at this we rejoiced as much as if the land we saw had been Portugal, for with the help of God we hoped to recover our health there, as we had done once before.[2]

This happened on January 2, 1499.[3] It was night when we came close to the land, and for this reason we put about ship and lay to. In the morning [January 3]

---

[1] From October 5 to January 2.

[2] At Mombaça.

[3] The MS. says "February" but this is an obvious mistake.

we reconnoitred the coast, so as to find out whither the Lord had taken us, for there was not a pilot on board, nor any other man who could tell on the chart in what place we were. Some said that we must be among certain islands off Moçambique, about 300 leagues from the mainland;[1] and they said this because a Moor whom we had taken at Moçambique had asserted that these islands were very unhealthy, and that their inhabitants suffered from the same disease which had afflicted us.

[*Magadoxo.*]

We found ourselves off a large town, with houses of several stories, big palaces in its centre, and four towers around it. This town faced the sea, belonged to the Moors, and was called Magadoxo.[2] When we were quite close to it we fired off many bombards,[3] and continued along the coast with a fair wind. We went on thus during the day, but lay to at night, as we did not know how far we were from Milingue [Malindi] whither we wished to go.

On Saturday, the 5th of the month, being becalmed, a thunderstorm burst upon us, and tore the ties of the *Raphael*. Whilst repairing these a privateer came out from a town called Pate[4] with eight boats and many men, but as soon as he came within reach of our bombards we fired upon him, and he fled. There being no wind we were not able to follow him.

---

[1] From Moçambique to Madagascar is only 60 leagues; 300 leagues would carry a ship as far as the Seychelles.

[2] Mukhdisho of the Arabs, Madisha of the Somal, in lat. 5° N. The town was founded by Arabs, perhaps on the site of a more ancient city, in 907, and attained the height of its prosperity under the dynasty of the El Mdofer, which was expelled by the Abgal Somal, probably in the sixteenth century.

[3] Whether merely as a sign of rejoicing or in wanton enmity is not clear.

[4] Pate is an island in 26° 5′ S., with a town of the same name.

[*Malindi.*]

On Monday, the 7th [of January][1] we again cast anchor off Milindy, when the king at once sent off to us a long boat holding many people, with a present of sheep, and a message to the captain-major, bidding him welcome. The king said that he had been expected for days past, and gave expresssion to his amicable and peaceable sentiments. The captain-major sent a man on shore with these messengers with instructions to bring off a supply of oranges, which were much desired by our sick. These he brought on the following day, as also other kinds of fruit; but our sick did not much profit by this, for the climate affected them in such a way that many of them died here. Moors also came on board, by order of the king, offering fowls and eggs.

When the captain saw that all this attention was shown us at a time when we stood so much in need of it, he sent a present to the king, and also a message by the mouth of one of our men who spoke Arabic, begging for a tusk of ivory to be given to the King [of Portugal], his Lord, and asking that a pillar be placed on the land as a sign of friendship. The king replied that he would do what was asked out of love for the King of Portugal, whom he desired to serve; and, in fact, he at once ordered a tusk to be taken to the captain and ordered the pillar to be erected.[2]

---

[1] The author says the 9th, but Monday was the 7th. The stay of five days extended from the 7th to the 11th.

[2] "Vasco da Gama's Pillar", now to be seen at Malindi, close to the town (to the left of it as seen from the sea) and at the extremity of a narrow rocky promontory of only a few feet in height, is certainly not the padrão erected by the great navigator, though it probably occupies its site. When Cabral arrived at Malindi in 1501 the pillar had been removed, it having proved a "stone of offence" to the people of Mombaça. The king, however, had stowed it away carefully, and

He also sent a young Moor,[1] who desired to go with us to Portugal, and whom he recommended strongly to the captain-major, saying that he sent him in order that the King of Portugal might know how much he desired his friendship.

We remained five days at this place enjoying ourselves, and reposing from the hardships endured during a passage

Vasco da Gama's Pillar at Malindi.
(From a photograph by Sir John Kirk.)

had even caused the royal arms to be repainted. João de Sá, who had been with Gama, identified it.

The existing pillar, of which we give an illustration, is built up of concrete made of coral rock and lime. It rises to a height of 16 feet, and is surmounted by a cross, bearing on the sea side the arms of Portugal, but no inscription. It is not the pillar put up at the request of Vasco da Gama, but Sir John Kirk feels sure that the cross is very ancient. The latter is of sandstone, and evidently of local make, whilst the other crosses discovered hitherto are of limestone or marble. See Introduction.

1 This ambassador returned with Cabral in 1501.

in the course of which all of us had been face to face with death.

[*Malindi to São Braz.*]

We left on Friday [January 11], in the morning, and on Saturday, which was the 12th of the month, we passed close to Mombaça. On Sunday [January 13] we anchored at the *Baixos de S. Raphael*,[1] where we set fire to the ship

The Figure-head of the *S. Raphael*.

of that name, as it was impossible for us to navigate three

[1] The figure-head of the *S. Raphael* was taken away by Vasco da Gama and treated as an heirloom by the family, several members of which carried it with them on their travels. It ultimately found a resting-place in the church of Vidigueira, founded by D. Francisco da Gama. When the church was desecrated in 1840, the figure was removed to another church, where Texeira de Aragão discovered it in 1853. It is now in the church at Belem. The figure is carved in oak, and about 24 inches in height (see *Texeira de Aragão*, in the Boletim of the Lisbon Geographical Society, VI, 1886, p. 621.)

vessels with the few hands that remained to us. The contents of this ship were transferred to the two other ships. We were here fifteen days,[1] and from a town in front of us, called Tamugate,[2] many fowls were brought to us for sale or barter in exchange for shirts and bracelets.

On Sunday, the 27th, we left this place with a fair wind. During the following night we lay to, and in the morning [January 28] we came close to a large island called Jamgiber [Zanzibar], which is peopled by Moors, and is quite ten leagues[3] from the mainland. Late on February 1, we anchored off the island of S. Jorge, near Moçambique. On the following day [February 2], in the morning, we set up a pillar in that island, where we had said mass on going out. The rain fell so heavily that we could not light a fire for melting the lead to fix the cross, and it therefore remained without one. We then returned to the ships.

On March 3 we reached the Angra de São Braz, where we caught many anchovies, seals and penguins, which we salted for our voyage. On the 12th we left, but when ten or twelve leagues from the watering-place the wind blew so strongly from the west, that we were compelled to return to this bay.

[*São Braz to the Rio Grande.*]

When the wind fell we started once more, and the Lord gave us such a good wind that on the 20th we were able to double the Cape of Good Hope. Those who had come so

---

[1] The author says five, but from January 13 to January 27, both included, is fifteen days.

[2] Barros says *Tangata*. It is Mtangata (see note, p. 33).

[3] Zanzibar is only twenty miles (six leagues) from the mainland.

far were in good health and quite robust, although at times nearly dead from the cold winds which we experienced. This feeling, however, we attributed less to the cold than to the heat of the countries from which we had come.

We pursued our route with a great desire of reaching home. For twenty-seven days[1] we had the wind astern, and were carried by it to the neighbourhood of the island of São Thiago. To judge from our charts we were within a hundred leagues from it, but some supposed we were quite near. But the wind fell and we were becalmed. The little wind there was came from ahead. Thunderstorms,[2] which came from the land, enabled us to tell our whereabouts, and we plied to windward as well as we could.

On Thursday, the 25th of April, we had soundings of 35 fathoms. All that day we followed our route, and the least sounding we had was 20 fathoms. We nevertheless could get no sight of the land, but the pilots told us that we were near the shoals of the Rio Grande.[3]

[Here the Journal ends abruptly. The succeeding events may be shortly stated. Vasco da Gama and Coelho were

---

[1] Twenty-seven days carry us from March 20 to April 16.

[2] The author here evidently refers to tornadoes or violent gusts of wind peculiar to the west coast of Africa, and more frequent at the beginning and termination of the rainy season. They generally blow off shore, their approach being indicated by an arch of clouds, from which lightning and thunder constantly proceed. At Sierra Leone the rainy season begins at the end of April (see *Africa Pilot*, 1893, Part II, p. 10).

[3] The Rio Grande of the Portuguese is an arm of the sea from five to thirteen miles in breadth, called Orango Channel on the Admiralty Chart. It lies between the mainland and the Bissagos islands.

separated in a storm, according to Resende. Coelho continued his voyage, arriving at Cascaes, below Lisbon, on July 10, 1499. Vasco da Gama, having waited one day for his consort, proceeded to the island of São Thiago, placed João de Sá in charge of the *S. Gabriel*, and chartered a caravel in which he conveyed his dying brother Paulo to the island of Terceira. João de Sá arrived soon after Coelho, and certainly anterior to August 28th, on which day the king addressed a letter to the Cardinal Protector of Portugal (see Appendix). Paulo died a day after he had landed at the Angra of Terceira, and was buried in the church of the Monastery of S. Francisco.[1] A resident of Terceira, one Arthur Rodriguez, at once started in a caravel to carry the news of Vasco da Gama's arrival to Lisbon.

The date of Vasco da Gama's return to Lisbon is not known with certainty. The commission appointed in 1871 to remove the remains of Vasco da Gama from the church of Vidigueira to Belem made every effort to ascertain the exact date, but in vain ; and whilst Barros, Goes, and Pero Barretto de Resende state that it happened on August 29th, Castanheda fixes upon September 8th, and a MS. in the Torre do Tombo, consulted by Texeira de Aragão, has September 18th. Herculano, in a note to the second edition of the "Roteiro", is content with saying that it happened at the end of August or at the beginning of September. Texeira de Aragão assumes (on the ground of a vague expression in De Barros) that he reached Terceira on August 29th, arrived at Lisbon on September 9th, and made his triumphal entry into the town on September 18th. This assumption is partly supported by the statement of Barros that Vasco da Gama, after his arrival at Belem, on account of the loss he had suffered

---

[1] This church was demolished in 1646 ; the place of burial can no longer be identified.

in the death of a beloved brother, spent nine days in retirement.[1]

I am myself inclined to believe that Vasco da Gama reached Lisbon on August 29th, and made his triumphal entry on September 8th.]

---

[1] See *Jose da Silva Mendes Leal* (Transactions of Lisbon Academy, 1871), and *Texeira de Aragão* (Boletim Lisbon Geogr. Soc., VI, 1886, p. 583).

[THE KINGDOMS TO THE SOUTH OF CALECUT.]

The following are the names of certain kingdoms on the coast to the south of Calecut, together with the productions of each, and what they are worth, all of which I have learnt in the most trustworthy manner from a man who spoke our language and who had come to those parts from Alexandria thirty years before.[1]

CALECUT, where we were. The articles of merchandise mentioned below are sent to it, and the vessels of Mecca take their cargoes to that city. The King, who is called Çamolim, can muster 100,000 fighting men, including auxiliaries, for the number under his proper jurisdiction is very small.

In the following we give the articles of merchandise brought thither in the vessels of Mecca, and their value throughout this part of India[2]:—

Copper, of which the frazila of nearly 30 pounds is worth 50 fanãos or 3 cruzados.

Stone of Baqua,[3] which is worth its weight in silver.

---

[1] This trustworthy man can have been no other than the "Moor" who was carried off from Anjediva (see Appendix E), and who, having been baptised, became known as Gaspar da Gama.

[2] The frazila of Calecut is equal to 10.4 kilogr.; the fanão is worth 25⅗ reis of 1555 (about 7.45*d.*) and the cruzado is worth 9*s.* 8*d.* But if 3 cruzados are accepted as the equivalent of 50 fanãos, the value of a fanão would be 6.96*d.*

[3] I have little doubt that instead of Baqua we ought to read Bezoar. In D. Manuel's letter to the King of Castile, the royal writer states that among the presents which the King of Cochin gave to Vasco da

Knives, worth one fanão each.

Rosewater, worth 50 fanãos the frazila.

Alum, worth 50 fanãos the frazila.

Camlot, worth 7 cruzados the piece.

Red cloth, worth 2 cruzados the *pequy*[1] of three spans (palmas).

Quicksilver, worth 10 cruzados the frazila.

QUORONGOLIZ [Corongolor][2] is a Christian country and the king is a Christian. Its distance from Calecut by sea, and with a favourable wind, is 3 days. The king can muster 40,000 fighting men. There is much pepper, the frazila being worth 9 fanãos, whilst at Calecut it is worth 14.

Gama (in 1502) there was a stone as large as a filbert, which was taken out of the head of a very rare animal, called Burgoldof, and which proved a specific against all poisons.

The Rev. J. J. Jaus, of the Basel Mission, informs me that the bezoar, in Malayalam, is called *Gōrōchanam*, which means "out of the cow's brain", *go* signifying cow. It still sells for its weight in silver, and is highly prized as a medicine and antidote. My esteemed correspondent is unable to enlighten me as to the meaning of *burgoldof*.

Bishop J. M. Speechly, in a letter addressed to me, suggests that "Baqua" (Bakwa) may be a corruption of "Bagawat", a common name for Shiva, and the "Stone of Baqua" a dedication to him.

The Arabic name of the bezoar (badesar) has the meaning of antidote. This "stone" is a calcareous concretion found in the intestines of some animals, more especially goats and antelopes, but also in those of monkeys. It varies in size from a pea to a fist. All through the Middle Ages, this oriental bezoar was looked upon as a most potent medicine against poisons, and it is still highly valued in the East. The Bezoar of Goa (Gowa) is an artificial product made up of musk, ambergris, and gum of tragacanth.

[1] The pequy (pik) is about 27 inches.

[2] This, according to Prof. Kopke, is meant for Crangalor, the modern Kodungalar in Cochin. The frazila there is equal to 8.314 kilo., and the fanão, when buying pepper, is valued at $22\frac{8}{18}$ reis (6.5*d.*).

COLEU [Colam, Coulão][1] is Christian. Its distance from Calecut by sea, and with a good wind, is 10 days. The king can muster 10,000 men. There is much cotton-cloth in this country, but little pepper.

CAELL [Cael],[2] the king of which is a Moor, whilst the people are Christians. Its distance from Calecut, by sea, is 10 days. The king can assemble 4,000 fighting men, and owns 100 war-elephants. There are many pearls.

CHOMANDARLA [Choramandel][3] is inhabited by Christians, and the king is a Christian. He can muster 100,000 men. There is much lac here, worth half a cruzado the frazila, and an extensive manufacture of cotton cloths.

CEYLAM [Ceylon] is a very large island inhabited by Christians under a Christian king. It is 8 days from Calecut, with a favourable wind. The king can muster 4,000 men, and has moreover many elephants for war as well as for sale. All the fine cinnamon of India is found here, as well as many sapphires, superior to those of other countries,[4] besides rubies, few but of good quality.

CAMATARRA [Sumatra] is Christian. It is 30 days from Calecut with a favourable wind. The king can muster 4,000 fighting-men, and has 1,000 horsemen and 300 war-

---

[1] It is the Coilum of Marco Polo, the Columbum of Friar Jordanus (1330), the modern Quilon. It is one of the principal seats of the Syrian Christians. The Portuguese built a fort there in 1503.

[2] Marco Polo's Cael has been satisfactorily identified by Dr. Caldwell with the decayed village of Kayal (Palaya Kayal), near the mouth of the Tamrapanni river; whilst our author's Caell is the Callegrande of Barros, now represented by Kayal Patnam, some distance to the south of that river. (Comp. Yule's *Marco Polo*, ii, p. 307.) The pearl fisheries are near it, on the coast of Ceylon.

[3] According to Prof. Kopke, it extended from Point Calymere to the Godavari.

[4] Barbosa (p. 214) says that "the best sapphires are found in Ceylon," as also "many rubies," but inferior to those of Pegu.

elephants. In this country much spun[1] silk is found, worth 8 cruzados the frazila. There is also much lac, worth 10 cruzados the bahar of 20 frazilas [208 kilo.].

XARNAUZ[2] is Christian and has a Christian king. Its distance from Calecut is 50 days with a good wind. The king can muster 20,000 fighting men and 4,000 horse, and owns 400 war-elephants. In this country is found much benzoin,[3] worth 3 cruzados the frazila, as also much aloes,[4] worth 25 cruzados the frazila.

TENACAR[5] is Christian with a Christian king. It is 40 days' sail from Calecut, if the wind is favourable. The king can muster 10,000 fighting men and possesses 500 fighting elephants. In this country is found much Brazil-wood[6] which yields a red dye, as fine as kermes, and is worth 3 cruzados the bahar, whilst at Quayro [Cairo] it fetches 60. There is likewise a little aloes.

---

[1] The silk referred to by the author, as also by Barbosa and Barros, is the produce of the silk cotton tree (*Bombax malabaricum*) and is much inferior in quality to true silk.—KOPKE.

[2] This, according to Prof. Kopke and Yule (*Marco Polo*, ii, p. 222), is Siam, the old capital of which (Ayuthia) is called Sornau or Xarnau by Varthema, Giovanni d'Empoli, and Mendez Pinto.

[3] Benzoin (Gum-Benjamin) is the produce of Styrax Benzoin, found in Siam, Cochin-China, Java and Sumatra, that of Siam being accounted the best.

[4] The odoriferous aloe-wood of the author is the wood of *Aquilaria Agallocha* (*Roxb.*), found in Further India, and more especially in Chamba. Its Sanscrit name, Aguru, was corrupted into Agila and Aquila; and hence its Latin and Portuguese name of "Eaglewood." (Yule's *Marco Polo*, ii, p. 215.)

[5] Prof. Kopke identifies Tenacar with Tenasserim, a great emporium at one time, through which the products of Siam reached the outer world.

[6] Brazil-wood first became known in Europe at the beginning of the fourteenth century under the designation of *Lignum presillum*. The most esteemed kind of this dye-wood is known as Sapan wood (*Caesalpinia sappan*), found more especially in Siam.

H 2

BEMGALA [Bengal].[1] In this kingdom there are many Moors and few Christians, and the king is a Christian. He can muster 20,000 fighting men on foot and 10,000 horse. In this country there is much cloth made of cotton and of silk, and much silver. The distance from Calecut is 40 days' sail, with a favourable wind.

MELEQUA [Malacca] is Christian with a Christian king. It is 40 days' sail from Qualecut [Calecut], with a good wind. The king can muster 10,000 fighting men, including 1,200 horse. All cloves[2] come from here, being worth on the spot 9 cruzados the bahar,[3] as also nutmeg, which is worth the like amount. There is also much porcelain, much silk and much tin, of which last they coin money ; but this money is heavy and of little value, 3 frazilas being worth only 1 cruzado. There are many big parrots in this country, whose plumage is red, like fire.

PEGUO [Pegu] is Christian and has a Christian king. The inhabitants are as white as we are. The king can muster 20,000 fighting men, *scilicet* 10,000 horse and the others on foot, besides 400 war-elephants. This country produces all the musk[4] of the world. The king possesses an island about four days' sail, with a good wind, from the mainland. In this island there are animals like deer, who have pouches

---

[1] This is no doubt Bengal, the capital of which was Chatigam (Chittagong).

[2] Cloves were originally found only in the Moluccas ; the true nutmeg (*Myristica moschata*) comes from the same islands and those further to the east. Tin was—and still is—a native product. The silk and porcelain came from China.

[3] The frazila was equal to 10.51 kilo., the bahar was 210.22 kilo. The cruzado was a silver coin and was valued at 360 reis (8*s.* 8*d.*).

[4] Barbosa (p. 186) gives a better account of musk, which really only reaches Pegu from the interior. It is the secretion of *Moschus moschiferus*, an animal resembling a deer, which lives in the mountains lying between the Amur river, China and India. The male has a pouch between the navel and the genitals which holds about 50 grammes of this secretion.

containing this musk, attached to their navels. At a certain period of each year they rub themselves against trees, when the pouches come off. It is then that the people of the country gather them. Their abundance is such that they give you four large pouches, or ten to twelve small ones, which would fill a large chest, for one cruzado. On the mainland many rubies[1] and much gold are found. For ten cruzados as much gold may be bought here as for twenty-five at Calecut. There is also much lac and benzoin of two kinds, white and black. The frazila of white benzoin is worth three cruzados, of black only a cruzado and a half. The silver to be obtained here for ten cruzados is worth fifteen at Calecut.

The distance of this country from Calecut is thirty days with a fair wind.

BEMGUALA [Bengal][2] has a Moorish king, and is inhabited by both Moors and Christians. Its distance from Calecut is thirty-five days with a fair wind. There may be 25,000 fighting men, *scilicet* 10,000 horse and the remainder on foot, as also 400 war-elephants. In this country the following merchandise is found:—much corn and much cloth of great value. Cloth which may be bought here for ten cruzados is worth forty at Calecut. There is also much silver.

CONIMATA[3] has a Christian king and Christian inhabitants. It is fifty days' sail from Calecut, with a good wind.

---

[1] Burma, above Pegu, is still famous for its rubies.

[2] This is evidently a duplicate account of what has been said above about Bemgala.

[3] Prof. Kopke would identify this with Timor, where there is a fort called Camanaça. This, however, is quite inadmissible, for there are no elephants in Timor. I am more inclined to think that "Conimata" stands for Sumatra, a small state in North Sumatra, adjoining Pedir. The voyage to Pater and Conimata is stated to occupy the same time, viz., fifty days. If this be so, there is a duplication of Sumatra as well as of Bengal.

The king can assemble five or six thousand men, and owns one thousand fighting elephants. In this country there are many sapphires and much brazil-wood.

PATER[1] has Christian inhabitants and a Christian king, and there is not a single Moor. The king can assemble four thousand fighting men, and has a hundred war-elephants. In this country is found much rhubarb, the frazila on the spot being worth nine cruzados. There are also many spinel rubies and much lac, a bahar of which is worth four cruzados. The distance from Calecut is fifty days with a fair wind.

[ABOUT ELEPHANTS.]

How the Elephants fight in this country.

They make a house of wood holding four men, and this house is put on the back of the elephant with the four men in it. The elephant has attached five naked swords to each of his tusks, being ten for the two tusks. This renders him so redoubtable that none awaits his attack if flight is possible. Whatever those seated on the top order to be done is done as if he were a rational creature, for if they tell him "kill this one, or do this thing or another", he does it.

How they capture Elephants in the Primeval Forests.

When they wish to capture a wild elephant they take a tame female, and dig a large hole on the track frequented by elephants, and cover its mouth with brushwood. They

---

1 This seems to be Pedir, a small kingdom in Northern Sumatra, which had a pagan king when Varthema was there, although many of the inhabitants were Mohammedans. Rhubarb (*Rheum officinale*) is, however, only to be found in W. and N.W. China and in Tibet. The lacca tree is a native of Sumatra.

then tell the female "Go! and if you meet with an elephant, entice him to this hole, in such a way that he falls into it, but take care that you do not fall into it yourself." She then goes away, and does as she has been told, and when she meets one she draws him on in such a way that he must fall into the hole, and the hole is so deep that unaided he could never get out of it.

How they are got out of the hole and broken-in.

After the elephant has fallen into this hole, five or six days are allowed to pass before he is given anything to eat. When that time has elapsed, a man brings him a very small supply of food, the supply being increased from day to day until he eats by himself. This is continued for about a month, during which time those who bring him food gradually tame him, until at last they venture to descend into the hole. This is done for several days until he permits the man to put his hands upon his tusks He then goes into the hole and puts heavy chains around the legs, and whilst in this condition they train him so well that he learns all but to speak.

These elephants are kept in stables like horses, and a good elephant is worth 2,000 cruzados.[1]

Prices at Alexandria.[2]

			[Value per Pound.] s.	d.
One quintal of cinnamon is worth	25	cruzados,	2	5
" " cloves "	20	"	1	11
" " pepper "	15	"	1	5
" " ginger "	21	"	2	0
(At Calecut one bahar, equal to 5 quintals, is worth 20 cruzados) . .			0	5

[1] Say £966.

[2] In calculating these values we have assumed the quintal to be

				[Value per Pound.] £	s.	d.
One quintal of nutmeg is worth	16	cruzados,		0	1	7
" " lac	"	25	"	0	2	5
" " Brazil wood	"	10	"	0	1	0
One ratel of rhubarb	"	12	"	5	16	0
One mitikal of musk	"	1	"	50	5	4
One ratel of aloe-wood	"	2	"	0	19	4
" " benzoin	"	1	"	0	9	8
One quintal of frankincense	"	2	"	0	0	2½
(At Mecca the bahar is worth 2 cruzados)			.	0	0	0½

equivalent to 100 pounds, the bahar = 460 pounds, the ratel = 1 pound. The cruzado is taken at 9*s.* 8*d.*

It is interesting to compare these prices with those given by Duarte Barbosa for Calecut. Assuming the fanão to be worth 6.5*d.* they were as follows per pound:—Cinnamon, 4.3*d.*; cloves, 7.2*d.* to 8.3*d.*; pepper, 2.9*d.* to 3.3*d.*; ginger, 0.5*d.* to 0.9*d.*; nutmeg, 3.0*d.* to 3.36*d.*; lac, 3.6*d.* to 5.2*d.*; rhubarb, 9*s.* 9*d.* to 11*s.*; musk, £15 11*s.*; aloe-wood, 24*s.* 7*d.*; frankincense, 0.9*d.* to 1.5*d.* A purchaser of one pound of each of these commodities would have paid at Calecut £17 13*s.* 6*d.*, and would have received at Alexandria £57 12*s.* 8*d.*, an increase of 210 per cent. (See Lord Stanley of Alderley's version of *Duarte Barbosa*, Hakluyt Society, 1866, p. 219.)

Present Retail Prices in London are as follows (per pound): cinnamon, 1*s.* 8*d.*; cloves, 1*s.* 6*d.*; pepper, 7½*d.* to 10½*d.*; ginger, 10*d.* to 1*s.* 4*d.*; nutmeg, 2*s.* 6*d.* to 3*s.*; lac, 8*d.*; rhubarb, 8*s.* to 12*s.*; musk, £117.

[A VOCABULARY OF MALAYALAM.]

THIS IS THE LANGUAGE OF CALECUT.[1]

See, look!	nocane [nōkka].
Hearest thou?	que que ne [kēlka].
Take him away	criane.
To draw	balichene [walikkān].
Rope	coraoo [kayara].
Largely	lacany.
Give me	cornda.
To drink	carichany [kutippān].
Eat	tinane [tinmān].
Take	y na.
I do not wish to	totenda.
To go	mareçane.
Go away!	poo [pō].
Come here!	baa [bā or wā].
Be silent!	pote.
Rise!	legany.
To throw	carecane [karikkān].
To speak	para ne [parane, speak thou].
Mad, silly	moto.
Serious	monday decany.
Lame	mura call [murakāl].
To fall	biamçe.
Many, much	balidu [walare].
Bad	betall [chītta].
Wind	clarle [kātta].
Little	chiredu [chiratu?].

---

[1] The words placed within brackets have been kindly furnished me by the Rt. Rev. J. M. Speechly, D.D., who was Bishop of Travancore, 1879-89. In a letter to me he remarks that, "at the sea-port towns generally the worst Malayālam is spoken. Many Malayālam words are the same in Tamil, and in this list there are some which a Tamil scholar would be able to point out. Also, it is not unlikely that there are some Arabic words Malayālamised in the list. The anonymous author's list is a very interesting one, and his journal, I have no doubt, will be so also. The 'ne' which ends so many words may stand for 'nī', 'thou'. Sometimes it is only an expressive ending".

Give him	criane.
Timber, wood	mara [maram].
Stone	calou [kallu].
Teeth	faley.
Lips	çire [chīra ?].
Nose	muco [mūkka].
Eyes	cana [kanna].
Forehead	necheim [nĭcha ?].
Hair	talanay [talla].
Head	tabu.
Ears	cadee [chewi].
Tongue	naoo [nākka].
Neck	caestez.
[Breast]	mulay [mula].
Breasts	nane.
Arms	carit.
Stomach	barri [wayara].
Legs	cali [kāla].
—	canay.
—	seyrim.
—	cudo.
Hands	lamguajem [kai].
Fingers	beda.
—	cula.
Fish	miny [mīna].
Mast	mana.
Light, fire	tiir [tī].
To sleep	teraquy.
Man	amoo [āna].
Women	pena [penna].
Chin, beard	tari.
Lobster	xame.
Parrot	tata [tatta].
Doves	cayninaa.
—	baly.
To kiss	mucane.
To bite	canchany [katikkān].
To see, look	noquany [nokkuwān].
To hear	çegade [kēlkawān].
To beat	catane.
Wound	morubo.
Sword	batany.
Shield	cutany.
Bow	cayny.
Arrow	ambum [anpa].

A VOCABULARY OF MALAYALAM.

Spear . .	concudoo.
To shoot with a bow .	heany.
Sun . . .	nerara.
Moon . . .	neelan.
Heaven . .	mana.
The earth . .	caraa.
The sea . .	caralu.
Ship . . .	capell [kappal].
Boat . . .	çambuco.
Night . .	erabut.
Day . . .	pagalala.
Eat . . .	tinane [tinmān].
— . . .	matara.
To mount . .	arricany.
To be on foot . .	anicany.
To go, travel . .	narecane.
To embrace . .	traigany.
Blows . . .	talancy.
To mourn, wail .	que ne.
To raise . .	alagany.
To dance . .	canechane.
To throw with stones or wood . .	ouriany.
To sing . .	fareny.
Rain . . .	ma jaa [mara].
Water . .	tany [tanni].
Blind . . .	curuge [kurutan, *blind man*].
Maimed of a hand .	muruquay [murukai].
— . . .	panany.
Take ! . .	ennay.
Let us go ! . .	pomga [pomka].
East . . .	careçache [kirakka].
West . . .	mecache [patinynyara].
North . .	barcangache [watakka].
South . . .	tycamgarche [tekka].
Dog . . .	naa [nāya].
Bitch . . .	pena [pennāya].
Young man . .	hum nee.
Girl . . .	co poo.
House . .	pura [pura]
Needle . .	cu doo.
Rod . . .	parima.
Oar . . .	tandii [tandu].
A great gun . .	ve dii.
Top-sail . .	talii.

Halyard . .	anguaa.
Anchor . .	napara.
Flag . . .	çoti [koti].
Rudder, helm . .	xoca.
Pilot . . .	cu pajaoo.
Shoe . . .	cacu paja.
Cap . . .	tupy [topi].

The following are some of the Names [of Persons].

Tenae.	Aja paa.	Anapa.
Pumi.	A rreco.	Canapa.
Paramganda.	A xirama.	Gande.
Uja pee.	Cuerapa.	Rremaa.
Quilaba.	Cutotopa.	Mamgala.
Gouaa.		

APPENDICES.

DOM MANUEL THE FORTUNATE, KING OF PORTUGAL, 1495-1521.
From "Leitura nova" (1° de Alemdouro) in the Torre do Tombo.
The signature is that of the King:—"Rey."

APPENDIX A.

TWO LETTERS OF KING MANUEL, 1499.

THE first of these letters is addressed to King Ferdinand and Queen Isabella, of Castile, whose daughter, Dona Isabella, King Manuel had married in October 1497.[1] The letter is dated July 1499, and may have been written immediately after the arrival of Coelho's vessel on July 10.

The draught, or copy, of this letter in the Torre do Tombo[2] has been published by A. C. Texeira de Aragão in the *Boletim* of the Lisbon Geographical Society, VI, 1886, p. 673. It was published a second time in *Alguns Documentos do Archivo Nacional da Torre do Tombo*, Lisbon, 1892, p. 95. There are several omissions in the latter version, due probably to the illegibility of the manuscript. In our rendering of this valuable document, all passages omitted in *Alguns Documentos* are printed in italics, while attention is directed to other differences by means of foot-notes.

---

[1] She died in childbed on August 24, 1498; and Dom Manuel, having been granted a dispensation from the Pope, married her sister, Dona Maria, on August 24, 1500, the second anniversary of his first wife's death.

[2] *Collecção de S. Vicente*, t. III, fol. 513; XIV, fol. 1.

The draught of the letter addressed to the "Cardinal Protector" also exists in the Torre do Tombo,[1] but is evidently very illegible, for the text published by Texeira de Aragão is full of blanks. The original, as also the letter to Pope Alexander VI, to which reference is made, may possibly be discovered in Rome. The letter is dated August 28, 1499, that is, the day before Vasco da Gama's supposed return to Lisbon. It was certainly written *after* the arrival of the *S. Gabriel*, for it refers to the "Moor of Tunis" or Monçaide, to the "Jew", who subsequently became known as Gaspar da Gama, and to the men carried off from Calecut, none of whom is likely to have been on board Coelho's small vessel.[2]

The "Cardinal Protector" can be identified with D. Jorge da Costa, a man of mean extraction, whom Dona Catharina, the virgin daughter of King Duarte, and sister of King Afonso IV, appointed her chaplain, and who subsequently rose to high dignities in the Church, until, finally, the Pope bestowed upon him a cardinal's hat. King John took a dislike to the cardinal, who went to reside at Rome; but King Manuel had a high opinion of his wisdom, and soon after his accession, in 1495, he invited him, through Pedro Correa,[3] his special ambassador to the Court of Rome, to return to Lisbon. The cardinal declined this invitation, pleading his great age and infirmities as an excuse, but ever afterwards attended most faithfully to the King's business with the Pope.

---

[1] *Collecção de S. Vicente*, t. XIV, fol. I.

[2] Gaspar da Gama certainly came in the *S. Gabriel* (see Sernigi's letter, Appendix B).

[3] The immediate business of Pedro Correa was to get Pope Alexander VI to grant permission to the Commanders and Knights of the Orders of Christ and Aviz to marry. In this he succeeded (Goes, *Chronica do D. Manuel*, I, c. 15).

I.—KING MANUEL'S LETTER TO THE KING AND QUEEN OF CASTILE, JULY 1499.

Most high and excellent Prince and Princess, most potent Lord and Lady!

Your Highnesses already know that we had ordered *Vasco da Gama, a nobleman of our household, and his brother Paulo da Gama, with* four vessels to make discoveries by sea, and that two years have now elapsed since their departure. And as the principal motive of this enterprise has been, with our predecessors, the service of God our Lord, and our own advantage,[1] it pleased Him in His mercy to speed them on their route. From a message which has now been brought to this city by one of the captains,[2] we learn that they did reach and discover India and other kingdoms *and lordships* bordering upon it; that they entered and navigated its sea, finding large cities, large edifices and rivers, and great populations, among whom is carried on all the trade in spices and precious stones, which are forwarded in ships (which these same explorers saw and met with in good numbers and of great size) to Mecca, and thence to Cairo, whence they are dispersed throughout the world. Of these [spices, etc.] they have brought a quantity, including cinnamon, cloves, ginger, nutmeg, *and pepper*, as well as other kinds, together with the boughs and leaves[3] of the same; also many fine stones of all sorts, such as rubies and others. And they also came to a country in which there are mines of gold, of which [gold], as of the spices and precious stones, they did not bring as much as they could have done, for they took no merchandise with them.[4]

---

[1] "e proveito nosso." This, in *Alguns Documentos*, is rendered "e principalemente nosso". It is just possible that the King meant to say that the "service of God" was his principal object, as it had been that of his predecessors.

[2] "By these same discoverers" (*Alguns Documentos*).

[3] This reference to "boughs and leaves" reminds us of what the author of the *Journal* says about gathering the branches and leaves of supposed cinnamon trees, p. 81.

[4] *Alguns Documentos* adds: "nor such as suited", that is, suited the requirements of the Indian market.

As we are aware that your Highnesses will hear of these things with much pleasure and satisfaction, we thought well to give this information. And your Highnesses may believe, in accordance with what we have learnt concerning the Christian people whom these explorers reached, that it will be possible, notwithstanding that they are not as yet strong in the faith or possessed of a thorough knowledge of it, to do much in the service of God and the exaltation of the Holy Faith, once they shall have been converted and fully fortified (confirmed) in it. And when *they shall have thus been fortified in the faith there will be an opportunity for destroying the Moors of those parts. Moreover, we hope, with the help of God, that* the great trade which now enriches the Moors of those parts, through whose hands it passes without the intervention of other persons or peoples, shall, in consequence of our regulations (ordenanços) be diverted *to the natives and ships of our own kingdom*, so that henceforth all Christendom, *in this part of Europe*, shall be able, *in a large measure*, to provide itself with these spices and precious stones. This, with the help of God, who in His mercy thus ordained it, will cause our designs and intentions to be pushed with more ardour [especially as respects] the war upon the Moors *of the territories conquered by us in these parts*, which your Highnesses are so firmly resolved upon, and in which we are equally zealous.

And we pray your Highnesses, in consideration of this great favour, which, with much gratitude, we received from Our Lord, to cause to be addressed to Him those praises which are His due.[1]

Most high *and excellent Prince and Princess, most potent Lord and Lady, may the Lord our God ever hold your persons and kingdoms in His holy keeping.*

Written at Lisbon, July 1499.

II.—King Manuel to the Cardinal Protector, August 28th, 1499.

Most Reverend Father in Christ, whom we love much as a brother!

We, Don Manuel, by the Grace of God King of Portugal and

---

[1] This paragraph only appears in *Alguns Documentos.*

of the Algarves on this side of and beyond the sea, in Africa, Lord of Guinea and of the Conquest the Navigation and Commerce of Ethiopia, Arabia, Persia and India, We send to recommend to your Reverence . . . . . very great news . . . . . Our Lord having ended our labours in the exploration of Ethiopia and India, of other countries, and eastern islands . . . . . we inform you with pleasure . . . . . and in order that you may know the progress of events we enclose the draught of a letter which we wrote to the Holy Father . . . . . Beyond what we wrote to his Holiness, your Reverence must know that those who have just returned from this investigation and discovery visited, among other ports of India, a city called Qualicut, whence they brought us cinnamon, cloves . . . . . the King looks upon himself and the major part of his people as Christian . . . . throughout the year there are found there cucumbers, oranges, lemons and citrons . . . . . there are great fleets . . . . . The island of Taprobane, which is called Ceilam,[1] is 150 leagues from Qualicut . . . . . Our people brought five or six Indians from Qualicut . . . . . moreover a Moor of Tunes . . . . . and a Jew,[2] who turned Christian, and who is a merchant and lapidary, and well acquainted with the coasts from Alexandria to India, and beyond with the interior (*sertão*) and Tartary as far as the major sea. . . . . . As soon as we had these news we ordered general processions to be made throughout our kingdom, returning many thanks to Our Lord . . . . . His Holiness and your Reverence must (*deve*) publicly rejoice no less and give many praises to God. Also, whereas by Apostolical[3] grants we enjoy very fully the

---

[1] The King, or his advisers, thus at once identified Ptolemy's Taprobane with Ceylon, whilst Ortelius, the professional geographer, seventy-six years later, still assigns that name to Sumatra (see his map *Indiae Orientalis*, in *Theatrum Orbis Terrarum*).

[2] Monçaide and Gaspar da Gama, see Appendix E.

[3] A Bull of Alexander VI, dated Rome 1497, kalendas of June, allows King Manuel and his successors to keep possession of the countries conquered from the infidels, without prejudice to any prior claims of other Christian powers, and prohibits all kings, not possessing such claims, from disturbing King Manuel in the enjoyment of these rights. Finally, the Pope requires the King to establish the Christian religion in all the countries he may conquer (quoted from *Alguns Documentos*, p. 90).

I 2

sovereignty and dominion of all we have discovered, in such manner that little or nothing else seems needed, yet would it please us, and we affectionately beg that after you shall have handed our letters to the Holy Father and the College of Cardinals, it may please you, speaking in this as if from yourself, to ask for a fresh expression of satisfaction with reference to a matter of such novelty and great and recent merit, so as to obtain His Holiness's renewed approval and declaration, in such form as may appear best to you, most Reverend Father, whom Our Lord hold in his keeping.

Written at Lisbon, August 28, 1499. The King.

APPENDIX B.

Vasco da Gama.

(From the Portrait in the Museu das Bellas Artes at Lisbon.)

This portrait formerly belonged to the Conde de Farrobo, who had it from the Casa de Niza. It was presented to the Museu in 1866 by King D. Ferdinand. It dates back, apparently, to the first quarter of the sixteenth century. In 1845 it was restored by Luiz Tirinanzi. The above is taken from a photograph kindly forwarded by Senhor José Bastos, of Lisbon. The signature attached (Ho Conde Almyrante) is that of Vasco da Gama.

The portrait in the possession of the Conde de Lavradio, which was published in Lord Stanley of Alderley's *The Three Voyages of Vasco da Gama*, is a copy of the above.

GIROLAMO SERNIGI'S LETTERS ON VASCO DA GAMA'S FIRST VOYAGE.

GIROLAMO SERNIGI was born in Florence in 1453. His father, Cipriano di Chimenti, was a member of the Clothiers' Guild, and was held in high respect by his fellow citizens. The family became extinct in 1680.[1]

Girolamo was residing at Lisbon, where he had settled as a merchant, when Vasco da Gama's expedition returned from India. He remained there for many years afterwards, and in 1510 commanded a vessel which went out to Malacca with the fleet of Diogo Mendez de Vasconcellos.[2]

In addition to the letters giving an account of the voyage of Vasco da Gama, he wrote others dealing with the trade between Portugal and India. Some of these will be found in the *Diari* of Marino Sanuto.

Manuscript copies of these letters exist in the Biblioteca Riccardiana, Florence (Codices 1910, f. 61, and 2112b), in the library of Mr. Ralph Sneyd, of Newcastle-under-Lyne, and possibly elsewhere. I am indebted to the mediation of Dr. R. Garnett and the kindness of Professor Biagi, chief librarian of the Biblioteca Mediceo-Laurenciana, at Florence, for a careful copy of Codex 1910. The MS. in the library of Mr. Sneyd formerly belonged to Count Soranzo of Venice, and Prof. Guglielmo Berchet of that city quotes passages from it in his valuable contribution to the "Raccolta Colombiana".[3] I regret to say that I failed in

---

[1] Canestrini, *Delle relazioni tra Firenze e il Portugallo* (Archivo Storico Italiano, Florence, 1846, App. III).

[2] Falcão, *Livro de toda a fazenda*, 1612, p. 144.

[3] See Parte III, *Fonti italiane*, vol. i, p. 215; vol. ii, p. 113.

my endeavours to secure a copy of this valuable manuscript. Fortunately, to judge from the few extracts given by Prof. Berchet, there seems to be no reason to suppose that it differs in any essential respect from the other documents of which I was able to avail myself.

The two letters addressed to a gentleman at Florence were published for the first time in Fracanzio di Montalboddo's famous *Paesi novamente retrovati*, Vicenza, 1507. This seems to be a faithful reproduction of the original, except that a few passages have been omitted, and that the letters have been divided into chapters, each with a distinctive heading. Ramusio,[1] who republished these letters in 1550, has taken much greater liberties with their writer. He has not merely improved his literary style, but has also condensed many passages, not always very happily, and suppressed others altogether. The more important of these omissions, and occasional additions, have been pointed out by me in the notes appended to the present translation.

The writer's name is not mentioned by Fracanzio or Ramusio. Bandini[2] rashly suggested it was Amerigo Vespucci, who addressed these letters to Dr. Lorenzo di Pierfrancesco de' Medici. Professor Kopke[3] devotes several pages to a refutation of this untenable hypothesis. It suffices to state that Vespucci was away with Alonzo de Hojeda in the West Indies, from May 1499 to February 1500, and cannot consequently have been at Lisbon in July 1499, when the first vessel of Vasco da Gama's fleet came back from India.[4]

---

[1] *Delle Navigationi e Viaggi*, i, Venice, 1550.

[2] *Vita e lettere d' Amerigo Vespucci*, Firenze, 1745, p. L.

[3] *Roteiro*, 2° ed., pp. 124-7.

[4] Markham, *The Letters of Amerigo Vespucci.* London (Hakluyt Society), 1894, p. x.

To Baldelli Boni is due the credit of having first made known the name of the actual writer, and of having directed attention to the copy of the first letter existing in the Riccardian library.[1]

The first of these letters was undoubtedly written immediately after the arrival of Coelho's vessel, on July 10th. The information it conveys was obtained from various members of the expedition, and there is at least one passage in it which shows that it was not all written on the same day.

The second letter was written some time afterwards, for it embodies information obtained from the "pilot", Gaspar da Gama, who had not come back when the first letter was written (see p. 136). This intelligent informant reached Lisbon on board the flag-ship, the *S. Gabriel*, the command of which had been entrusted by Vasco da Gama to his clerk, João de Sá, when he himself left São Thiago in a caravel for Terçeira.

Both these letters are addressed to a gentleman at Florence with whom the writer was not on terms of familiarity, and whom he consequently addresses as "Vossignoria". This need not, however, be translated as "your Lordship", for that style of address was customary in the case of persons of much humbler degree.

The third letter is undoubtedly by the same writer. An abstract of it, in German, was discovered among the papers of Conrad Peutinger, of Augsburg, the antiquarian, and at one time the owner of the famous *Tabula Peutingeriana.* It was first published, together with other documents dealing with early voyages to the New World and to India, by Dr. G. Greiff, in 1861.[2]

---

[1] *Il Milione di Marco Polo*, Firenze, 1828, i, p. liii.

[2] *Sechs-und-zwanzigster Jahresbericht des historichen Kreisvereins von Schwaben*, Augsburg, 1861, pp. 113-170.

Peutinger[1] was shown this letter during a temporary visit to Rome, and made the abstract thus published. He states explicitly that the letter was addressed to the author's *brother*. Covering the same ground as the preceding letters, and written about the same time, it is only natural that there should occur many similar passages; and this would in all probability be even more apparent if we were in a position to collate the letter seen by Peutinger at Rome with that preserved in the "Riccardiana". But the letter, notwithstanding, is quite distinct from the letters addressed to a gentleman in Florence. The arrangement of the subjects dealt with is different, and whilst we meet with paragraphs not to be found in either of the other letters, there are numerous omissions. Among these latter we may direct attention to the speculation about the Chinese being Germans, which would most certainly not have been passed over by a German.

The Peutinger letter was written after the captain had come back "*a salvamento*" to Lisbon with the "one vessel" of 90 tons, not previously accounted for. This definite statement is rather puzzling, for if Vasco da Gama really came home in his flagship, we are either compelled to reject the statements of such well-accredited historians as De Barros, Goes, and Castanheda, who affirm that the captain-major ordered João de Sá to take his flagship, the *S. Gabriel*, to Lisbon, whilst he himself chartered a swift caravel which conveyed himself and his dying brother to the Azores; or we must assume that João de Sá, having refitted the *S. Gabriel* at São Thiago, joined his chief at

---

[1] Peutinger studied at Padua and other cities of Italy, 1483-6. He is supposed to have paid a flying visit to Rome early in the sixteenth century. His brother-in-law, Christopher Welser, was at that time resident there, and perhaps the abstract was made by him.

Terçeira, and returned with him to Lisbon.[1] We are inclined to believe that we have before us an inaccurate statement made by the writer of the letter, or else an erroneous rendering of his meaning by Peutinger. The letter was certainly written after the arrival of João de Sá in the *S. Gabriel*, but Vasco da Gama himself, coming direct from Terçeira, may have reached Lisbon a day or two later: these two distinct events becoming thus blended, as it were, in the mind of a man not thoroughly informed of the matter.

We have contented ourselves with printing a few extracts from Peutinger's letter.

GIROLAMO SERNIGI'S FIRST LETTER TO A GENTLEMAN AT FLORENCE.[2]

[*The Start.*]

The most illustrious Lord Manuel of Portugal sent 3 new vessels to discover new countries, namely 2 vessels[3] (balonieri) of 90 tons each, and one of 50 tons, in addition to which there was a ship (navetta), of one hundred and ten tons, laden with provisions. Between them they took away cxviij men,[4] and they left this city of Lisbon on July 9 1497.[5] Vasco da Gama went as captain of this fleet.

---

[1] Sailing vessels going from the Cape Verde Islands to Lisbon frequently shape their course by the Azores. See p. 94.

[2] Translated from Codex 1910 in the Riccardian Library at Florence.

[3] Literally, "whalers", or "vessels having the shape of a whale", called "barinels" by the Portuguese, and not caravels.

[4] According to the *Paesi novamente retrovati* and Ramusio, there were 180, but Peutinger says there were 118, of whom 55 died and 60 came back.

[5] According to the *Paesi*, etc., July 11th.

[*The Voyage.*]

On July x 1499 the vessel of 50 tons came back to this city.[1] The captain, Vasco da Gama, remained at the Cape Verde islands with one of the vessels of 90 tons in order to land there his brother Paulo da Gama, who was very ill.[2] The other vessel of 90 tons was burnt because there were not people enough to navigate and steer her. The store-ship also was burnt, for it was not intended she should return.

In the course of the voyage there died 55 men from a disease which first attacked the mouth, and thence descended to the throat; they also suffered great pain in the legs from the knee downwards.

They discovered 1800 leagues[3] (each league being equal to 4¼ of our miles) of new land beyond the cape of Good Hope, which cape was first discovered in the time of King John. Beyond that cape they followed the coast for about 600 leagues[4] and met with a dense population of black people. And when they had made these 600 leagues they discovered a large river,[5] and at the mouth of that river a great village inhabited by black people, who are, as it were, subject to the Moors. These Moors live in the interior of the country, and continually make war upon the blacks. And in this river, according to these blacks, are found immense quantities (infinite) of gold; and they told the captain that if he would tarry a moon,[6] that is a month, they would give him gold

---

[1] This was the vessel commanded by Nicolau Coelho.

[2] "*Molto amalado*". The *Paesi* says "amallato a morte", sick unto death, the very expression used by Peutinger.

[3] Ramusio says 1,300 leagues, but even this is a gross exaggeration. If we allow 17½ leagues to a degree, the new land actually discovered beyond the Rio de Infante amounted to 860 leagues, viz.., 800 leagues along the African coast and 60 leagues in India.

[4] From the Cape to the Rio dos Bons Signaes is only 460 leagues.

[5] The Rio dos Bons Signaes, or Kiliman River.

[6] Peutinger says: "if they would stay till new moon, when the waters would grow small, they would give them gold in plenty in exchange for their money or merchandise."

The Zambezi begins to subside in the beginning of April. Vasco da Gama left on February 25th. This is a very satisfactory confirmation of the writer's information.

in plenty. But the captain would not wait, and went about 350 leagues[1] further, and discovered a great walled city, with very good stone houses in the Moorish style, inhabited by Moors of the colour of Indians. There the captain landed, and the Moorish king of this city received him with much feasting (chon gran festa), and gave him a pilot for crossing the gulf. This city is called Melinde, and lies at the entrance of a gulf, the whole of which is peopled by Moors. This pilot spoke Italian.[2]

[*The Arabian Sea.*]

This gulf is above 700 leagues across,[3] and they crossed it from side to side, and came to a very large city, larger than Lisbon, inhabited by Christians, and called Chalichut.

On both sides of this gulf there is a dense population of Moors, with great towns and castles.[4] At the termination of this gulf there is a strait[5] like that of Romania,[6] and having passed through this strait there is another and greater gulf, which is the Red Sea. And from the right hand of this to the house of Mecca, where is the tomb of Mohammed, is 3 days' journey by land. At the said house of Mecca is a very great town of Moors. I am of opinion that this is the Gulf of Arabia,[7] concerning which Pliny wrote that Alexander the Great went there, to make war, as also did the Romans, who took all by war.

[*Chalichut.*]

Let us return to the above-named city of Chalichut, which is bigger than Lisbon, and peopled by Christian Indians, as said.[8]

---

[1] From the Kiliman River (Zambezi) to Melinde is 330 leagues.

[2] The writer must have misunderstood his informants. Gaspar da Gama is evidently referred to. See Appendix E.

[3] From Melinde to Calecut is about 2,340 miles, or 682 leagues.

[4] This sentence is omitted by Ramusio.

[5] The "Bab el mandeb".

[6] The Strait of Romania is the Bosporus, ancient cartographers (Ortelius and others) very properly writing "Romania" for the Turkish "Rum-ili", instead of the corrupt "Roumelia" of most modern authors.

[7] The "Sinus Arabicus" of Pliny (vi, 28) is a gulf of the Erythrean, identical with our Red Sea.

[8] Peutinger adds that the people of Calecut were neither black nor white; and that they were Christians, although bad ones.

In this city are churches with bells,[1] but there are no priests, and the divine offices are not performed nor sacrificial [masses] celebrated, but in each church there is a pillar holding water, in the manner of the fonts holding our holy water, and a second pillar with balm. They bathe once every 3 years in a river which is near the city.[2] The houses in this city are of stone and mortar, in the Moorish style, and the roads laid out and straight as are these.[3]

[*An Audience.*]

And the king of this city is waited upon in grand style (molto altamente), and keeps regal state, having his chamberlains, doorkeepers, and barons,[4] as also a very sumptuous palace. When the captain of the said vessel arrived at the city the king was away at a castle at a distance of about 6 leagues, and having been informed that Christians had arrived he at once came to the city attended by about 5000 persons.[5] After the lapse of 3 days the king sent for the captain, who had stayed in his vessel. The captain, with xii of his men, went at once, and about 5000 persons accompanied him from the shore as far as the palace of the king, at the gate of which stood x doorkeepers with silver-mounted sticks. Having entered he proceeded to a chamber where the king reposed upon a low couch. The whole of the floor was covered with green velvet,[6] whilst around it was drapery of variously-coloured damask. The couch had a very fine white coverlet, all worked with gold thread, and above it was a canopy, very white, delicate and sumptuous.

---

[1] Peutinger says: "churches and convents."

[2] Peutinger's version of this sentence is as follows: "Large and small are baptized in a state of nudity, once every three years, in a river near the town."

[3] The writer evidently refers to the roads in Portugal, but Ramusio says "as in Italy".

[4] Ramusio: "Esquires, doorkeepers and chamberlains."

[5] Ramusio and Peutinger say: "by about fifty persons."

[6] Peutinger says the couch "was hung round (umhangen) with blackish-green velvet, and had a white coverlet, all worked with gold, and above it a sumptuous curtain. The walls were hung with fine velvet of various colours."

The king at once asked[1] the captain what he had come to seek. The captain replied that it was the custom among Christians that when an ambassador had to deliver his message to a prince he should do so in secret and not in public. The king, upon this, ordered all his people outside. The captain then said that the King of Portugal had long since heard of his Highness (alteza) and that he was a Christian king. Being desirous of his friendship he had been ordered to visit him, as was the custom between Christian kings.

The king received this message (ambascata) most graciously, and ordered the Christian captain to be lodged in the house of a very rich Moor.

[*Moorish Merchants.*]

In this city there reside many very wealthy Moorish merchants, and all the trade is in their hands.[2] They have a fine mosque[3] in the square of the town. The king is, as it were, governed by these Moors because of the presents which they give him; and owing to their industry[4] the government is wholly in their hands, for these Christians are coarse people.

[*Spice Trade.*]

All kinds of spices are to be found in this city of Chalichut, such as cinnamon, pepper, ginger, frankincense, lac: and brazil-wood abounds in the forests. These spices do not grow here, but[5] in a certain island at a distance of 160 leagues from this city, near the mainland. It can be reached overland in xx days and is inhabited by Moors.[6] All the above spices are brought to this city as to a staple.[7]

---

[1] Peutinger: "the king had the captain asked what he wanted or sought."

[2] Ramusio: "carried on in their vessels."

[3] Peutinger translates: "Irrkirche," *i.e.*, heterodox church.

[4] Industria: The word in Peutinger's letter, "gescheidigkeit", or intelligence, seems more appropriate.

[5] Ramusio adds here "partly". The island is Ceylon.

[6] Ramusio adds: "and not by Christians, and the Moors are the masters (signori)."

[7] The Italian original has "stapola".

[*Coins.*]

The coins most in circulation in this city are serafins of fine gold, coined by the Sultan of Babylonia,[1] which weigh 2 or 3 grains less than a ducat, and are called serafins.[2] There also circulate some Venetian and Genoese ducats, as also small silver coins, which must likewise be of the coinage of said sultan.

[*Merchandise.*]

There is abundance of silken stuffs, namely, velvets of various colours,[3] satins, damask, taffetas, brocades worked in gold, scarlet cloth, brass and tin ware.[4] In fine, all these things are to be found in abundance, and it is my opinion that the cloths worked in gold and the silks are brought thither from Cairo.

[*Shipping.*]

The Portuguese remained three months at that town, namely, from May 21[5] to August 25, and during that time there arrived about 1,500 Moorish vessels in search of spices. The largest of these vessels did not exceed 800 tons.[6] They are of all sorts, large and small. Having only one mast they can make headway only with the wind astern, and sometimes are obliged to wait from four to six months for fair weather [the monsoon or season].

---

[1] Babylonia of Egypt. Ramusio omits "Babylonia". Peutinger has Alkeiro (Cairo).

[2] The xerafins of Portuguese authors, worth about 7*s.* 10*d.* (at Calecut).

[3] The *Paesi* and Ramusio add "zetanini velutati"; and Ramusio introduces also "damasked Lucca cloth", in place of "scarlet cloth". Prof. Dalla Vedova suggests that "cetanini" may stand for "setini", a silken stuff of narrow width used in decorating the columns of churches. Bandini says it means "zendado, a kind of cloth". Lucca was famous in the sixteenth century for its silks and woollen cloths.

[4] Tin, from Malacca.

[5] The *Paesi*, Ramusio, and Peutinger say May 19. According to the "Roteiro", Vasco da Gama anchored off Capua on May 20.

[6] Ramusio says 200 tons; Peutinger 1,200.

Many ot these vessels are lost.[1] They are badly built,[2] and very frail. They carry neither arms nor artillery.

The vessels which visit the islands to carry spices to this city of Chalichut are flat-bottomed, so as to draw little water, for there are many dry places (shoals). Some of these vessels are built without any nails or iron,[3] for they have to pass over the loadstone.

All the vessels, as long as they remain at this city, are drawn up on the beach, for there is no port where they would be safe otherwise.[4]

[*Prices.*]

A load of cinnamon equal to 5 Lisbon cantars[5] is worth in that city between x and xii ducats, or serafins, at most; but in the islands where it is collected it is worth only half that sum. Pepper and cloves are rated similarly. Ginger[6] and cinnamon are worth more than any other spices, but lac is worth next to nothing, and they ballast their vessels with it, that is calk them.[7] Brazil-wood abounds in the forests.

---

[1] This sentence is omitted by Ramusio; but Peutinger says "many of these vessels are drowned in the sea".

[2] Ramusio says: "are of curious build".

[3] Ramusio adds: "but with wooden bolts", but omits the allusion to the loadstone.

Peutinger locates the "calamito or loadstone" near Ceylon. The myth of magnetic mountains and islands originated in India or China, and was widely credited during the Middle Ages. It was believed that the magnet pulled out the iron bolts and nails of passing ships, which then fell to pieces and were lost.

[4] Ramusio adds: "The sea rises and falls alternately every six hours, as elsewhere, and sometimes between 500 and 700 vessels may be seen there—a great sight".

[5] Peutinger adds that the cantar is equal to 250 pounds, when in fact it is only a hundredweight. Five cantars were equal to 1 bahar =208 kilo=460 pounds.

[6] Ramusio and Peutinger say that ginger is worth only one half. They say nothing about cinnamon.

[7] Ramusio says nothing about "calking". The writer seems to look upon "ballasting" and "calking" as identical operations. Or has he made use of a Portuguese term (alastrar), the meaning of which he did not know? Or are we to understand that lac was employed as a substitute for pitch?

In payment they only take gold and silver; coral and other merchandise of our parts they esteem but little,[1] linen-cloth excepted, which I believe would find a ready market, as the sailors bartered some of their shirts very profitably for spices, although very fine white linen cloth, probably imported from Cairo, is found there.

There is a custom-house in this city as elsewhere, and merchandise pays a duty of 5 p. c.

The Portuguese who returned home brought a few precious stones of little value, for, in truth, they had neither gold nor silver to buy any. They say that these jewels are very dear there, as also are pearls, but I believe they are to be had cheap. This is my opinion, but those they bought were in the hands of Moorish brokers, who sell at a fourfold profit. They have brought some balasci,[2] sapphires and very small rubies, as also many garnets. They say that the captain brings some valuable jewels, which he bought with the silver which he had at his disposal, but as he has not yet come back it is not known what he brings.[3]

[*Trade with Egypt and East Africa.*]

Most of the vessels which lade spices at Chalichut cross the large gulf, mentioned above, over which the pilot took them; they then pass through the strait.[4] The Red Sea is crossed in smaller vessels, after which they proceed by land to the House of Mecca, which is a journey of 3 days. They then take the route for Cairo, past the foot of Mount Sinai, and through a desert of sand where, they say, high winds sometimes raise the sand in such a manner that it covers them. Some of the spice-vessels visit all the cities of the gulf, others go to the mouth of the great

---

[1] Ramusio and Peutinger say that they also take corals in payment, and this seems more probable.

[2] "Balasci" are the pink rubies named after the country of their origin, Badakhshi, which was usually known, according to Ibn Batuta, as Al-balaksh (Yule's *Marco Polo*, I, p. 169; Heyd, *Geschichte des Levante-Handels*, 1879, I, p. 582). Badakhshi is Badakhshan, and not a kingdom near Pegu and Bengal, as supposed by Duarte Barbosa (Hakluyt Society's edition, 1866, p. 212).

[3] The latter part of this sentence is omitted by Ramusio.

[4] Bab el Mandeb.

river,[1] where gold is found and a Moorish population, and there discharge their cargoes.

They found in this city of Chalichut barrels of Malvasia[2] from Candia, and I believe that they were brought from Cairo, as is other merchandise.

[*Chinese Visitors.*]

It is now about 80 years since there arrived in this city of Chalicut certain vessels of white Christians, who wore their hair long like Germans, and had no beards except around the mouth, such as are worn at Constantinople by cavaliers and courtiers.[3] They landed, wearing a cuirass, helmet, and vizor, and carrying a certain weapon [sword] attached to a spear. Their vessels are armed with bombards, shorter than those in use with us. Once every two years they return with 20 or 25 vessels. They are unable to tell what people they are, nor what merchandise they bring to this city, save that it includes very fine linen-cloth and brass-ware. They load spices. Their vessels have four masts like those of Spain. If they were Germans it seems to me that we should have had some notice about them; possibly they may be Russians if they have a port there. On the arrival of the captain we may learn who these people are, for the Italian-speaking pilot, who was given him by the Moorish king,[4] and whom he took away contrary to his inclinations, is with him, and may be able to tell.[5]

---

[1] The Rio dos Bons Signaes, or Zambezi.

[2] Malvasia (Malmsey) is a luscious Greek wine, named after the town of Napoli di Malvasia, in Laconia. The vines were transplanted to Crete, Madeira, and other places.

[3] Ramusio says: "they had a beard between the nose and the mouth, such as is worn by the courtiers at Constantinople, who call it a moustache."

[4] Ramusio adds: "of Melinde". The "pilot" here referred to was Gaspar da Gama. See Appendix E.

[5] This information was apparently never asked for. The "strangers" were undoubtedly Chinese. Marco Polo (*Yule*, I, p. lxvi, and II, pp. 197, 327) already mentions their four-masted vessels. In his time, Chinese vessels regularly visited the west coast of India. The vizor in the guise of a mask, distinctly points to the Chinese, and the sword attached to a spear is a Chinese weapon. Up to the introduc-

[*Food.*]

Corn in abundance is found in this city of Chalichut, it being brought thither by the Moors. For 3 reals,[1] which are smaller than ours, bread sufficient for the daily sustenance of a man can be purchased. Their bread is unleavened, resembling small cakes, which are baked daily in the ashes. Rice, likewise, is found in abundance. There are cows and oxen. They are small, but yield much milk and butter. Oranges of indifferent flavour[2] are plentiful, as also lemons, citrons and limes, very good melons,[3] dates, fresh and dried, and great variety of other kinds of fruit.

The king of this city of Chalichut eats neither of meat nor fish nor anything that has been killed, nor do his barons, courtiers, or other persons of quality, for they say that Jesus Christ[4] said in his law that he who kills shall die. For this reason they refuse to eat anything that has been killed, and it is a great thing that they should be able to support themselves without eating meat or fish.[5] The common people eat meat and fish, but they do not eat oxen or cows, for they hold these animals to be blessed (benedetto), and when they meet an ox on the highway they touch him, and afterwards kiss their hand, as a sign of great humility.

The king lives on rice, milk and butter,[6] and so do his barons

---

tion of pig-tails by the Manju, in 1644, the Chinese wore their hair long. A punitive fleet of sixty-two Chinese vessels was sent to Ceylon in 1401. In 1417 an embassy was sent from Mu-ku-tu-su (Magadoxo) to China (Bretschneider, *On the Knowledge possessed by the Ancient Chinese of the Arabs*, London, 1871), and in 1431 Chinese junks might be seen at Jedda (Hirth, *Verhandlungen*, Berlin Geographical Society, 1889, p. 46).

During the second half of the fifteenth century the intercourse between China and Malabar seems to have become rare, until at last it ceased altogether (Richthofen, *China*, I, p. 10, 5).

Ramusio contemptuously suppresses the writer's speculations about these curious strangers being Germans or Russians.

[1] Less than a penny.

[2] "di mezo sapore". Ramusio has "tutte dolci".

[3] "Poponi": Ramusio says "pomi", apples.

[4] Or rather Buddha.

[5] Ramusio has suppressed this passage.

[6] Ramusio adds: "And bread made of corn and other things of the kind".

and some of the other men of quality. And the king is waited upon right royally at table. He drinks palm-wine out of a silver cup. This cup he does not put to his mouth, but holds at some distance and pours the wine down his throat.

[*Fish.*]

The fish are of the same kinds as are those of Portugal, namely, perch,[1] soles,[2] bream,[3] salmon, mullets, and so of all other kinds. And there are fishermen who go a-fishing[4] [soles and salmon].

[*Elephants.*]

The Christians ride on elephants, of whom there are many: they are domesticated. When the king goes to war most of his people go on foot, but some are mounted on elephants; but when he goes from place to place he causes himself to be carried by some among the principal men of his court.[5]

[*Dress.*]

All or most of these people are clothed in cotton-cloths from the waist down to the knee, but from the waist upwards they go naked. Courtiers and men of condition dress in the same manner, but make use of silk-stuffs, reddish or scarlet or of other colours, as seems good to them.[6] The wives (ladies) of men of condition are clothed above the girdle in very white and delicate linen; but the wives of lower degree are naked above the

---

[1] Professor Dalla Vedova suggests that the "pescotto" of the original may be the "Pesce persico" (*Perca fluviatilis*), or perch. Ramusio, in his edition of 1563, however, has "pescietti", which means "small fishes" (sardines).

[2] Lenguazzi: perhaps the modern "linguattole", or sole.

[3] Bisuccho, in Portuguese Besugo, the sea-bream (*Sparus cantabricus*).

[4] The words within brackets are only to be found in the *Paesi*.

[5] Ramusio adds: "There are also horses as with us, and they are highly valued by Christians and Moors alike". Peutinger and the *Paesi* say the same.

[6] Ramusio says: "silk-stuffs and bocassins". He does not mention the colours.

waist.[1] The Moors dress according to their custom in *jubbi* and *balandrau*.[2]

[*Distance to Lisbon.*]

From this city of Chalichut to Lisbon is a distance of 3800 leagues,[3] and at the rate of 4½ miles to the league this makes 17,100 miles, and as much again for the return voyage. From this the time in which such a voyage can be made may be judged, it requiring from 15 to 16 months.

[*Native Navigation.*]

The mariners of that part, namely the Moors, do not guide themselves by the Pole in navigating this gulf, but trust to quadrants of wood.[4] When they cross the gulf to that side, so they were told by the pilot, they leave a thousand or more islands[5] to the right; and whoever gets among these will be lost as there are many rocks (shoals), and I am inclined to think that they be those which were discovered by the King of Castile.[6]

[*Prester John.*]

At the city of Chalichut they have some knowledge of Prester John,[7] but not much, as he is far away. These Christians believe that Jesus Christ was born of the Virgin Mary, without sin, was crucified and killed by the Jews, and buried at Jerusalem. They also have some knowledge of the Pope of Rome, but know

---

1 Peutinger adds: "They are decent, quiet (fromm) people at his court, and dress according to their condition and rank (adel)".

2 *Jubbi* (Arabic) is a long coat or caftan; the *balandrau* (Portuguese) is a surtout worn by the Brothers of Mercy in Portugal. Ramusio calls the latter garments *palascani*.

3 The actual distance is about 10,500 nautical miles, or 3,060 Portuguese leagues.

4 In his second letter the writer recurs to this subject.

5 These are the Laccadive islands, fourteen in number: but, as their name implies (Laksha Dwipa = the Hundred Thousand Islands), supposed to be much more numerous. Mr. Sneyd's *Codex* says there were 11,000 of these islands. The Maldives were known as Narikela Dwipa.

6 That is the West Indies!

7 Ramusio adds: "through vessels which go to Mecca".

nothing of our faith beyond this. They [the people of Prester John] have letters and a written language.

[*Articles of Commerce.*]

In this city are found many tusks of elephants, also much cotton, sugar and sweetmeats, and all the wealth of the world seems now to have been discovered.

I presume that wine would prove a good article in these parts, and very acceptable to these Christians. Oil, too, is in demand.

Justice is strictly administered in this city. Robbers, murderers, and other malefactors are incontinently impaled in the Turkish fashion; and whoever defrauds the king's excise (customs) is punished by having his merchandise confiscated.

Civet, musk, ambergris and storax are met with.[1]

[*Spice Islands.*]

The island where the spices grow is called Zilon, and is 60[2] leagues from said city. In that island grow the trees which yield very good cinnamon; as also pepper.[3] However, there is still another island [in which spices grow]. Cinnamon and pepper also grow on the mainland, around this city, but the quality is inferior to the products of the islands. Ginger grows on the mainland, and is of very good quality. Cloves grow at a great distance. Of rhubarb there is much, and many other kinds of spices are found there, as also many almonds.[4]

[*The Arabian Sea.*]

I stated above that the gulf was wholly peopled by Moors, but I have since[5] learnt that this is not the case. Only the shore on this side [the west], where is the city of Melinde, is wholly inhabited by white Moors, whilst the further [eastern] shore is

---

[1] Ramusio adds: "benzoin".

[2] It should be 160.

[3] Ramusio adds: "many sapphires and other jewels". He then says: "Pepper and ginger grow around the said city of Calicut". The paragraph is worded obscurely, but my version seems to be preferable. Sapphires are mentioned at the end of the letter.

[4] Ramusio does not mention almonds, nor does Peutinger.

[5] This expression proves that the letter was not written at one sitting, but by degrees.

peopled by Christian Indians, who are white as we are. Along the coast and throughout the mainland much corn, meat and fruit are produced.

The country around the city of Melinde is very fertile, and many of these provisions are shipped from it to Chalichut, for most of the land around the latter is sandy and yields no fruit.[1]

[*The Monsoons.*]

There are only two dominant winds in those parts, namely westerly and easterly winds, and it is winter during the former and summer during the latter.

[*Artists.*]

There are many excellent painters in this city of Ghalinde,[2] of figures as well as of other subjects.

[*Architecture.*]

Neither Ghalinde nor any of the other cities is enclosed within walls or otherwise, but there are many good houses, built in the Moorish style, of stone and mortar, and streets regularly laid out (ordinate).[3]

[*Ceylon.*]

In the island of Zilon, where the cinnamon grows, are found many precious stones and the biggest sapphires.

GIROLAMO SERNIGI.

Lisbon.

---

[1] Ramusio has much condensed the whole of this paragraph, and seems to have misunderstood the writer. The statement that provisions were sent from Melinde to Calecut can hardly be accepted, and it was perhaps for this reason that Ramusio suppressed the name of that town. The country around Calecut is certainly sandy, but it is not as sterile as the bald statement of the writer would lead one to believe, for the city lies in the midst of extensive groves of palm, mango, and jack trees.

Peutinger thus summarises this passage: "The country around Kalekut is mostly sand, and neither corn nor any other fruit grows there. These are imported by sea."

[2] Should be Chalechut, as Bandini prints it.

[3] The last two paragraphs have been omitted by Ramusio.

GIROLAMO SERNIGI'S SECOND LETTER TO A GENTLEMAN OF FLORENCE.[1]

Since I sent you full particulars about India and its discovery there has arrived here the pilot whom they took by force. He appeared to be a Sclavonian and turns out to be a Jew, born at Alexandria, or in those parts, and thence went to India when very young. At Calichut he has a wife and children. He owned a ship and went several times to sea.

[*Spices.*]

This man told wonderful things about those countries, and their wealth in spices. The best and finest cinnamon is procured from another island [Ceylon], about 150 leagues beyond Calichut and very near the mainland. This island is inhabited by Moors. Pepper and cloves come from more distant parts.

[*Jews.*]

He says that there are not many Jews there; and that there is a King of the Jews of the ten tribes of the Jewish people which went out of Egypt.[2]

[*Christians.*]

He says that in those countries there are many gentiles, that is idolaters, and only a few Christians;[3] that the supposed churches

---

[1] Translated from the *Paesi novamente retrovati*, Vicenza, 1507.

[2] The true history of the Jewish colony in Malabar has been written by Claudius Buchanan (*Christian Researches in Asia*, Edinburgh, 1812). Ritter (*Erdkunde*, v, pp. 595-601) gives an excellent summary.

[3] Gaspar da Gama was quite right. There were no Christians at Calecut when Vasco da Gama first visited that town, nor are there many now. Cochin, and not Calecut, was the chief seat of the Syrian Christians of Malabar. They were an offshoot of the church of Persia, which recognised the Nestorian patriarch of Babylon (Mosul). After the condemnation of their dogmas by the Council of Ephesus (431) they sought a refuge in distant countries. After 1599 many of them recognised the Pope, but after the ascendency of the Dutch (since 1653) some turned Protestants, whilst others recognised the Jacobite bishop of Antioch as their head. Popularly they are

and belfries are in reality temples of idolaters, and that the pictures within them are those of idols and not of Saints. To me this seems more probable than saying that there are Christian but no divine administrations, no priests and no sacrificial mass. I do not understand that there are any Christians there to be taken into account,[1] excepting those of Prester John, whose country is far from Calichut, on this [*i.e.*, the western] side of the Gulf of Arabia, and borders upon the country of the King of Melinde, and, far in the interior, upon the Ethiopians, that is the black people of Guinea, as also upon Egypt, that is the country of the Sultan of Babylon [Cairo]. This Prester John has priests, who offer sacrifices, respect the Gospels and the Laws of the Church, much as is done by other Christians.

[*Trade with Egypt.*]

The Sultan has a port on the Red Sea, and the route from Alexandria to that port passes throughout through his territories, it being a journey of quite lxxx days.[2] At that port all spices coming from Calichut are discharged.

[*A Pearl Fishery.*]

There is an island about a league from the mainland,[3] inhabited by fishermen, who do nothing but fish for pearls. There is no water in the island, and many barges go daily to a large river on the mainland where they are filled with water—no tubs or barrels being used. When the animals of the island see these barges return, they immediately hasten to the shore to drink out of these barges. Pearls are not fished at any island except this

---

known as S. Thomas Christians, although there exists not the slightest evidence of that Apostle ever having visited India. Their worship is of a simple nature : they admit no images to their churches, reject the doctrine of transubstantiation, and allow their priests to marry (G. Milne Rae, *The Syrian Church in India*, 1892 ; Percy Badger, *The Nestorians and their Ritual*, 1852 ; German, *Die Kirche der Thomaschristen*, 1877).

[1] Ramusio says : "excepting those called Jacobites and those of Prester John."

[2] Ramusio says forty days.

[3] Ramusio adds : "towards the Gulf of Persia".

one which lies quite 60 leagues[1] this side of Calichut. It is inhabited by gentiles, who set great store by cows and oxen, whom they almost worship, so that anyone discovered to have eaten beef is adjudged guilty of death.[2]

[*Taprobana.*]

Taprobana, concerning which Pliny wrote so fully, was not known to the pilot, for it must be quite out at sea, far away from the mainland.[3]

[*A Pagoda.*]

At Calichut there is a temple and whoever enters it before noon on a seventh Wednesday dies[4] because of diabolical apparitions. The Jewish pilot affirms that this is most certainly true, and that on a certain day of the year some lamps in this same temple begin to burn spontaneously and cause many deformities of nature to appear.

[*Moorish Navigation.*]

He, moreover, stated that in those seas they navigate without compasses, but with the aid of quadrants of wood. This seems to be a difficult thing to do, especially during a fog, when it is impossible to see the stars. They also have a kind of very small anchor, but I do not know how it is used.[5] The planks of their vessels are held together by cords, and they are three palms longer than the beam. All the vessels of that country are built at Calichut, for no wood is found elsewhere.

---

[1] Ramusio says 300 leagues. The real distance of Bahrein is about 550 leagues. There may be some confusion with the Manar pearl fishery.

[2] Varthema (p. 95) and Duarte Barbosa (p. 37) refer to the pearl fishery of the Bahrein islands. They both describe the islanders as Mohammedans. Mr. Bent (*Journal Royal Geographical Society*, xii, 1890) visited the islands in 1889, and states that there is a good supply of water. Indeed, a river such as is described in the letter only exists some 250 miles away.

[3] King Manuel was better advised (see p. 115, note).

[4] Ramusio says: "is frightened".

[5] These "anchors", according to Varthema (p. 153), consist of a block of marble, which has two ropes attached to it. On the African coast a box fitted with stones is used for the same purpose.

[*Suitable Exports.*]

The articles of merchandise most suitable for that country seem to be coral, copper kettles and thin plates of the same metal; tartar, spectacles (for there are countries where a pair of them fetches a high price), coarse linens, wine, oil, thin brocades, and also boccasins, that is cloths. The said Jew has thrown much light on all these matters.

[*Plans of King Manuel.*]

Our King of Portugal is very keen in this matter and has already ordered four vessels to be got ready, besides two caravels, well armed, to sail in January with plenty of merchandise.[1] Should the King of Calicut not allow the Portuguese to trade in those countries, the captain of these vessels is instructed to capture as many native craft as he can. In my opinion he will be able to capture as many as he chooses, for they are frail, and so badly constructed that they can only sail before the wind. Of these native vessels, engaged in the spice trade, there are very many.

[*Elephants.*]

The principal animals of this country are elephants, which they employ in war. On the back of the animal they place a kind of castle sheltering three or four fighting men, in addition to whom there is one man, and he the most important, who guides the animal, as described by Pliny.[2] Some kings there are who have 1500 elephants each, others a thousand and others eight hundred, according to the extent of their dominions. When they wish to beach their ships they do so by the strength of these animals, and they make them run, which seems fabulous, but is nevertheless true.

[*Precious Stones.*]

Those who have returned say that precious stones (jewels) are plentiful, but dear in comparison with other merchandise. Neither the captain nor the others have brought back jewels worth taking

---

[1] The next expedition was that sent out under Pedralvarez Cabral, who left Lisbon in March, 1500, with thirteen vessels.

[2] In Book VIII of his *Natural History*.

into account, and this makes me think that they are not found there, but come from afar. The princes and kings of those countries value precious stones very much.

Storax, benzoin, civet and similar things are not as plentiful there as I was led to believe.

[*The Royal Title.*]

Our king has taken a title from those countries, *viz.* King of Portugal and Algarve on this and on the other side of the sea, in Africa, Lord of Guinea, and of the conquest, the navigation and commerce of Ethiopia, Arabia, Persia and India.

This is what I was able to learn from some persons of intelligence who returned with this fleet. And if I have written it down somewhat at random you, Sir,[1] will pardon and excuse me.

EXTRACTS FROM GIROLAMO SERNIGI'S LETTER TO HIS BROTHER, 1499.

From an Abstract made by Conrad Peutinger at Rome.

. . . .

The four vessels left Lisbon on July 10, 1499 . . . . The captain remained behind with three vessels, because his brother Paulo da Gama, was sick unto death. He landed him at an island called Capo Verde, far from Lisbon, and burnt two vessels, the one of 110 tons and one of 90 tons, so that they might not fall into the hands of the heathen [Mohammedans], for 55 of his people had died, and he was unable to bring these ships home with the remaining 63 men. Afterwards the captain came *a Sambameno* (*a salvamento*, safely) back to Lisbon with the one ship.[2]

---

[1] This last paragraph is not found in the *Paesi novamente retrovati*, and is taken from Ramusio.

[2] This paragraph is rather puzzling. July 10th, 1499, was the date of Coelho's arrival. Of the four vessels, two are correctly stated to have been burnt, though not near Cape Verde, namely, the store ship of 110 tons, and one of the vessels of 90 tons (the *S. Raphael*). Coelho brought home the small vessel of 50 tons, and the "captain" himself is stated to have returned in the remaining vessel of 90 tons.

. . . . . On the voyage out from Lisbon the vessels came to some distant islands where they [the Portuguese] had been before.[1] Beyond these islands they came to a gulf, or arm of the sea, which they crossed, having the land always to the left and the broad sea to the right. . . . . .

Various kinds of spices are brought from distant islands to Colokutt. Pepper, brazil-wood, *grao*,[2] cinnamon, frankincense, lac, are to be found there. These things abound and are worth next to nothing. Of brazil-wood there is plenty. There are likewise many ivory tusks and various other kinds of merchandise, such as variously-coloured silk-stuffs, costly cloth worked in gold, fine white linen, and woollen-stuffs, such as bocassins of various colours, and also much cotton. It is thought that the silver stuffs and cloths, as also the linens, come from Alkeiro (Cairo).

. . . . . . Most of the spices brought to Kalikut are said to come from the island of Zelong (Ceylon). Only heathen live in that island, and the king is a heathen [Moor]. It is at a distance of 160 leagues from Kalekutt, and only one league from the mainland. By land it is a journey of twenty days. In the island are forests of brazil-wood and roseberries,[3] and other spices, including cloves and rhubarb, are found. Some minor spices come from more distant islands. Cinnamon is imported from Ceylon . . . .

---

[1] The Cape Verde islands.

[2] Grão or gran (Portuguese), kermes-grain, anciently scarlet, is not mentioned by Ramusio.

[3] Rosebeeren (Roseberries) seems to stand for Rose mallus, or Rossamalha, an aromatic resin containing benzoic acid, yielded by the majestic Rasamala tree (*Altingia excelsa*) of Java, where it is used as a substitute for benzoin.

APPENDIX C.

VASCO DA GAMA.
(From a Paris MS. of Barretto de Rezende.)

THREE PORTUGUESE ACCOUNTS OF VASCO DA GAMA'S FIRST VOYAGE (1608-1646).

I.—JORNAL DAS VIAGENS DOS PORTUGUEZES ÁS INDIAS, 1608.

THE late Visconde de Santarem, in his *Noticia dos Manuscriptos*, 2nd edition, Lisbon, 1863, p. 93, draws attention to the existence of a MS. in the Bibliothèque Nationale at Paris, which in his opinion furnishes most valuable chronological information on the Portuguese voyages to India, from 1497 to 1632. We have translated from this codex all that refers to the first voyage of Vasco da Gama; and a perusal of the translation will, we think, convince the reader that he has before him, not a document based upon authentic sources, but a compilation of very doubtful value.

We have examined three copies, or rather editions, of this *Jornal das Viagens dos Portuguezes ás Indias*, viz.:—

1. *Bibl. Nat. Port.* 8, *No.* 85. This is the earliest of the three MSS., for it only extends to the year 1608. On folio 206[b] is a statement to the effect that it was copied in 1618 from a MS. in the possession of the Conde de Vidigueira.

2. *Bibl. Nat. Port.* 46. This, formerly, bore the number 10023, and is the MS. described by Santarem. It is identical with Port. 8, except that its information is extended to the year 1632.

3. *British Museum Add. MSS.* 20902. This is the MS. quoted by Dr. Walter de Gray Birch (*The Commentaries*

of the Great Afonso Dalboquerque, ii, p. xvi). It is still more recent than the preceding, having been extended by an unknown author to the year 1653. A list of the Viceroys up to 1610 is appended. The marginal notes are derived from Pedro Barretto de Rezende's *Livro das Armadas*.

THE YEAR 1497.

On the second of June, 1497, there set sail from Lisbon for the discovery of Oriental India, Vasco da Gama, the second son of Estevão da Gama, comptroller (veador) of the household of the King Don Affonso V, and of Dona Isabel Sodré, his wife, as captain-major of four vessels: himself in the *São Raphael;* Paulo da Gama, his elder brother, in the *São Gabriel;* Nicolao Coelho in the *São Miguel.*

Gonçalo Nunes was captain of a vessel carrying provisions, which this side (*antes*) the Cape of Good Hope were transferred to the other vessels, when he returned to this kingdom [of Portugal]. And the vessel *S. Gabriel*, in which went Paulo da Gama, being much dilapidated, so as to be unable to continue the voyage, was broken up for the purpose of repairing the other vessels, in a river of Cafraria, beyond the Cape of Good Hope, which was named the river of Mercy. And Paulo da Gama went over to the vessel of his brother, while his people were distributed among the two vessels. Thence they continued their voyage.

Having come to an anchor at Moçambique, where the Sheikh attempted to take the vessels by treachery, they disembarked at the island of São Jorge, where was celebrated the first mass beyond the Cape of Good Hope. Thence they went to Quiloa and Mombaça, and the kings of all these islands attempted to act treacherously, but God would not permit their success.

At Melinde the King made them honestly welcome, and gave them trustworthy pilots, who guided them to Angediva, where they fought the fustas of the Sabayo, the governor of Goa, over whom they gained the victory. And thence they went to Calicut, where the Samori planned many treacherous acts which took no effect. Thence they went to Cochim, where the King received them well, and to Cananor, in the same manner. There they completed the loading of the two vessels, and returned to this kingdom, arriving safely at Lisbon on September 18th, 1499.[1]

Paulo da Gama died of an illness in the island of Terçeira, at the city of Angra, and lies buried in the monastery of São Francisco of that city.[2]

II.—Luiz de Figueiredo Falcão, 1612.

Luiz de Figueiredo Falcão was secretary of King Philip II of Portugal (Philip III of Spain), and is the compiler of a *Livro em que se contem toda a Fazenda, & Real Patrimonio dos Reynos de Portugal, India, ilhas adjacentes de sua coroa*, which was printed by order of the Portuguese Government in 1859.

The Preface is dated "Madrid, October 20, MDC.VII", but this is evidently a misprint, for reference is made in it to a list of captains who went to India since 1497 as containing information up to the year 1612; and instead of VII, we ought therefore to read XII, the date of the book being thus 1612.

The author had access to the original records in the India House, and claims to have expended three years upon the compilation of his work, which certainly contains a mass of information of the highest interest. Neverthe-

---

[1] I need hardly direct the reader's attention to the fact that the fustas of the Sabayo were fought *after* Vasco's return from Calecut, and that he visited neither Cochin nor Cananor in the course of this first voyage.

[2] A MS. in the Torre do Tombo quoted by Texeira de Aragão (*Boletim*, VI, 1886, p. 580), ornamented with the coloured coats of arms of the *Counts* of Vidigueira, and extending to 1641, seems to be identical in several respects with the MS. from which the above is quoted. The concluding portion, beginning with "returned to this kingdom", is taken word for word from the earlier *Jornal*. Vasco da Gama is stated to have gone in the *S. Raphael*, whilst Paulo's vessel, the *S. Gabriel*, is said to have been destroyed on the homeward voyage near Cabo de S. Vicente.

less, his book is not free from errors, many of which have already been pointed out by Cunha Rivara in an Appendix to a translation of the *Viagem de Francisco Pyrard*, published at Nova Goa in 1858. Texeira de Aragão (*Boletim*, Lisbon Geographical Society, vi, p. 578) also warns against accepting without question all the statements made by this author.

We quote the following information on Vasco da Gama's first voyage from a "List of Captain-majors and Captains who went to India since 1497", p. 137:—

1497.

In the year 1497 there departed for India Vasco da Gama, the first discoverer, as captain-major of four vessels. He left Lisbon on July 8th, 1497.

São Miguel, flagship .	Pilot: Pero d'Alenquer.
São Raphael . .	Captain: Paulo da Gama, brother of Vasco da Gama. Pilot: João de Coimbra.
Berrio . .	Captain: Nicolao Coelho. Pilot: Pero Escovar.
A ship (*nao*) . .	Captain: Gonçalo Nunez, a retainer of Vasco da Gama. She carried provisions.[1]

The *Berrio*, with her captain, returned and reached the bar of Lisbon on July 10th, 1499.

Vasco da Gama went from India to Cape Verde, where he remained with his brother, Paulo da Gama, who died there, and whose body he conveyed to the island of Terçeira, and he sent one of his servants with the *São Raphael* to Lisbon.

Vasco da Gama himself reached Lisbon in a caravel on August 29th, two years and nearly two months after he had left that port.

It is scarcely necessary to point out that the flagship was

---

[1] Paulo da Gama came back in this vessel, his own having been burnt by order of Vasco da Gama, off Tangáta. [*Note by the author.*]

the *São Gabriel*, and that Paulo da Gama came back in that vessel and not in the store-ship. It was, indeed, Paulo's own ship, the *São Raphael*, which was burnt off Tangáta.

As an instance of the author's inconsistencies, we need only quote the following passage from a "Summary Statement of Vessels which left Portugal for India", p. 194:—

> Between July 10th, 1499, on which day there arrived in the port of Lisbon the ship *São Raphael*, in which Vasco da Gama had gone to India in 1497, and 1612, there came back from India 425 vessels.

It was the *Berrio* which came back on July 10th, the *São Raphael* having been burnt off Mtangata; and Vasco da Gama did not go in the *S. Raphael*, by the author's own (erroneous) statement.

III.—PEDRO BARRETTO DE REZENDE, 1646.

Captain Pedro Barretto de Rezende, a professed Knight of the Order of St. Benedict of Aviz, and a native of Pavia,[1] is the author of a *Livro do Estado da India*, consisting of three Parts and an Appendix, of which MS. copies exist in the British Museum (Sloane Collection, No. 197) and the Bibliothèque Nationale (Port. 1, and Port. 36). Part I of this work contains a succinct account of the doings of the Viceroys of India up to 1634, and gives portraits of all of them; Parts II and III contain plans of the Portuguese forts between the Cape of Good Hope and China, with descriptions; whilst the Appendix furnishes an account of the "armadas" or fleets which were sent to India up to 1605.

Dr. Walter de Gray Birch (*Commentaries of the Great*

---

[1] Pavia, a small town twenty miles to the north of Evora.

Afonso Dalboquerque, i, pp. vii-xiii) has given an account of the MS. of this work existing in the British Museum.

If this valuable document should ever be printed, it will be necessary to collate the copies existing in London, Paris, and probably also elsewhere, for they are not in all respects identical. Port. 36 seems to me to deserve the preference as far as respects Part I, but Part II (the description of the forts) has been abridged, as compared with Port. 1. The portraits in this latter are more neatly done

Vasco da Gama as Viceroy.
(*After Correa's portrait in the Palacio do Governo, at Goa.*)

than in Port. 36. No reference to the source of these full-length portraits is made by the author. They certainly differ from the portraits designed in 1547 by a native artist under the supervision of Gaspar Correa, and published in the Lisbon edition of his *Lendas* (see t. iv, p. 596). Lord Stanley (*Vasco da Gama*, p. ix) says that Correa's portraits are "better" than those in Rezende's work. All that we can say is that they are not worse. Our full-length portrait is from a MS. of Barretto de Rezende in the Bibliothéque Nationale, as reproduced in Charton's *Voyageurs anciens et modernes.* The small oval portrait is from a copy of

Correa's painting which was made by order of D. Francisco da Assumpção de Brito, who was installed Archbishop of Goa in 1774. It was first published in 1817 in a work entitled *Retratos e Elogios de Varões e Donas.*

FIRST VOYAGE, 1497; FOUR SAILS.

King John II of Portugal having died without a legitimate son, Dom Manuel was proclaimed King on October 27th, 1495; and as this fresh dignity entailed that he should prosecute the undertakings initiated by his predecessors, he proposed to himself to go on with the discovery of Oriental India by sea, which, seventy-five years before, had been set going.

In 1496 he had many councils on this affair, and in consequence of the resolutions arrived at he agreed (*assentou*) to despatch on this enterprise one Vasco da Gama, and forthwith arranged for the fleet to be sent, the work upon which was carried on with such expedition that rigging and all was ready by Saturday, July 8th, 1496.

The fleet (*armada*) only included three ships of from 100 to 320 tons, and there went in them, between sailors and soldiers, 260 persons. In addition there was a ship carrying provisions.

The flag-ship, in which Vasco da Gama, the captain-major, embarked, was called the *São Gabriel*, and Pero de Alemquer was the pilot. The second ship was called the *São Raphael;* Paulo da Gama, the brother of said Vasco, was captain, and João de Coimbra, pilot.

The third vessel was called the *Berrio;* Nicolao Coelho was her captain and P^{o}. Escolar her pilot.

Gonsalo Nunes, a retainer (*criado*) of Vasco da Gama, was captain of the cargo-ship (*nao*); only provisions went in her. These, as also the crew, having been transferred to the other ships at the Cape of Good Hope, they set fire to her.

They set sail from the bar of Lisbon on July 8th, 1497, arrived at Moçambique on March 1st, 1498, made Mombasa on Palm Sunday, the 7th of April,[1] and Melinde on the 15th of the same month.

There he took pilots to guide him to India, and on May 16th

[1] The 7th of April was a Saturday (see p. 34).

of the same year, '498,[1] he made the land at a port on the coast of Mallavar (Malabar), in the kingdom of the Samorim, two leagues below Callecut, which is the principal city and capital of that kingdom. There he remained seventy-four days, in the course of which, induced thereto by the Moors who live in that country, he practised upon us a thousand deceits. But having discovered that for the sake of which he had been sent, namely, India, of which he was able to take home such good intelligence, he determined to return to Portugal, and set sail on August 29th of this same year, namely, '498. At the Anjediva islands he careened the ships and took in water, and there he took a Jew who, by order of Sabayo, the King of Goa, had visited him, it being the intention, immediately after the return of this Jew, to send a fleet against him (Vasco da Gama).

Vasco da Gama departed thence and made the coast of Melinde. Wishing to depart thence for this kingdom, the ship *São Raphael*, in which was his brother, was lost on the same shoals on which she had already once grounded on the way out to India. The loss of this ship did not give much concern to Vasco da Gama, for he was short of men, and those in her were distributed among the two other vessels. He passed Moçambique, doubled the Cape of Good Hope on March 20th, 1499; when near the Cape Verde Islands a severe storm separated the two vessels, namely, that in which he (Vasco) was from her consort in which was Nicolau Coelho, who, leading, lost sight of Vasco da Gama, and reached the bar of Lisbon[2] on July 10th of said year.

Vasco da Gama only arrived on August 29th in a caravel, for his brother, Paulo da Gama, being very ill, he went from the island of Saõ Thiago to that of Terçeira, allowing his ship to be taken to Lisbon by João de Sá.

And Vasco da Gama buried his brother, whose death much afflicted him, in the island of Terçeira, and after that landed at Lisbon on August 29th, as stated above, or two years after he had started on his discovery.

---

[1] The preceding dates agree with those in the *Journal*, but the anchorage, two leagues from Calecut (see p. 48) was only reached on May 20th, and the stay at or off Calecut was certainly much longer than the seventy-four days allowed by Rezende. In fact, seventy-four days would only carry us from May 20th to August 1st.

[2] That is, the mouth of the Tagus.

From the *Livro das armadas e capitaes que forão a India*, which, as already stated, forms an Appendix to Rezende's *Livro do estado da India*, we take the following:—

Vasco da Gama, captain-major, 1497.

He departed on July 8th, by order of King Dom Manuel, with four ships to discover India, viz.:

Vasco da Gama in the *S. Gabriel*.
Paulo da Gama, his brother, in the *S. Raphael*.
Nicolao Coelho in the ship *Berrio*.
Gonçalo Nunes in a store-ship.

The people and provisions in the ship of Gonçalo Nunes were distributed among the other ships after the Cape of Good Hope had been passed, and beyond the Aguada (watering-place) of S. Braz, and this ship, having been stripped, was set on fire.

The ship of Paulo da Gama stranded on the voyage home to Portugal on the shoals between Guilva [Kilwa] and Mombaça, and these shoals were named after the *S. Raphael* which had now run aground upon them. Her people were distributed among the two companion-ships.

APPENDIX D.

THE "SÃO GABRIEL".

(From a Model designed by Captain A. A. Baldaque da Silva, drawn by Herbert Johnson.)

VASCO DA GAMA'S SHIPS AND THEIR EQUIPMENT.

ALL authorities agree that the fleet, or armada, fitted out for Vasco da Gama's voyage numbered four vessels, but they are not agreed as to the names which these vessels bore. We are not, however, likely to be misled if we accept the unanimous testimony of the author of our *Roteiro*, of João de Barros, Lopez de Castanheda, Pedro Barretto de Rezende, and Manuel Faria y Sousa: according to whom the names of the ships and of their principal officers were as follows:—

S. Gabriel (flag-ship).—Vasco da Gama, captain-major; Pero d'Alenquer, pilot; Gonçalo Alvarez, master; Diogo Dias, clerk.

S. Raphael.—Paulo da Gama, captain; João de Coimbra pilot; João de Sá, clerk.

Berrio.—Nicolau Coelho, captain; Pero Escolar, pilot; Alvaro de Braga, clerk.

Store-ship.—Gonçalo Nunes, captain.

Correa and the unknown author of the *Jornal das Viagens* (p. 145) call the "Berrio" *S. Miguel*, and make the *S. Raphael* the flag-ship; whilst L. de Figueiredo de Falcão (p. 147) substitutes a *S. Miguel* for the *S. Raphael.* It is just possible that the vessel popularly called *Berrio*, after its former owner, had been re-christened *S. Miguel.*

The *Berrio* was one of those swift lateen-rigged vessels for which Portugal was famous from the thirteenth to the beginning of the sixteenth century, and which, after the *barinel*[1] had been discarded, were exclusively employed in

[1] A sailing vessel occasionally propelled by oars.

the exploration of the African coast. Their burthen did not exceed 200 tons, and they had two or three masts, and occasionally even four.[1] The *Berrio* is stated to have been a vessel of only 50 tons. She was named after her former owner and pilot,[2] of whom she was purchased expressly for this voyage.

The store-ship was of more considerable size. Sernigi (p. 123) says she measured 110 tons; Castanheda credits

A Caravel.

(*After a Painting of the sixteenth century, in the Monastery of the Mother of God at Lisbon.*)

her with 200. She may have been a so-called *caravela redonda*, that is a caravel which carried square sails on the main and fore-masts and triangular ones on the mizzen-mast and the bowsprit. This vessel was purchased of Ayres Correa, a shipowner of Lisbon.

---

[1] Henrique Lopes de Mendonça, *Estudos sobre navios Portuguezes*, Lisbon (Ac. Real), 1892, p. 58.

[2] A pilot, Fernando Rodriques Berrio, resided at Lagos in 1502, and there were other members of the same family (Varnhagen).

The *S. Gabriel* and *S. Raphael* were specially built for this voyage. Bartholomeu Dias, who superintended their construction, discarded the caravel in which he himself had achieved his great success, in favour of square-rigged vessels of greater burthen, which, although slower sailers and less able to ply to windward, offered greater safety and more comfort to their crews. He took care, at the same time, that the draught of these vessels should enable them to navigate shallow waters, such as it was expected would be met with in the course of the voyage. The timber for these two vessels had been cut during the last year of the reign of King John, in the Crown woods of Leiria and Alcacer. The vessels having been completed, the King ordered them to be equipped by Fernão Lourenço, the factor of the house of Mines, and one of the most "magnificent" men of his time.[1]

No contemporary description or picture of these vessels has reached us, but there can hardly be a doubt that their type[2] is fairly represented on a painting made by order of D. Jorge Cabral, who was Governor of India from 1549 to 1550. This painting subsequently became the property of D. João de Castro. A copy of it was first published by the Visconde de Juromenha, who took it from a MS. dated 1558.[3] The fine woodcut in W. S. Lindsay's *History of Merchant Shipping* (II, p. 5), from an ancient picture which also belonged to D. João de Castro, seems to be derived from the same source, but as the vessel carries the flag of the Order of Christ at the main, and not the Royal Standard, it cannot represent the flag-ship. At all events,

---

[1] Goes, *Chronica do Rei D. Emanuel*, 1790, I, p. 10.

[2] Only their type, for the legend below N. Coelho's ship ("which they broke up") shows that these are not portraits of the actual vessels, but fancy sketches. Coelho's vessel was the first to return to Lisbon; it was the store-ship which was broken up.

[3] *Obras de Luiz de Camões*, VI.

it is not more authentic than either of the ships delineated in the drawing first published by Juromenha.

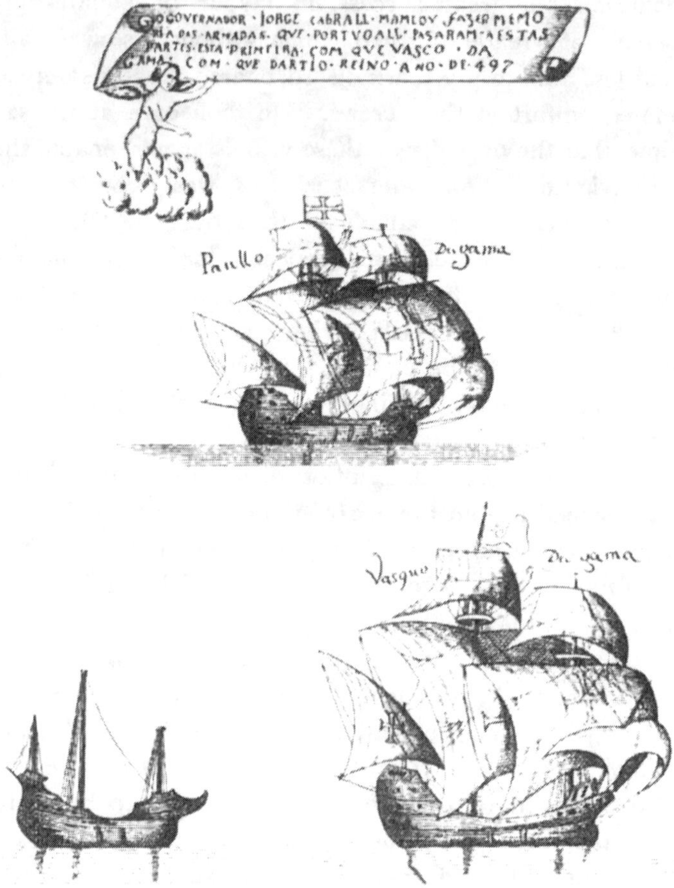

The supposed Armada of Vasco da Gama.

(*From a Painting made by order of Jorge Cabral* (1549-50.)

Authorities differ very widely as to the tonnage of these two vessels. Sernigi (see p. 123) says they were of 90 tons each, thus partly bearing out Correa, who states that the *three* ships (including the *Berrio*) were built of the same size and pattern.[1] D. Pacheco Pereira[2] states that the largest of them did not exceed 100 tons; J. de Barros gives them a burthen of between 100 and 120 tons; whilst Castanheda allocates 120 tons to the flag-ship and 100 to the *S. Raphael*.

But whilst the authorities quoted dwell upon the small size of the vessels which for the first time reached India from a European port, and even give reasons for this limitation of burthen,[3] there is some ground for believing that the tonnage of Vasco da Gama's ships, expressed according to modern terminology, was in reality much greater than is usually supposed. Pedro Barretto de Rezende (p. 151) may therefore have some justification when he states that these vessels ranged from 100 to 320 tons. Mr. Lindsay (*loc. cit.*) would go even further. The *S. Gabriel*, according to him, was constructed to carry 400 pipes, equivalent to 400 tons measurement, or about 250 to 300 tons register. He adds that Sr. E. Pinto Bastos agrees with him.[4]

In considering this question of tonnage, it must be borne in mind that "ton", at the close of the fifteenth century, was a different measure from what it is at present. We learn from E. A. D'Albertis[5] that the *tonelada* of Seville was supposed to afford accommodation for two pipes of 27½ arrobas (98 gallons) each, and measured 1.405 cubic metres, or about 50 cubic feet. The *tonel* of Biscay was 20 per cent. larger. According to Capt. H. Lopez de

---

[1] Stanley's *Vasco da Gama*, p. 26.

[2] *Esmeraldo de Situ Orbis*, Lisbon, 1892, p. 99.

[3] *Esmeraldo*, p. 99.

[4] A ton register is of a capacity of 100 cubic feet; a ton measurement is usually assumed to have a capacity of 40 cubic feet. Hence 400 tons measurement would be equivalent to 160 tons register, instead of 250 to 300.

[5] *Le construzione navali* (*Raccolta Colombiana*), Rome, 1893, p. 76.

Mendonça, the *tonel* at Lisbon measured 6 palmos de goa in length (talha), and 4 such palmos in breadth and height (parea), that is, about 85 cubic feet.[1] This, however, seems excessive, for my wine merchant tells me that two butts of sherry of 108 gallons each would occupy only 75 cubic feet. At any rate, these data show that the ton of the fifteenth century was considerably larger than the ton measurement of the nineteenth.

Two attempts have been made recently by distinguished officers of the Portuguese Navy, Captains João Braz d'Oliveira[2] and A. A. Baldaque da Silva,[3] to reconstruct Vasco da Gama's flagship, or rather to design a ship of a type existing at the close of the fifteenth century, and answering as nearly as possible to the scanty indications to be found within the pages of the historians of this memorable voyage. In this reconstruction good use has been made of an early manuscript on shipbuilding by Fernando Oliveira (*O livro da fabrica das Nãos*), which Captain Lopez de Mendonça proposes to publish.

The designs produced by the two naval officers differ widely in several respects, and more especially as regards the relation between the total length of the ship and the breadth of beam. In Captain B. da Silva's ship the beam is equal to one-third of the length, whilst the proportion in Captain J. Braz d'Oliveira's ship is as one to five. The former of these ships is broad-beamed, as befits the period, whilst the latter is almost as slim as a modern clipper. It must be remembered that, until comparatively recent times, it was held that the length of a sailing ship should not

---

[1] The palmo de goa was equal to 293 m.m., and the *tonel* consequently measured 2.42 cubic metres or 85 cubic feet. "Goa" has nothing to do either with *agoa*, or with the town of that name in India, but is a corruption of "gouê", a measure anciently used by shipbuilders in the Mediterranean (see Lopez de Mendonça, *loc. cit.*, p. 118).

[2] *Os Navios de Vasco da Gama*, Lisbon, June, 1892.

[3] *Noticia sobre e Não S. Gabriel*, Lisbon, August, 1892.

exceed four times the breadth of beam; and this maxim was undoubtedly acted upon by the shipbuilders of the fifteenth century.

Captain Baldaque da Silva's design of the *S. Gabriel* has been embodied in a model, and from a photograph of this model Mr. Herbert Johnson has produced the illustration placed in front of this Appendix.

The dimensions of the ship designed by Captain Baldaque da Silva are as follows:—[1]

Length over all	84.1 feet.
Water-line (when laden)	64.0 "
Keel	56.7 "
Breadth of beam	27.9 "
Depth	17.1 "
Draught, abaft	7.5 "
" forward	5.6 "
Metocentric height above the water-line (laden)	7.4 "
Displacement	178 tons.
Tonnage . . 4,130 cubic feet, or	103 "

This, as I learn from a private letter of Captain B. da Silva, is supposed to be the gross under-deck tonnage, but on calculating the tonnage according to the Builders' Old Measurement Rule, I find it to amount to 230 tons of 40 cubic feet each, whilst the "expeditive" method practised at Venice[2] during the fifteenth century yields 896 botte of 28 gallons, or about 250 toneladas.

The ship was flat-bottomed, with a square stern and bluff bow, the latter ornamented with a figure of her patron saint. Wales were placed along the sides to reduce

---

[1] Captain Braz d'Oliveira gives the following dimensions: length, 106 ft.; keel, 54.5 ft.; beam, 20 ft.; draught, aft, 10.5 ft.; depth, 18 ft.

[2] This consists in multiplying length of keel, breadth and depth, and dividing by thirty. The result is expressed in *botte*.

her rolling when going before the wind. Formidable "castles" rose fore and aft, having a deep waist between them. These "castles," however, had not then grown to the portentous height attained at a subsequent period, when they rendered it difficult to govern the ship in a gale, and it often became necessary to cut down the fore-mast and dismantle the forecastle to enable them to keep her head to the wind.

These "castles" were in reality citadels, and enabled the crew to make a last stand after the vessel had been boarded. A notable instance of this occurred in the course of the fight with the *Meri* in 1502.[1]

The captain was lodged in the castle rising upon the quarter-deck, the officers were accommodated in the room below his and in the forecastle, whilst the men had their quarters beneath the gang boards which ran along the top-sides from castle to castle. The men were each allowed a locker, to contain such goods as they might obtain by barter with the natives. Ladders led from the main deck up to the fighting decks (*chapitéo de ré* and *de vante*) of the two castles, and these were defended against boarders by nettings. The tiller of the rudder entered the battery abaft the captain's apartments, where also stood the binnacle. The armament consisted of twenty guns. The lower battery of the "castle" rising on the quarter-deck was armed with eight breech-loaders made of wrought-iron staves, held together by hoops and mounted on forked props. The upper battery held six bombards, and the forecastle the same number.[2] We may at once state that

[1] See J. de Barros, dec. I, l. vi, c. 3.

[2] Barros and Castanheda, in addition to bombards, mention spingards (wall-pieces) and one-pounder matchlocks. Correa (Stanley's *Vasco da Gama*) says that the ships, or some of them, in Vasco da Gama's second voyage were armed with six heavy guns below, four smaller guns and four falconets on deck, and several swivel guns.

the men carried no firearms. Their arms included cross-bows, spears, axes, swords, javelins, and boarding-pikes. Some of the officers were clad in steel armour, whilst the men had to be content with leather jerkins and breast-plates.

Amidships stood the *batel,* or long boat, in addition to which there was available a yawl rowed with four or six oars.

There were three masts and a bowsprit. The main-mast rose to a height of 110 ft. above the keel and flew the Royal Standard at its head, whilst the captain's scarlet flag floated from the crow's-nest, nearly 70 ft. above deck. A similar crow's-nest was attached to the foremast. In the case of an engagement these points of vantage were occupied by fighting men, who hurled thence javelins, grenades, and powder-pots upon the enemy. The sails were square, with the exception of that of the mizzen, which was triangular. When spread they presented 4,000 square feet of canvas to the wind; this was exclusive of the "bonnets" which were occasionally laced to the leeches of the mainsail, and served to some extent the same purpose as a modern studding-sail.[1] The Cross of the Order of Christ was painted on each sail.

The anchors, two in number, were of iron, with a wooden stock and a ring for bending the cable.

The hold was divided into three compartments. Amid-ships were the water barrels, with coils of cable on the top of them—a very inconvenient arrangement; abaft was the powder-magazine, and most arms and munitions, including iron and stone balls, were kept there; the forward com-partment was used for the storage of requisites, including spare sails and a spare anchor.

The caravels, though only manned by thirty men, carried four heavy guns below, six falconets and twelve swivel guns.

[1] Note by Sir Clements R. Markham.

The lower deck was divided by bulkheads into three compartments, two of which were set apart for provisions, presents, and articles of barter. The "provisions", according to Castanheda, were calculated to suffice for three years, and the daily rations were on a liberal scale, consisting of $1\frac{1}{2}$ pounds of biscuit, 1 pound of beef or half a pound of pork, $2\frac{1}{2}$ pints of water, $1\frac{1}{4}$ pints of wine, one-third of a gill of vinegar, and half that quantity of oil. On fast days, half a pound of rice, of codfish, or cheese was substituted for the meat. There were, in addition, flour, lentils, sardines, plums, almonds, onions, garlic, mustard, salt, sugar and honey. These ships' stores were supplemented by fish, caught whenever an opportunity offered, and by fresh provisions obtained when in port, among which were oranges, which proved most acceptable to the many men suffering from scurvy.

The merchandise was not only insufficient in quantity, but proved altogether unsuited to the Indian market. It seems to have included *lambel* (striped cotton stuff), sugar, olive-oil, honey, and coral beads. Among the objects intended for presents, there were wash-hand basins, scarlet hoods, silk jackets, pantaloons, hats, Moorish caps; besides such trifles as glass beads, little round bells, tin rings and bracelets, which were well enough suited for barter on the Guinea coast, but were not appreciated by the wealthy merchants of Calecut. Of ready money there seems to have been little to spare. All this is made evident by the letters of D. Manuel and Signor Sernigi.

The scientific outfit of the expedition, it may safely be presumed, was the best to be procured at the time. The learned D. Diogo Ortiz de Vilhegas[1] furnished Da Gama

---

[1] D. Diogo Ortiz de Vilhegas was a native of Calçadinha, in Leon, and came to Portugal as father-confessor and spiritual director of that "excellent lady", D. Joanna. King Manuel held him in high respect, and appointed him Bishop of Tangier in 1491. Jointly with Masters

with maps and books, including, almost as a matter of course, a copy of Ptolemy, and copies of the information on the East collected at Lisbon for years past. Among these reports, that sent home by Pero de Covilhão found, no doubt, a place,[1] as also the information furnished by Lucas Marcos,[2] an Abyssinian priest who visited Lisbon about 1490.

The astronomical instruments were provided by Zacut, the astronomer, and it is even stated that Vasco enjoyed the advantage of being trained as a practical observer by that learned Hebrew. These instruments included a large wooden astrolabe, smaller astrolabes of metal, and, in all probability, also quadrants; and they were accompanied by a copy of Zacut's *Almanach perpetuum Celestium motuum cujus radix est 1473*, a translation of which, by José Vizinho, had been printed at Leiria in 1496.[3] These

---

Rodriguez, the physician, and Jose Vizinho, he is responsible for reporting adversely on the bold projects of Columbus. In 1500, he was transferred to the See of Ceuta, and, in 1505, to that of Vizeu. He never resided in his African dioceses. When Gama took leave of the King at Montemór ó novo, Vilhegas is said to have celebrated Mass. He died in 1519 at Almeirim.—(Paiva Manso, *Historia Ecclesiastica*, Lisbon, 1872, I, pp. 40, 47, 62.)

[1] Pero de Covilhão and Affonso de Paiva were despatched from Santarem in 1487 to spy out the countries of the east. Covilhão, in the course of his extensive travels, visited Hormuz, Calecut, and the east coast of Africa as far as Sofala. He ultimately reached the court of Prester John, and was never again allowed to leave it. These travellers, too, received a map and instructions from D. Diogo de Vilhegas. The best account of Covilhão's adventures is that furnished by Alvarez, c. 103 (see Lord Stanley's translation, published by the Hakluyt Society).

[2] Lucas Marcos visited Rome and Lisbon. The information furnished by him included a vocabulary.—(Barros, *Da Asia*, dec. I, l. iii, c. 5.)

[3] Abraham ben Samuel Zacuto was professor of astronomy and mathematics in the University of Salamanca when King John II called him to Portugal in 1492, and appointed him Astronomer Royal.

tables enabled the navigator to calculate his latitudes by observing the altitude of the sun.

There was, of course, a sufficient supply of compasses, of sounding leads and hour-glasses, and possibly also a *catena a poppa*, that is, a rope towed at the stern to determine the ship's leeway, and a *toleta de marteloia*, a graphical substitute for our modern traverse tables, both of them contrivances long since in use among the Italians. It is also possible that Vasco was already provided with an equinoctial compass for determining the time of high water at the ports he visited, and with a variation compass. This instrument consisted of a combination of a sun-dial with a magnetic needle. It had been invented by Peurbach, *c.* 1460, was improved by Felipe Guillen, 1528, and by Pedro Nunes, 1537, and used for the first time on an extensive scale by João de Castro, during a voyage to

---

He is the author of *Ephemerides*, originally written in Hebrew, a Latin translation of which, by José Vizinho, one of his pupils, was first printed in 1496—on the eve of Vasco da Gama's departure—although there can be no doubt that these useful tables previously circulated in MS. José Vizinho is perhaps identical with the physician José whom King John had charged, jointly with Master Rodrigo, to prepare tables of the declination of the sun, which would enable navigators to determine their latitude after they had lost sight of the Pole star. Rudolf Wolf (*Geschichte der Astronomie*, p. 97) credits Regiomontanus with having produced the first set of "practical" tables for the use of mariners. He does not even once mention Zacuto in his history, and states that the tables of the great German astronomer were those made use of by Dias and Vasco da Gama. As the *Ephemerides* of Regiomontanus were printed in 1474, they naturally became more widely known than those of Zacuto, which only circulated in MS., and they were, perhaps, brought to Portugal by Martin Behaim. It cannot, however, be doubted that the tables which Vasco da Gama took with him were those of Zacuto.

For the contents of the first printed edition of Zacuto's *Almanach Perpetuum*, see Antonio Ribeiro dos Santos in *Memorias de Litteratura Portugueza*, 2 edição, VIII, p. 46; for later reprints of the Tables of the Declination of the Sun, see Luciano Cordeira in the *Boletim* of the Lisbon Geographical Society, 1883, p. 163.

India and the Red Sea, in 1538-41.[1] We are inclined to think that Vasco had such a variation compass, for the Cabo das Agulhas, or "Needle Cape", thus named because the needle there pointed, or was supposed to point, due north, has already found a place on Cantino's Chart, and can have been named only as the result of an actual observation, however inaccurate.

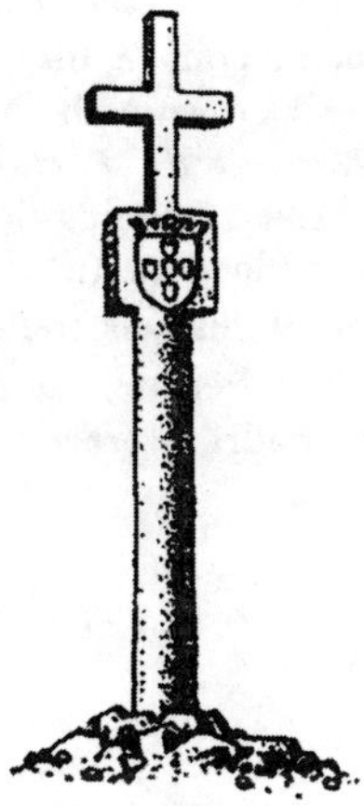

Cão's Padrão at Cape Cross.

Lastly, there remain to be noticed the Padrãos, or pillars of stone which were on board the vessels, and three of which, by the king's express desire, were dedicated to S. Raphael, S. Gabriel, and S. Maria (see p. 80). Barros and Castanheda tell us that these pillars resembled those set up by Cão and Dias in the time of D. João II; and in a series of pictures which D. Manuel desired to have painted in celebration of the discovery of India, the Padrão to be shown at the Cape of Good Hope, or "Prasum promontorium", was to have been surmounted by a cross, and to bear the Royal Arms and a Pelican, with an inscription giving the date.[2]

Correa, on the other hand, affirms in his *Lendas* that the pillar set up at the Rio da Misericordia (the Rio dos Bons Signaes of the *Roteiro*) was of marble, with two escutcheons, one of the arms of Portugal, and the other (at the back) of a sphere, and that the inscription was "Do senhorio de Portugal reino de Christãos". The pillar at Melinde had

---

[1] See Hellmann, in *Zeitschrift für Erdkunde*, 1897. The *Roteiros* of João de Castro, containing these observations, were published at Lisbon, 1833 and 1882.

[2] The description of this proposed series is of historical interest (see *Alguns documentos*, 1892, p. 516).

the same escutcheons, but the inscription was limited to the words "Rey Manoel".[1] As Correa had an opportunity of seeing these pillars, his description of them may be correct, though he is an arrant fabulator.

---

[1] See Stanley's *Vasco da Gama*, pp. 73 and 144. The "Sphere" was a device bestowed upon D. Manuel by King João II. A coin called an "Esphera de Ouro" was coined in Portuguese India. M. B. Lopez Fernandes (*Memoria das moedas*, Lisbon, 1856, p. 121) had such a coin in his possession. It had the device on the face, and a royal crown with the word MEA on the obverse. Manuel de Faria (*Noticias de Portugal*, Disc. IV, § 31) thinks that MEA stands for "Mine", meaning that the whole sphere was Manuel's; but Fernandes is inclined to think that it stands for MEIA, that is, "Half". The coin in his collection had an intrinsic value of about six shillings.

The Pelican was the device of King João II. It may have been on the padrãos erected by Dias, but has not been discovered on those of Cão.

APPENDIX E.

VASCO DA GAMA.

(*From A. Morelet's French version of the "Roteiro"*, 1864.)

After a Portrait formerly the property of Conde de Farrobo, now in the *Museu das Bellas Artes*, Lisbon.

MUSTER-ROLL OF VASCO DA GAMA'S FLEET.

THE officers and men in Vasco da Gama's *armada* were carefully selected. Several of them had been with Bartholomeu Dias round the Cape; all of them, as appears from this "Journal", justified by their conduct under sometimes trying circumstances the selection which had been made.

Authorities widely differ as to the number of men who embarked. Sernigi (p. 124) says there were only 118, of whom 55 died during the voyage and only 63 returned. Galvão says there were 120, besides the men in the store-ship. Castanheda and Goes raise the number to 148, of whom only 55 returned, many of them broken in health. Faria y Sousa and San Ramon say there were 160, and the latter adds that 93 of these died during the voyage, thus confirming a statement made by King Manuel in his letter of February 20th, 1504, to the effect that less than one-half returned.[1] According to Barros there were 170 men, including soldiers and sailors. Correa raises the number to 260, for he says that in each of the three ships there were 80 officers and men, including servants, besides six convicts and two priests.[2] He says nothing of the store-ship. By the time Vasco da Gama had reached the Rio da Misericordia only 150 out of this number are said to have been alive.

Correa, no doubt, exaggerates. On the other hand, Sernigi's numbers seem to us to err quite as much on the

[1] See Texeira de Aragão (*Boletim*, VI, 1886, p. 562).

[2] See Stanley's *Vasco da Gama*, pp. 38, 73, 94, 96.

other side. It is quite true that a Mediterranean merchant-man of 100 tons, in the sixteenth century, was manned by 12 able and 8 ordinary seamen ;[1] but in the case of an expedition sent forth for a number of years and to unknown dangers, this number would no doubt have been increased. We are, therefore, inclined to believe that the number given by De Barros—namely, 170—may be nearer the truth, namely 70 men in the flag-ship, 50 in the *S. Raphael*, 30 in the caravel, and 20 in the store-ship. The men in the flag-ship may have included 1 captain, 1 master, 1 pilot, 1 assistant pilot, 1 mate (contramestre), 1 boatswain (guardião), 20 able seamen (marinheiros), 10 ordinary seamen (grumetes), 2 boys (pagens). 1 chief gunner or constable, 8 bombardiers, 4 trumpeters, 1 clerk or purser (escrivão), 1 storekeeper (dispenseiro), 1 officer of justice (meirinho), 1 barber-surgeon, 2 interpreters, 1 chaplain, 6 artificers (ropemaker, carpenter, calker, cooper, armourer and cook), and 10 servants. One or more of these servants may have been negro slaves. The "Degradados", or convicts on board, to be "adventured on land" (p. 48), are included in the total. Whether private gentlemen were permitted to join this expedition as volunteers history doth not record.

The following "muster-roll" contains short notices of all those who are stated to have embarked at Lisbon in Vasco da Gama's fleet, or who subsequently joined it, either voluntarily or upon compulsion.

Apart from natives, thirty-one persons are mentioned, and with respect to twenty-six of these no reasonable doubt can be entertained that they were actually members of the ships' companies.

---

[1] According to J. de Escalante de Mendoso (1575), quoted by D'Albertis, *loc. cit.*, p. 84.

Those among them whose names appear in the "Journal" are distinguished by an asterisk.[1]

Captains.

**Vasco da Gama*, Captain-Major in the *S. Gabriel.*

**Paulo da Gama*, his brother, commanding the *S. Raphael.*

**Nicolau Coelho*, Captain of the *Berrio* or *S. Miguel.* He subsequently went out to India with Cabral (1500), and for a third time with Francisco d'Albuquerque, in 1503.

On February 24, 1500, the King granted him a pension of 70,000 reis. He also received a coat-of-arms, viz.: a field *gules*, charged with a lion rampant between two pillars (*padrãos*), *silver*, standing upon hillocks by the sea *vert;* and two small escutcheons charged with five *bezants* (Severim de Faria, *Noticias de Portugal*, Disc. 3, § 15). He seems to have been dead in 1522, for on December 19 of that year, his son, Francisco, begged the King to transfer the pension of his late father to himself.—(Cunha Rivara, *Arch. Port. Oriental*, fasc. v, p. 254; and Texeira de Aragão, *Boletim*, 1886, p. 573.)

Gonçalo Nunes, Captain of the store-ship (Barros, I, pt. 1, p. 279; Castanheda, I, p. 7). Castanheda, 1st edition, erroneously calls him Gonçalo Gomez. He was a retainer of Vasco da Gama.

Pilots and Masters.

**Pero d'Alenquer*, pilot of the *S. Gabriel* (Barros, I, pt. 1, p. 279; Castanheda, I, p. 7; Goes, I, 69; Faria y Sousa, p. 29). He had been with Dias in the discovery of the Cape of Good Hope, and with the Congo mission in 1490.

**João de Coimbra*, pilot of the *S. Raphael* (Barros, I, pt. 1, p. 279). A negro slave belonging to him deserted at Moçambique (see p. 30).

Pero Escolar, pilot of the *Berrio* (Barros, *ib.*; Faria y Sousa, p. 29). On February 18, 1500, the King granted him a pension of 4,000 reis. He went as pilot with Cabral.

---

[1] In quoting authorities I refer to the following editions:—João de Barros, *Da Asia*, Lisbon, 1788; Castanheda, *Historia da India*, Lisbon, 1833; Manuel de Faria y Sousa, *Asia Portuguesa*, Lisbon, 1666; Gaspar Correa, *Lendas da India*, Lisbon, 1858-64; Damião de Goes, *Chronica do Rei D. Manuel*, 1790.

Gonçalo Alvares, master of the *S. Gabriel* (Barros, *ib.*). He subsequently held the office of pilot-major of India (Correa, *Lendas*, I, p. 570). On January 26, 1504, the King granted him a pension of 6,000 reis (Texeira de Aragão, *Boletim*, 1886, p. 674).

André Gonçalves. According to Correa (*Lendas*, I, p. 148), he had been with Vasco da Gama, whose interest had procured him an appointment in Cabral's fleet. The same untrustworthy author states (p. 152) that Cabral sent him back from Brazil with the news of his discovery, and that the King, immediately after his arrival, fitted out a fleet to continue the explorations in the New World. Barros (I, pt. 1, p. 384) and Castanheda (I, p. 97) state that Cabral sent back Gaspar de Lemos. Neither they, nor, as far as I am aware, any other authority, mention an André Gonçalves in connection with Gama's or Cabral's expeditions.

Pursers or Clerks.

**Diogo Dias*, clerk of the *S. Gabriel* (Barros, I, pt. 1, p. 279; Castanheda, I, pp. 54, 80; Goes, I, p. 90; Faria y Sousa, I, p. 29). He was a brother of Bartholomeu Dias, the discoverer of the Cape of Good Hope.

João de Sá, clerk of the *S. Raphael* (Barros, I, pt. 1, p. 370; Castanheda, Goes, Faria y Sousa). He again went to India with Cabral (Barros, I, pt. 1, p. 403), and subsequently became treasurer of the India House (Castanheda, I, p. 54).

Alvaro de Braga, clerk of the *Berrio* (Barros, Castanheda, Goes). Vasco appointed him head of the factory at Calecut. Correa (*Lendas*, I, pp. 89-91) erroneously calls him Pedro de Braga. He was rewarded by the King, February 1, 1501 (*Boletim*, 1886, p. 675).

Interpreters.

**Martim Affonso* (Barros, I, pt. 1, p. 289; Castanheda, I, p. 15; Goes, I, p. 74; Faria y Sousa, p. 29). He had lived in Congo.

Fernão Martins (Barros, I, pt. 1, p. 290; Castanheda, I, pp. 51, 54; Goes, I, p. 89). Vasco sent him to the King of Calecut, and he was present at the audience which Vasco had of the King (Goes, I, p. 95). Subsequently he filled several positions of trust in India. He is the "African slave" who spoke Arabic, referred to by Correa (Stanley's *Vasco da Gama*, pp. 76, 203).

João Martins, see João Nunez, *infra*.

Priests.

Pedro de Covilhã, called Pero de Cobillones by Faria y Sousa (I, p. 29), who refers to ancient documents and the assertion of F. Christoval Osorio, of the Order of Trinity, as his authorities. He was Prior of a monastery of the Order of the Trinity at Lisbon, and went out as Chaplain of the Fleet and Father Confessor. According to Francisco de Sousa's *Oriente Conquistado*, I, p. 477, he died a martyr on July 7, 1498, and this statement is accepted by P. Francisco de S. Maria (*Anno historico*, II, Lisbon, 1794, p. 323). Fr. Jeronymo de São Jose (*Historia chronologica da Ordem da S. Trindade*, Lisbon, 1789-94) enlarges upon this by stating that this apocryphal "protomartyr" of India "was speared whilst expounding the doctrines of the Trinity". At the date of his alleged death, Vasco da Gama was still at Calecut. He may have died of disease. Neither Barros, Castanheda, nor Correa mentions the name of this priest.

João Figueiro. Correa claims to have derived much information from a diary kept by this priest, of which only fragments appear to have come into his possession. Other authors ignore the name (see Stanley's *Vasco da Gama*, pp. ii, vi, 260).

Sailors and Soldiers.

João d'Ameixoeira or *Dameiroeiro.* According to Correa (I, p. 136), he was one of the mutineers who returned to Portugal. No other writer mentions him.

Pedro de Faria e Figueiredo, died at Cabo das Correntes (Faria y Sousa, I, p. 29).

Francisco de Faria e Figueiredo, brother of the preceding. He wrote Latin verses. He, too, died at Cabo das Correntes (Faria y Sousa, I, p. 29).

**Sancho Mexia*, incidentally mentioned in the *Roteiro* (see p. 6).

João Palha, one of the thirteen who attended Vasco da Gama to Calecut (Correa, I, p. 96).

Gonçalo Pirez, a mariner and retainer of Vasco da Gama (Castanheda, I, p. 54). On May 31, 1497, he had been appointed master of a caravel recently built at Oporto (Texeira de Aragão, *Boletim*, 1886, p. 563).

Leonardo Ribeyro. According to Manuel Correa's commentary on the *Obras do grande Camões*, Lisbon, 1720, this, on the authority of the poet himself, is the full name of the "Leonardo" mentioned in Canto VI, stanza 40. Faria y Sousa (*Asia Portuguesa*, I, p. 29) identified this "Leonardo" with Francisco de Faria e Figueredo, but subsequently (*Commentos aos Lusiadas*, 1639) he gave up the point.

João de Setubal, according to Correa (I, pp. 96, 104, 107), was one of the thirteen who accompanied Vasco da Gama to Calecut (see Stanley's *Vasco da Gama*, pp. 119, 213).

Alvaro Velho, a soldier (Castanheda, I, p. 54; Goes, I, p. 90; Faria y Sousa). Perhaps this is the Alvaro Velho de Barreyro mentioned by Valentin Ferdinand (Valentino de Moravia or Alemão), in his *Description of Africa* (1507), as having resided eight years at Sierra Leone (see Kunstmann, in *Abhdlgn. d. bayer. Ak. d. W.*, *Cl. iij*, t. IX, Abt. 1).

**Fernão Veloso*, a soldier (Barros, I, pt. 1, p. 283-6; Castanheda, I, p. 9; Goes, I, p. 71; Faria y Sousa; Camoens, Canto VI, stanza 41).

Convicts or Banished Men (Degradados).

Pedro Dias, nicknamed "Northeasterling". Correa (*Lendas*, I, p. 46) says that Vasco da Gama left him behind at Moçambique, and that subsequently he came to India (compare Stanley's *Vasco da Gama*, p. 106).

Pero Esteves. Correa (*Lendas*, I, p. 236) says that Vasco da Gama left him behind at Quiloa, and that when J. da Nova reached that port in 1501, he came out to meet him. Barros (I, pt. 1, p. 467) says that the convict who met J. da Nova had been landed by Cabral, and that his name was Antonio Fernandez.

João Machado, according to Correa (*Lendas*, I, pp. 41, 160), was left behind by Vasco da Gama at Moçambique, but according to Barros (I, pt. 1, p. 406) it was Cabral who left him at Melinde, with instructions to make inquiries about Prester John. Cabral may have transferred him from Moçambique to the more northern port. He subsequently did good service, and Affonso de Albuquerque appointed him alcaide mór of Goa. He was slain in battle, 1515 (see Stanley's *Vasco da Gama*, pp. 93-5).

Damião Rodriguez was a friend of João Machado, and a seaman on board the *S. Gabriel*, from which vessel he deserted at the shoals of S. Raphael. When Cabral came to Moçambique, his grave was pointed out. All this is stated on the sole authority of Correa (*Lendas*, I, p. 160). Compare Stanley's *Vasco da Gama*, p. 94.

João Nunez, a "new" Christian (*i.e.*, a converted Jew), who knew a little Arabic and Hebrew, and was landed at Calecut. In the Portuguese edition of Correa (I, p. 78) he is erroneously called João Martins (see Stanley's *Vasco da Gama*, pp. 159, 180, 206).

Natives and others Embarked in the East.

**Gaspar da Gama*. This is the "Moor", or renegade, who joined Vasco da Gama at Anjediva Island. Our anonymous author describes him as about forty years of age, and as being able to speak "Venetian" well. He claimed to have come to India in early youth, and was at the time in the service of the Governor of Goa. Vasco da Gama carried him to Portugal, where he was baptized and received the name of Gaspar da Gama. In the *Commentaries of Afonso Dalboquerque* (Hakluyt Society, 1884) he is frequently referred to as Gaspar da India. Correa (*Lendas da India*) usually refers to him as Gaspar da Gama, but also calls him Gaspar de las Indias, or Gaspar d'Almeida. King Manuel, in his letter to the Cardinal Protector, calls him a "Jew, who turned Christian, a merchant and lapidary". Sernigi (see p. 136) held a conversation with him at Lisbon. He speaks of him as a Sclavonian Jew, born at Alexandria.

According to the information given by Barros and Goes, the parents of Gaspar fled from Posen, in Poland, at the time when King Casimir cruelly persecuted the Jews (about 1456). After a short residence in Palestine they removed to Alexandria, where Gaspar was born (Barros, I, pt. 1, pp. 364-5; Goes, pt. 1, c. 44).

He accompanied Cabral as interpreter. Vespucci met him on his homeward voyage at Cape Verde, and in his letter of June 4, 1501, published by Baldelli (*Il Milione*, 1827), he speaks highly of Gaspar's linguistic attainments, and refers to his extensive travels in Asia.

Gaspar repeatedly accompanied Portuguese expeditions to India, and was last heard of in 1510. Goes (*loc. cit.*) says that King Manuel liked him, and appointed him a cavalier of his household.

Correa (Stanley's *Vasco da Gama*, p. 247) describes this Gaspar as a Jew, who, "at the taking of Granada was a very young man; and who, having been driven from his country, passed through many lands . . . on to India". But, as Granada was only taken in 1492, this is absurd.

Lunardo da Chá Masser, who came to Lisbon in 1504 as ambassador of the Signoria, in a letter written about 1506 and first published in the *Archivio Storico Italiano* (Florence, 1846), says that Gaspar married a Portuguese lady,[1] and was granted a pension of 170 ducats annually, in recognition of the valuable information which he furnished respecting the Oriental trade.

**Monçaide*, who came on board Vasco da Gama's vessel at Calecut, is stated by Barros (I, pt. 1, pp. 330 *et seq.*) and Goes (I, p. 98) to have been a native of Tunis, who, in the time of King John II had done business with the Portuguese at Oran, and spoke Castilian. He accompanied Vasco da Gama to Portugal and was baptised. In King Manuel's letter to the Cardinal Protector he is referred to as a "Moor of Tunis". The author of the *Roteiro* calls him a "Moor of Tunis" whom the Moors of Calecut suspected of being a Christian and emissary of the King of Portugal (p. 75).

Correa (Stanley's *Vasco da Gama*, pp. 162-5, 221) says that he was a native of Seville, who, having been captured when five years old, turned Moslem, although "in his soul he was still a Christian". He generally refers to this man as "the Castilian", and says that his true name was Alonso Perez.

Castanheda (I, p. 50) tells us that the Portuguese corrupted Monçaide into Bontaibo, a combination of the Portuguese *bom*, "good", and the Arabic *tayyib*, having the same meaning. Mon-

---

[1] If Correa (I, p. 656) can be trusted, he still had a wife at Cochin in 1506. Sernigi (see p. 136) credits him with a wife and children at Calecut.

çaide is probably a corruption of El Masud, the "happy-one (Burton's *Camoens*, iv, p. 432).

**Malemo Canaqua*, or *Cana*, the pilot who guided Vasco da Gama from Melinde to Calecut. He was a native of Gujarat (Barros, I, pt. 1, pp. 319, 328, 330; Goes, I, c. 38; Castanheda, I, p. 41). Malemo stands for "muallim" or "mallim", "master" or "teacher", the usual native designation of the skipper of a vessel, whilst "Kanaka" designates the pilot's caste.

Davane, of Cambay, said to have been taken out of a dhau to the south of Moçambique, to have agreed to accompany Vasco da Gama to Calecut as broker, and to have been ultimately discharged with good testimonials in November 1498 at Cananor, is only mentioned by Correa (Stanley's *Vasco da Gama*, pp. 79, 84, 113, 128, 235). No other historian knows anything about this mythical personage.

**Baltasar*, and the four other Moors, forcibly carried away from Calecut (see pp. 73, 75, and 79, and King Manuel's letter to the Cardinal Protector, p. 115) were taken back by Cabral, as was also the Ambassador of the King of Melinde (*Alguns Documentos do Archivo nacional*, 1892, p. 97).

Vasco da Gama originally detained eighteen "Moors". He is stated in the "Journal" to have subsequently liberated six, and to have sent one with a letter to the Zamorin. This would leave eleven, not five. The number of those liberated must, therefore, have been twelve, and not six.

APPENDIX F.

Calecut in 1876.

(*From a Sketch by Mr. Herbert Johnson.*)

THE VOYAGE.

THE King was at Montemór o novo[1] when he despatched Vasco da Gama and his fellow-commanders upon the momentous expedition which was to place Portugal for a time in the forefront of maritime and commercial powers. It was summer, and His Majesty did not, therefore, desert the beautiful hills of Monfurado for the stifling heat of the capital, in order that he might witness the embarkation of his "loyal vassal" whom, on account of his proved valour and past services he had deemed worthy of the honourable distinction of being entrusted with the conduct of so important an enterprise.[2] Vasco da Gama and his officers, the night before their departure, kept vigil in the chapel of Our Lady of Belem, which was not then a stately pile such as that which now occupies the site of the original unostentatious *ermida* founded by Prince Henry for the convenience of mariners.

On the following morning, which was Saturday, the 8th of July, 1497,[3] Vasco da Gama and his companions were

---

[1] Barros, *Dec. I*, IV, c. 1; Goes, I, c. 23; Castanheda, I, c. 2.

[2] Correa gives a circumstantial account of the embarkation in the King's presence, but the description of the paintings which were to have been executed by the King's order in illustration of the discovery and "conquest" of India, shows very conclusively that the King was *not* there (*Alguns documentos*, p. 516).

[3] This, without a doubt, is the correct date. The author of our "Journal", Barros, Goes, Castanheda, and Faria y Sousa, they all agree in this. Sernigi gives July 9th; Correa fixes upon March 25th as the day of departure.

We may say, once for all, that the dates given in the "Journal" may confidently be accepted as correct, allowing for a few *lapsi calami* (or

escorted to the beach by a procession of priests and friars. They all carried lighted tapers, and an excited crowd muttered responses to the litany which was being intoned by the priests. On reaching the place of embarkation, the vicar of the chapel celebrated mass and received a general confession; after which, in virtue of a Bull published by Pope Nicholas V in 1452, he absolved the departing adventurers of their sins. And thus they left on their errand with the blessings of the Church, in the favour of their King, and amidst the acclamations of a sympathising people.

Lisbon to the Cape Verde Islands.

Winds and currents being favourable, the voyage to the Cape Verde Islands was accomplished in good time, and the flag-ship, notwithstanding some delay caused by a dense fog on the Saharan coast, reached the Ilha do Sal, 1,590 miles from Lisbon, in the course of fourteen days, if not earlier, and on July 27th the little armada lay snugly in the harbour of São Thiago.

The Voyage across the Southern Atlantic.

The accounts of Vasco da Gama's remarkable voyage across the Southern Atlantic are of so scanty a nature that it is quite impossible to lay down his track with certainty. What we learn from the "Journal" may be condensed into a few words. The little armada left São Thiago on August 3rd, *going east!* On the 18th of that month, when 200 leagues (680 miles) out at sea, the main-yard of the flagship sprung in a squall, and this necessitated laying to for a couple of days and a night. On the 22nd

---

errors of the copyist), which can fortunately be rectified in nearly every instance, as the Author names the day of the week, and often even the name of the Saint to whom the day is dedicated.

of October,[1] when 800 leagues (2,700 miles) out at sea, going S. by W.,[2] large birds were seen flying to the S.S.E. as if making for the land, as also a whale.[3] On October 27th more whales were seen, besides seals. On November 4th, at 9 A.M., the main land was sighted, probably about 150 miles to the north of St. Helena Bay (30° S.).

In these days of hydrographic offices and sailing directories we know how a sailing vessel desirous of proceeding from the Cape Verde Islands to the Cape would shape her course. She would endeavour to cross the equator about long. 22° W., pass to the leeward of Trinidad Island (20° S.), and then, gradually gaining a higher latitude, trust to the "brave" westerly winds carrying her beyond Tristão da Cunha to the Cape, or beyond.[4]

But Vasco da Gama had none of this information to guide him in shaping his course. He was informed, as a matter of course, about the winds and currents prevailing off the Guinea coast, but of what might be experienced in the open sea beyond he knew nothing.

It is just possible that he may have considered the possibility of reaching the Cape by a direct course of 3,770 miles, and he may even have attempted to carry out such a scheme. In the end, however, he would never have been able to work down against the strong S.E. "trades"

---

[1] This date is doubtful. See p. 3, note 3. The wrong date is not August 18th, but August 22nd.

[2] The variation being about 19° E., according to João de Castro, the true course would have been nearly S. by E.

[3] See p. 4, note 1.

[4] See Admiralty "Chart showing the tracks of sailing vessels with auxiliary steam power"; the valuable track-charts by Capt. A. Schück in the *Jahresbericht* of the Hamburg Geographical Society, for 1874; Dr. G. Schott, "Die Verkehrswege" in *Zeitschrift für Erdkunde*, 1895, with maps; the sailing directories of all ages since Duarte Pacheco wrote his *Esmeraldo* in 1505.

and northern currents, for his ships could not be laid nearer than six points to the wind, and even then they would have made considerable leeway.

His actual course, in any case, must have been a circuitous one, and we may suppose it to have been as follows :—Having left São Thiago in an easterly direction,[1] he kept in the direction of the coast for a considerable distance, but when he came within the influence of the dreaded *doldrums* he met with unpleasant weather in the shape of calms, baffling winds, and squalls, which prevail more especially during the months of June, July, and August. One of these squalls sprung the mainyard of the flagship, and heaving up a new yard necessitated a delay of two days and a night. When attempting to make southing he was driven to the westward, but managed to cross the equator in about 19° west.

Thence he followed a circuitous course, which brought him within 600 miles of the coast of Brazil. The northern part of this assumed course lies to the west of a track recommended by Captain Horsburgh as being most favourable for vessels proceeding between April and October from the Cape Verdes to St. Helena, whilst its southern part lies to the west of the usual track of sailing vessels going from Ascension to the Cape. In this manner we suppose Vasco da Gama to have reached lat. 30° S. long. 15° W., by October 22nd. This point lies about 800 leagues, or 2,700 miles, in a direct line from São Thiago; but by the track assumed by us the distance is 1,030 leagues, or 3,480 miles. As Vasco da Gama spent eighty days in making this distance, including the time lost in repairing his yard, his daily run only amounted to 44 miles.

It was here that Vasco da Gama saw birds flying to the

---

[1] According to Barros, Bartholemeu Dias kept in his company until he took the direction of Mina.

S.S.E. They were no doubt making for Tristão da Cunha, which lies at a distance of about 400 miles in that direction. He also saw a whale, a very common sight in these latitudes.[1]

Thus far the course followed had been more or less southerly, but Vasco da Gama had now passed beyond the S.E. "trades", and found himself under the welcome influence of "brave" west winds and of an eastern current, running at the rate of a knot in the hour. This speeded him on his course, and he covered the 500 leagues, or 1,700 miles, which still separated him from the west coast of Africa, in the course of thirteen days, making his first landfall on November 4th in about 30° S. His average daily run on this course must, therefore, have amounted to 131 miles.[2]

This may seem a high rate, but it is by no means an exceptional one. Vasco himself made at least 114 miles daily during his passage from Lisbon to the Cape Verdes, and 125 between the Cape and the Guinea coast when homeward bound. Columbus, during his first voyage, averaged 84 miles[3] daily between Gomera and Guanahani, but on nine days his daily run exceeded 150 miles, and on one day—the 4th of September—he actually covered 210 miles, although he had to take into account the bad sailing qualities of one of his vessels, the *Niña*.

We have laid down Vasco da Gama's hypothetical track with a considerable amount of diffidence. The passage might, of course, have been effected in various

---

[1] See, for instance, *The Voyage of François Leguat*, by Capt. Pasfield Oliver (Hakluyt Society, 1891), i, p. 25.

[2] Modern sailing vessels do much better. The passage from São Thiago to the Cape by way of Trinidad (5,140 miles) is made on an average in forty-six days, being a daily run of 125 miles, as compared with 54 miles daily, with which we have credited Vasco da Gama (see the Table at the end of this Appendix).

[3] One league of Columbus = 4 Italian miles = 3.38 nautical miles.

other ways.[1] When Cabral started for India in 1500 he was instructed by Vasco da Gama himself to sail southward from the Cape Verde Islands, until he should have reached the latitude of the Cape, and then to head to the east. Cabral, however, was carried by winds and currents towards Brazil, which he made in lat. 17° 20′ S., and thence followed a track which took him past Trinidad and Fernão Vaz,[2] and does not differ much from that now recommended to sailing vessels.

João da Nova, who left for India in March 1501, did not follow the route of his predecessor, perhaps on account of the terrible disaster which overtook Cabral when in the vicinity of Tristão da Cunha. Nova seems to have attempted a direct passage; for following perhaps the eastern route recommended to a later generation by Laurie's *Sailing Directory for the Ethiopic Ocean* (4th edition, by A. G. Finlay, p. 74), he discovered the island of Ascension on the outward voyage, and is generally credited with having reached the Cape without coming within sight of the coast of Brazil.[3]

---

[1] In note 3, p. 3, we have assumed a somewhat shorter course, but after due consideration we now give the preference to the track laid down upon our chart. On an old map of Africa, by H. Moll, a "tract" passing to the east of Ascension and St. Helena is recommended as "a good course of sailing from Great Britain to the East Indies in the Spring and Fall". What would Admiral Wharton say to this?

[2] These islands are distinctly shown on the Cantino Chart, but unfortunately not named. They are not, however, the *Ys. Tebas* of Juan de la Cosa, as is supposed by the Editor of Spruner's *Historical Atlas*, for the chart of the Spanish pilot which contains this name was completed before Cabral's return. If we can credit a statement of Correa (Stanley's *Vasco da Gama*, p. 825), who quotes Gaspar da Gama as his authority, Cabral also discovered Tristão da Cunha. He certainly must have been very near these islands when several of his vessels foundered.

[3] King Manuel, in his letter of 1505, to King Ferdinand of Castile ("Centenario do descobrimento da America", Lisbon, 1892),

Vasco da Gama, during his second voyage in 1502, seems to have seen no land from the time he left Cape Verde until he arrived at Sofala, that is, during ninety-nine days, viz., from March 7th to June 14th: a remarkably quick passage. He seems on that occasion to have given the Cape of Good Hope a wide berth.

His nephew, Estevão da Gama, who left Lisbon on April 1st, took the western route. He passed the Cape Verde Islands on April 15th, Trinidad,[1] in the Southern Atlantic, on May 18th, doubled the Cape about the beginning of June, and first made land, on July 11th, at the Cabo Primeiro, on the coast of Natal, one hundred and two days after his departure from Lisbon.

When Affonso de Albuquerque reached Cape Verde on his voyage to India, in 1503, he took counsel with his pilots whether to follow the "usual route" along the coast of Africa, or to make boldly for mid-ocean. The latter course was decided upon. After a voyage of twenty-eight days, the Island of Ascension[2] was reached, at an estimated distance of 750 to 800 leagues from the Cape. Subsequently de Albuquerque touched the coast of Brazil, and then stood across the Atlantic for the Cape of Good Hope, which

---

says that João da Nova sailed to the Terra de Santa Cruz (Brazil), and thence to the Cape. He does not mention Ascension (Conceiçao). This, however, is not conclusive, for Kings, unlike Popes, are not infallible. Barros, Goes, and Galvão are our authorities for the discovery of the island of Concepçao in 8° S.

[1] There is no doubt that the island referred to by Thome Lopes (see Ramusio) as being 330 leagues from the Ilha dos Papagaios (Brazil), 775 leagues from the Ilha da Boa Vista (Cape Verdes), and 850 leagues from the Cape, is the island now known as Trinidad. This island, on early Portuguese charts, is called Ascenção menor.

[2] If the distance given by Giovanni da Empoli, who writes as an eye-witness, can be trusted, this must be the Ascenção menor (Trinidad), and not the island discovered by João da Nova, which is only 400 leagues from Cape Verde.

he made on July 6th, having thus accomplished the passage from Lisbon in the course of ninety-one days.

Duarte Pacheco, who wrote his *Esmeraldo de Situ Orbis* in 1505, recommends vessels to go south from Cape Verde for 600 leagues, to lat. 19° S., and thence to make for a point 40 leagues to the S.W. of the Cape of Good Hope, in lat. 37. Such a course would take a vessel to the windward of Trinidad.

These notes prove that the Portuguese, in the course of a few years, must have acquired a remarkably correct knowledge of the winds and currents of the Southern Atlantic; for the tracks laid down and followed by their pilots in the beginning of the sixteenth century differ but little, if at all, from those recommended in our modern sailing directories.

Doubling the Cape.

Three days after his landfall we find Vasco da Gama in the Bay of St. Helena, where he careened his ships, took in a fresh supply of water, and observed the latitude.[1]

He left this anchorage on November 16th. Two days afterwards he sighted the Cape, but the wind being from the S.S.W. he was obliged to stand off and on until the 22nd, when he succeeded in getting beyond it "without encountering the storms and perils expected by the mariners"; and following the coast he cast anchor in the Bay of S. Braz on the 25th, and there set up his first padrão. In that run he must have been favoured by the wind, which along the coast and in November blows generally from the S.E., although westerly winds and even gales are not infrequent.

Barros, Castanheda, and Goes give the same account of

---

[1] On Canerio's chart St. Helena's Bay is placed 32° 30′ S., the true latitude being 32° 40′ S. Cantino, whose *outline* is far more correct places the Bay in 31° S.

the doubling of the Cape, but Correa would have us believe that Vasco da Gama, after having made a landfall to the north of the Cape, stood out for the open sea for a month, until there were scarcely six hours of sunlight in the day; and that, even after that, and after he had once more failed to reach the southern extremity of Africa, he continued south for two more months. Then at last he turned again to the east, and found that he had doubled the Cape. Beyond it he discovered lofty mountains and many rivers, one of which was ascended by Coelho for twenty leagues.[1] The utter absurdity of this account is evident, and it is surprising that it should have been accepted by serious historians. A day of six hours may be experienced in lat. 58° 30′ S. in mid-winter—that is in June—but nowhere in the southern hemisphere during summer. In November the duration of daylight in that latitude is about sixteen hours, and to talk about "darkness" under these circumstances seems absurd. It would, moreover, have been impossible to reach so high a latitude without coming amidst masses of drift-ice, which surely would have proved a stranger experience to Vasco's companions than "tremendous seas" and "high winds", and better worth recording.

Along the East Coast of Africa.

On December 8th Vasco left the Bay of S. Braz, and four days afterwards experienced a heavy westerly gale (p. 18).

Barros, Goes, and Castanheda refer to this gale, but Correa, not content with a gale, conjures up a succession of storms, continuing for days, so that the crews clamoured to be taken back to Portugal. The men in Coelho's ships

[1] See Stanley's *Vasco da Gama*, p. 48. Compare Introduction, p. xviii.

are actually said to have conspired to mutiny at the earliest opportunity. Their intention, we are expected to believe, was made known to the captain-major by a mysteriously-worded message shouted from ship to ship by Coelho. Vasco at once summoned his people, declared to them that "if the bad weather came again he had determined to put back; but to disculpate himself with the King" it was necessary for some among them to sign a document giving the reasons for putting back. Having invited on this pretence his pilot, his master and three leading seamen into his cabin, he treacherously put them in irons, and, flinging all the instruments necessary for navigating the ship into the sea, declared that God would henceforth be their master and pilot. The men were released on reaching the River of Mercy, but on their return to Portugal they were ironed once more, to be presented in that degrading state to their King![1]

Osorio[2] likewise gives an account of a mutiny, but says that it occurred before the Cape was doubled. He differs in other respects from Correa, stating, for instance, that "*all* the pilots were put in chains." As Osorio's book was published in 1571, whilst Correa's MS., although written in 1561, only reached Lisbon in 1583, it is not probable that the former borrowed from the latter. They may both have derived their information from the same impure source, and accepted an idle tradition as the record of a fact. That there may have been some discontent among the men is quite possible, but we cannot believe that the pilots intended to head a mutiny. We quite agree with Professor Kopke,[3] when he prefers the authority of Barros, Goes, and Castanheda, and of the author of this "Journal",

---

[1] See Stanley's *Vasco da Gama*, pp. 62, 67, 270.

[2] *The History of the Portuguese during the Reign of Emmanuel* London, 1752, I, p. 48.

[3] *Roteiro*, first edition, p. 143.

to that of Osorio. This applies with still greater force to the absurdly elaborate account of Correa. Professor A. Herculano, in the second edition of the *Roteiro* (p. viii), discredits Professor Kopke's notes on the insufficient ground that the eminent authorities referred to above refrained from every allusion to a mutiny from a "fear of tarnishing the fame of Vasco da Gama's companions." But Herculano believed in Correa—we do not.

Early on December 15th, Vasco once more made for the land, and found himself abreast the Ilhéos Chãos (Bird islands) in Algoa Bay, having thus covered only a couple of hundred miles in the course of seven days. Fair progress was made for a couple of days after this. The vessels kept near the coast, and being favoured by the wind, and also by an inshore counter-current, were able to pass beyond the pillar set up by Dias and the furthest point reached by that navigator. But on December 17th the wind sprang round to the east. Vasco da Gama stood out to sea, and was thus made to experience the full force of the Agulhas current, which here runs at a distance of about ten miles from the land. He was unable to make head against the combined forces of wind and current, and when, on December 20th, he again approached the land he found himself at the Ilhéo da Cruz, 27 miles to the westward of the group of islets from which he had started on the 15th (see p. 15).

Henceforth, for a number of days, the wind proved propitious, and by December 25th our voyagers, clinging all the while to the coast, had proceeded 240 miles beyond the furthest point reached by Dias (as estimated by the pilots); and three days afterwards they cast anchor and took a quantity of fish. This locality we identify with Durnford Point—the Ponta da Pescaria of the old charts—300 miles beyond the Rio de Infante (which was Dias's furthest), and 370 miles beyond the Ilhéo da Cruz. The daily run since December 20th had thus averaged 46 miles.

Vasco da Gama then stood off the land, for reasons not given by any of the historians. Whether it was from fear of being driven upon a lee-shore by a strong easterly wind, or the hope of being able to shorten his passage by a more direct north-easterly course, we are unable to tell. However that may be, a fortnight passed before the vessels returned to the land, so that drinking-water began to fail, and the men had to be put on short rations. It was on the 11th of January that Vasco da Gama found himself off the mouth of a small river, the Rio do Cobre, where he established friendly relations with the "good people" of a country ruled by petty chiefs.[1] The distance of this river from the "Fishing Point" is only 315 miles, and contrary winds must therefore have driven the little flotilla far out of its direct course, but not as far as the neighbourhood of Madagascar, for southerly winds would have been picked up there, which would have carried it more speedily towards its destination than was possible in the face of the south-easterly winds prevailing along the coast of Africa.

After a stay of five days, Vasco da Gama left the Rio do Cobre on January 16th, and without further incident, and leaving Sofala far to the west, he arrived off the mouth of the Rio dos Bons Signaes (Kilimani) on January 24th, having thus accomplished a distance of 480 miles in eight days. Coelho's caravel at once crossed the bar to take soundings, and the two ships followed on the next day. In this river Vasco da Gama stayed 31 days, careening his vessels, refreshing his crews, and erecting a padrão dedicated to S. Raphael (see p. 19). It was here that he heard the glad tidings of more civilised regions in front of him.

On February 24th the vessels once more gained the

---

[1] For a discussion of these sites, see p. 18, *note*.

open sea, and following the coast for six days arrived off Mozambique on March 2nd. During this voyage of 330 miles they kept outside the islands which here skirt the coast, and lay to at night, as usual, which accounts for the slow rate of progress made during this coasting voyage. Coelho, as before, led the way, and entered by the shallow southern channel, between the islands of S. Thiago and S. Jorge. The three vessels anchored in front of the town (see p. 23). Later on they removed to the island of S. Jorge, where mass was read on March 12th, after which the little flotilla set sail for the north. Two days afterwards, the Soriza Peaks rose in the distance. In the course of that day they were becalmed. A light easterly wind arose, and at night on the 14th they stood off shore; and when in the morning of the 15th they looked about them, they found that the Mozambique current, which here frequently runs at the rate of two to four knots to the southward, had swept them twelve miles abaft Mozambique. Sailing vessels are advised,[1] under such circumstances, to stand to the eastward for sixty miles or more, and regain their northing beyond the influence of the southerly current. Of course, Vasco da Gama knew nothing about all this. Fortunately, he was able to recover his old anchorage at the island of S. Jorge in the course of the afternoon.

A fresh start was made on March 29th. This time the wind was favourable. The Moorish pilot whom Vasco da Gama had on board took him past Kilwa, which the captain would have liked to have visited, and shaped a course outside Mafia, Zanzibar and the other islands lying off that coast. Early on April 7th the *S. Raphael* ran aground near Mtangata, but was speedily got off; and on April 7th Vasco da Gama cast anchor in the outer road of

---

[1] *Africa Pilot*, iii, p. 241.

Mombasa, the finest port on the whole coast of Eastern Africa. The distance thus accomplished in the course of nine days was 690 miles (see p. 34).

Sixty miles more brought the Portuguese to the roadstead of Melinde, where they cast anchor on April 14th, and remained until the 24th. This was the only town at which they met with a cordial reception (p. 40).

Across the Arabian Gulf to Calecut.

On April 24th Vasco da Gama, who had secured the services of a Gujarati pilot, started for India. By that time the S.W. monsoon was blowing steadily, though not as yet very strongly. The African coast was kept in sight for a couple of days, after which the vessels stood boldly across the "Great Gulf." They passed in all probability to the south of the *Baixos de Padua*. They had been twenty-one days at sea, and were still 24 miles from the land, when there rose in front of them a lofty wooded mountain. This was Mount Eli, 2,220 miles from Melinde, and the day on which India was first beheld by Europeans who had come direct from a European port was May 18th, a Friday (see p. 47).[1]

Galvão[2] is the only author who mentions the "Flats of Padua,"[3] as having been discovered by Vasco da Gama on his outward voyage, and we freely accept his statement, for the Portuguese must either have crossed the Laccadives or passed to the north of them. As these islands are very low, the author of the *Roteiro* may not have thought it

---

[1] Vasco da Gama thus took 24 days to cross from Melinde to India. Cabral, João da Nova, Estevão da Gama and Affonso de Albuquerque effected this passage in from 15 to 18 days. They crossed in August, when the S.-W. monsoon blows freshly.

[2] *The Discoveries of the World* (Hakluyt Society), p. 93.

[3] These "Flats" are a submerged coral reef lying between 12° 30′ and 13° 40′ N. The native name is Maniyal Par.

worth while to mention them. It is evident, however, from what Sernigi says (p. 134), as also from the evidence of the earliest maps illustrating this voyage, that the Portuguese learnt a good deal about them from the pilots whom they employed.

On the following day, having stood off during the night, the captain-major again approached the land, but the western Ghats were wrapped in clouds, and it rained heavily, so that the pilot failed to identify the locality. The day after, however, the 20th of May, having passed Monte Formosa (see p. 47, note 6), he recognised the lofty mountains above Calecut, and in the evening of that day the little fleet was riding at anchor about five miles off Capocate, or Capua, a small town only seven miles to the north of the much-desired city, which was pointed out to the expectant Portuguese (p. 48). Soon afterwards Vasco da Gama took up a position right in front of that city;[1] but on May 27th a pilot of the Zamorin guided him to an anchorage off Pandarani, thirteen miles to the north, on the ground of its greater safety, and at that anchorage the Portuguese remained no less than 88 days, until August 23rd, when Vasco da Gama once more took up a position four leagues to the leeward of Calecut. From that time to the day of his final departure, in the afternoon of August 30th, he hovered about that city, standing off and on, as the state of the weather or the exigencies of his relations with the Zamorin required.

The Voyage Home.

In the afternoon of August 30th, a tornado carried Vasco da Gama out to sea (p. 77), and when making his way along the coast he was obliged to tack, depending for

[1] According to the author of Add. MS. 20901 (British Museum), Vasco da Gama "cast anchor in front of the most noble and rich city of Calecut on May 22". The date of this MS. is about 1516.

his progress upon land and sea breezes, and laying-to when becalmed. At Cananor he sent ashore one of his captives (p. 79), but held no communication with the town himself. On September 15th he landed on a small island, and erected the padrão dedicated to St. Mary (p. 80).[1]

On September 20th Vasco da Gama arrived at the Anjediva Islands, about 14° 45′ N., having thus spent twenty-one days in accomplishing 240 miles. He seems, first of all, to have anchored near the Oyster Rocks, off the Kalipadi river, but on September 24th he landed on the largest of these islands, where he remained until October 5th, waiting for a propitious wind, and availed himself of the enforced leisure to careen the flagship and the *Berrio* (p. 83).

The passage across the gulf proved a fearful trial for the Portuguese. Foul winds and calms impeded their progress, whilst a renewed outbreak of scurvy carried off thirty victims and prostrated the remaining men, so that only seven or eight were fit to do duty in each vessel. Vasco da Gama had left Anjediva on October 5th (a Friday !), although the N.E. monsoon only sets in at the end of the month, and ninety days elapsed before the African coast came within sight, near Magadoxo, and five more before the hard-proved mariners once more found themselves with the friendly Sultan of Melinde (p. 89).

The remainder of the voyage home calls for little comment. Having left Melinde on January 11th, Vasco da Gama, passing between the mainland and Zanzibar,

[1] On page 80, note 2, we have identified the island upon which this padrão was placed with Pigeon Island, 14° 1′, on the ground of its answering better to the description given by the author of the *Roteiro*; but we see reasons for accepting the general opinion that one of the islands off Mulpy (perhaps Coco Nut Island) must be meant, although none of these islets is more than a mile from the coast, instead of two leagues. Barros (Dec. 1, l. iv, c. ii.) locates the Ilhéos de Santa Maria between Bacanor and Baticala.

stopped for a fortnight at the "baixos" upon which the *S. Raphael* had run in the outward voyage, and there that doomed ship was set on fire, as there were no men left to sail her. Late on February 1st the remaining two vessels hove to in front of S. Jorge Island, where a padrão was erected on the following morning in drenching rain. The voyage was continued without communicating with the town of Moçambique, and on March 3rd Vasco once more found himself in the Bay of S. Braz.

The Cape was doubled on March 20th. The wind proved fair during twenty-seven days—that is, to April 16th or 17th—but after came calms and foul winds; and on April 25th, when the wearied mariners already believed themselves to be near S. Thiago, the pilots told them that they had only reached the shoals off the Rio Grande (p. 93).

Here the two consorts appear to have parted company, under circumstances not known; and whilst Vasco da Gama accompanied his dying brother to Terçeira, Coelho is said to have made straight for Lisbon, where he arrived, after a voyage of seventy-six days, on July 10th. The distance along the coast of Africa is only 1,900 miles, and that by way of the Azores, the only route at all suitable for sailing vessels, is 2,920 miles. The passage ought certainly to have been accomplished in forty days.[1] What did he do during the remaining thirty-six days? We cannot suppose for one moment that an experienced sailor like Coelho would have faced the head-winds of the coast for the sake of shortening the distance to be run. Still, such things *have* happened.

From the following statement of distances run it will be seen that from July 8th, 1497, the day of Vasco da

[1] Cabral, on his homeward voyage in 1501, reached Lisbon from Cape Verde in twenty days, but Juan Sebastian del Cano, in the *Victoria*, took fifty-seven days to reach San Lucar from the Cape Verde Islands.

Gama's departure from Lisbon to the return of Coelho on July 10th, 1499, there elapsed 732 days, or two years and two days. Of this time 316 days were expended before Calecut was reached, 102 at Calecut and in its vicinity, and 314 on the homeward passage.[1]

Dates and Places.	Days.	Old Portuguese Leagues [1]	Nautical Miles.	Average Daily Run, Miles.
Lisbon to S. Thiago, July 8 to 27, 1497 .	19	515	1740	90
S. Thiago to First Landfall, 30° S., Aug. 3 to Nov. 4	93	1533	5180	54
To S. Helena Bay, Nov. 4 to 7 . .	3	49	165	55
S. Helena Bay to Cape of Good Hope, Nov. 16 to 22	6	34	115	19
Cape to Bay of S. Braz, Nov. 22 to 25 .	3	59	200	67
S. Braz to Rio do Cobre, Dec. 8 to Jan. 11, 1498	34	259	875	26[2]
Rio do Cobre to Rio dos Bons Signaes, Jan. 16 to 24	8	142	480	60
Rio dos Bons Signaes to Moçambique, Feb 24 to March 2	6	98	330	55
Moçambique to Mombaça, March 29 to April 7[3]	9	204	690	77
Mombaça to Melinde, April 12 to 14 .	2	18	60	30
Melinde to Mount Eli, April 24 to May 18	24	657	2220	93
Mount Eli to Capocate near Calecut, May 18 to 20	2	16	53	26
Total Outward Passage . .	209	3584	12108	58
Calecut to Anjediva, Aug. 30 to Sept. 20, 1498	21	71	240	11
Anjediva to Melinde, Oct. 5 to Jan 7, 1499	94	710	2400	25
Melinde to Moçambique, Jan. 11 to Feb. 1	21[4]	219	740	35
Moçambique to S. Braz, Feb. 2 to March 3	30	500	1690	56
S. Braz to Cape, March 12 to 20 . .	8	59	200	25
Cape to Rio Grande, March 20 to April 25	36	994	3360	93
Rio Grande to Lisbon (Coelho's vessel), April 25 to July 10, 1499	76	864	2920	25
Total Homeward Passage . .	286	3417	11550	40

[1] In converting legoas into nautical miles we have assumed 100 legoas to be the equivalent of 338 miles. See *League* in Index and Glossary.

[2] Or thirty miles, if we exclude the five days wasted in a vain effort to stem the Agulhas current (see p. 15).

[3] No account is taken of the four days lost in an attempt to sail north (see p. 28).

[4] This includes a delay of fifteen (? five) days when burning the *S. Raphael*.

APPENDIX G.

EARLY MAPS ILLUSTRATING VASCO DA GAMA'S FIRST VOYAGE.

IT must ever be matter for regret that none of the sailing charts prepared by Vasco da Gama's pilots should have reached us. In tracing the progress of his expedition with the aid of charts we are consequently dependent upon compilations which, although contemporary, embody also materials brought home by other navigators.

One great drawback of all the charts available for our purpose is their small scale.[1] This compelled their compilers to make a selection from the names which they found inserted upon the larger charts at their disposal, and this selection may not always have been a judicious one. The compilation of a map from discordant materials presents difficulties even in the present day, and these difficulties

[1] Charts on a larger scale, but of a later date, are available, and enable us to trace the physical features of the coast, but their nomenclature is not always that of the original discoverers. Nor are we so fortunate as to possess such full descriptions of the coast as are to be found in the "Africa Pilot", for the *Esmeraldo de Situ Orbis* (1505) of the famous Duarte Pacheco Pereira stops short at the Rio de Infante; whilst works such as Linschoten's *Itinerarium ofte Schipvaert*, belong either to a much later epoch, or are of too general a nature to prove of use when attempting to identify the more obscure place-names. I think it was Admiral Ignacio da Costa Quintella, the author of the *Annaes da marinha Portugueza*, who regretted that the task of writing the history of Portuguese exploration should have devolved almost exclusively upon landsmen, who neglected to give satisfactory accounts of the routes followed by the early navigators. This regret we fully share.

were much greater at a time when the compiler had not at his command trustworthy observations for latitude which would have enabled him to check the positions of intermediate places, and bring into agreement the records brought home by successive explorers. As an instance, we may mention that in the five maps which we shall bring more fully under notice, the latitude assigned to the Cape of Good Hope varies between 29° and 34° S., its true position being 34° 22′ S. As to longitudes, they had to be determined by dead reckoning, and it need not therefore surprise us if, on the maps referred to, the Cape is placed from 3° 50′ to 10° 20′ too far to the eastward. Nay, this near approach to the truth, in at least one instance, compels our recognition of the skill of the men who piloted the first ships around that long-sought *Cabo desejado.*

Another difficulty arises from the crabbed characters employed by the map draughtsmen of the early part of the sixteenth century: a difficulty all the more serious when these illegible characters had to be reproduced by Italians having no knowledge of the language of the documents they used, or the meaning of the uncouth names which they were called upon to copy. It is one of the great merits of Mercator to have caused these characters to be banished from the maps of his countrymen; but a second Mercator is still wanted to do the same good work for their printed books.

I now proceed to a consideration of the charts which illustrate more especially Vasco da Gama's first voyage.

The first of these charts is by Henricus Martellus Germanus. It is one of many in a MS., *Insularium illustratum*, now in the British Museum (Add. MS. 15760). It is a map of the world, very roughly drawn and without a scale, and is dated 1489, that is almost immediately after the return of Dias in the December of the preceding year. The author, no doubt, was an Italian, and other maps by his skilful hand are known to exist.[1] Unfortunately for our purpose, the coast beyond the Cape is very incorrectly drawn, and there are but six names, viz., Golfo dentro delle serre (False Bay), Rio della vacche (Gouritz), Cavo dalhado (talhado, Seal Point), Golfo de Pastori (St. Francis Bay), Padrom de S. George (instead of Gregorio), and Ilha de fonte (instead of infante).[2]

The first map illustrating, or rather attempting to illustrate, Vasco da Gama's voyage is that compiled by Juan de la Cosa, the famous pilot of Columbus, in 1500. The author was fairly well informed of the discoveries made by his own countrymen, but knew apparently but little about those of the Portuguese. Thus, although Vicente Yanez Pinzon only returned to Spain on September 30th, 1500, the coast explored by him to the westward of the Rostro hermoso (the Cabo de Agostinho of the Portuguese) is laid down properly; whilst Santa Cruz, discovered by Cabral in April 1500, is incorrectly indicated,[3] although Gaspar de Lemos, whom Cabral sent back with the news of his discovery, arrived in Portugal three months before the Spanish navigator. As to two groups of islands in the southern Atlantic, namely, "thebas, yslas tibras etiopicas yn mare oceanum austral" (lat. 1° 40′ S.), and "Y. tausens, ylas tausens montises etiopicus oceanas" (lat. 15° S.), they seem to be quite imaginary, and I only refer to them here because they kept their place on later maps,

---

[1] See, for instance, A. Mori, in *Atti IIº Congresso Geogr. Italiana*, Rome, 1895, who describes maps by him in a "Ptolemy" in the Biblioteca Nazionale at Florence.

[2] The late Dr. Kohl published a facsimile of this map in the *Zeitschrift für Erdkunde*, I, 1856, but it is not very accurate. That portion of the map which lies between the Guinea islands and Dias's furthest accompanies my Paper on "Cão, Dias and Behaim", in the *Geographical Journal*.

[3] A legend (near the southern tropic and on the meridian of Lisbon) refers to Santa Cruz as "ysla descubierta por portugal".

and might be mistaken for the islands discovered by João da Nova in 1501-2. Of the results of Vasco da Gama's expedition Juan de la Cosa must have been very ill-informed; among the many uncouth and incomprehensible names inserted by him along the Eastern coast of Africa there is not one which can be traced to Gama. Not even such places as Sofala, Quiloa, Moçambique and Mombaça can be identified, whilst Zanzibar and Madagascar lie far out in the Indian Ocean.[1]

The coastline of the Indian Ocean is Ptolemaic; there is no hint at the peninsular shape of India, the map being in that respect inferior to that of the Catalan, more than a hundred years older, and the only indication of Vasco da Gama's visit to these seas is the name "Calicut", placed on the south coast of Caramania (Kerman), with a legend to the east of it: "tierra descubierto por el reÿ dom Manuel rey de Portugal."[2]

Our next chart shows a great advance upon the preceding. It was purchased at a sale in London, and is now the property of Dr. Hamy, who published a description of it, with facsimiles, in his *Études historiques et géographiques*, Paris, 1896. The author is not known. His chart places on record the discoveries made by Vicente Yanez Pinzon, Cabral, Sancho de Toar, and Cortereal, and by the expedition which King Manuel sent to Brazil in 1501, and which returned at the beginning of September, 1502.[3] This expedition, which was accompanied by Vespucci, explored the American coast as far as the Rio de Cananea, in lat.

[1] There are flags at Abaran, c. etiopico and quinonico.

[2] A fine facsimile of this map was published at Madrid, in 1892, by Antonio Cánovas Vallego and Prof. Traynor, together with a biographical sketch of Juan de la Cosa by Antonio Vasáno.

[3] A. Galvano, *The Discoveries of the World*, London (Hakluyt Society), 1862, p. 98; and *The Letters of Vespucci*, translated by Sir C. R. Markham, *ib.* 1894.

25° 45′ S. The author knows nothing of the discoveries of João da Nova, who returned to Lisbon on September 11th, 1502. We may therefore safely date his map "1502", as is done by Dr. Hamy.

One curious feature of this map is its double equator: that for the western half of the map being the 'new' equator, to which the recent discoveries of the Spaniards and Portuguese are to be referred, whilst that for the east lies four degrees to the north of the former, and is taken from Ptolemy. Indeed, the outline of the Indian Ocean is Ptolemy's, and so is the nomenclature, with a few exceptions to be noticed presently. In the south-east, however, the author has broken through Ptolemy's encircling barrier, and has thus opened a way from the *Indicum mare* to an outer ocean where room has been found for Seilam, Iava and far Quinsai. The eastern edge of his Oekumene lies 205° to the east of Lisbon (196° E. of Greenwich).[1] The only original features within the Indian Ocean are a peninsular India, which is made to project from Ptolemy's old coast-line to the west of Taprobana, with a town, "Colochuti", and the islands of Madagascar and Tangibar lying far out at sea in lat. 20° S. The only other modern name within this wide area is "Malacha", which is placed in the Aurea Chersonesus.

The nomenclature along the African coast is fairly full, and evidently taken from original sources,[2] but the spelling is so corrupt, and the letters are frequently so illegible, that I failed to make out many of the names, although I had that portion of the map which specially interested me enlarged from Dr. Hamy's facsimile by photography. An examination of the copy, which I give, will show that the drawing of the coast-line leaves very much to be desired.

---

[1] This carries us almost to Hawaii.

[2] The words "questo avemo visto", to the south of Moçambique, point to the use of an original sailing chart.

A very great advance upon the preceding is shown by a chart which Alberto Cantino, the correspondent of Hercules d'Este, Duke of Ferrara, caused to be specially designed for his patron, at Lisbon, and for which he paid twelve golden ducats. There can be no doubt about the date of this map. It was begun after Cortereal's return, October 11th, 1501, and had been completed some time before November, 1502. The MS. of this valuable chart is deposited in the Biblioteca Estense at Modena. The American portion of it has been published by Mr. Harrisse (*Les Cortereals*, Paris, 1888[1]), and the Indian Section by the Vienna Geographical Society.[2] Through the kindness of Signor M. C. Caputo, librarian of the Biblioteca Estense, who procured for me an excellent photograph, I am enabled to publish Africa from the Gulf of Guinea to Makhdesho. An examination of this reproduction will at once establish the superiority of this chart over those already noticed, as also over later charts. The outline of Africa is wonderfully correct, considering the age of the chart, and the broad face presented by that continent to the south is brought out most satisfactorily. Unfortunately, several of the names along the south coast are rendered illegible, even on the original, owing to the coloured Table Mountain, and I have failed to decipher these satisfactorily, notwithstanding the kind help afforded me by Signor Caputo. Along the east coast there is a paucity of names. It should be observed that the padrões and Portuguese flags have been located somewhat at haphazard.

Whilst the African coast is taken exclusively from recent Portuguese sources, that of India and Further India

---

[1] Reproduced in Sir Clements R. Markham's *Journal of Christopher Columbus*, London, 1893, where also see Cantino's letters.

[2] *Die topographischen Capitel des Indischen Seespiegels Mohit*, von Dr. M. Bittner, Vienna, 1897, with thirty maps by Dr. Tomaschek.

is largely based upon native information. This is proved by some of the legends. At Çatiguam we read "esta em xi pulgados a o norte," but these "pulgados" or inches are clearly the "isbas" of the "Mohit," a mode of expressing the latitude which is peculiar to the Indian Ocean and has been explained by me on p. 26, note 4.

In order to enable the reader to judge of the extent to which the compilers of early Portuguese maps were in-

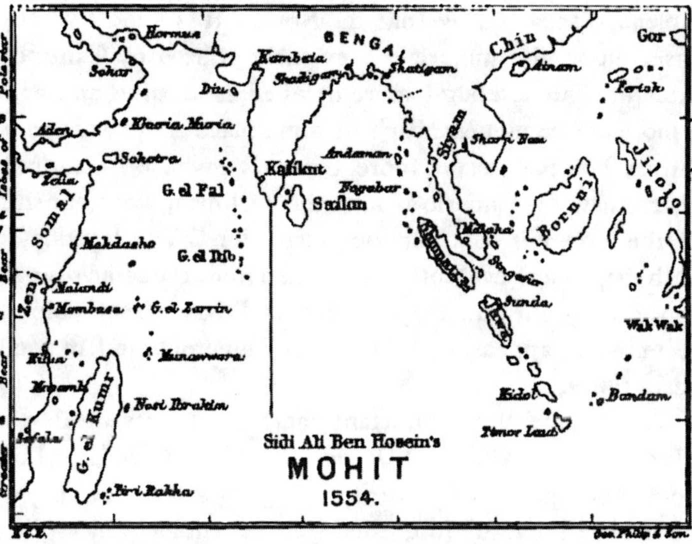

debted to native sailing directories and charts, and of the judgment exercised by them in their use, I insert here a reduction of Dr. Tomaschek's elaborate reconstruction of a chart in accordance with the data contained in Admiral Sidi Ali ben Hosein's "Mohit," or "Encyclopædia of the Sea," which, although only written in 1554, embodies the local knowledge gained in the course of centuries, and is not indebted to Portuguese charts for its superiority.[1]

[1] Even Ptolemy seems to have been in possession of some of these Indian sailing charts, and Dr. Tomaschek suggests that the monstrous size of his Taprobana, or Ceylon, is due to his having mistaken the

The next chart to be considered is by Nicolas de Canerio, of Genoa. Its date is undoubtedly the same as that of the Cantino Map, that is, it was drawn before the results of João da Nova's voyage had become available. This is proved by finding "y. tebas, iste insulle chamada secular" in the mid-Atlantic (9° S.), with a Portuguese flag, for these islands are borrowed from Juan de la Cosa, and have nothing to do with Conceiçao (Ascension) or St. Helena, discovered by João da Nova. It is almost wholly based upon the materials previously utilised by Cantino's draughtsman, although more detailed in outline and with a more ample nomenclature in some places. The shape of Africa, however, is far more correctly given on Cantino's chart than on Canerio's,[1] and the technical workmanship of the former is of a superior character. The legends on both maps have evidently been taken from the same source: those on Cantino's map, as far as I have been able to examine it, appearing to be more numerous and in some cases fuller.

The MS. of this important chart is at present in the Hydrographic Office at Paris. Prof. L. Gallois, whose contributions to the history of geography are highly appreciated by all interested in the subject, has given an account of it in the *Bulletin* of the Geographical Society of Lyons.[2] This account is accompanied by a reproduction of two sections of the map, viz., America and Africa. Prof. Gallois has had the extreme kindness to supply me with a tracing of the Asiatic portion of the map, and has thus enabled me to produce Map VII, illus-

---

horizontal lines crossing these charts for parallels drawn at intervals of a degree.

[1] Africa to the north of Mozambique measures 28° across on Canerio's chart, and 25° on Cantino's, the actual breadth being 26°.

[2] *Le Portulan de Nicolas de Canerio* (Bulletin de la Soc. de Géogr. de Lyon, 1890).

trating this volume. My reproduction contains all the names of the original to the east of the Cape of Good Hope, whilst the legends for which there was no room upon the Reduction are given at the end of this Appendix.

On examining this chart it will at once be seen that the author—not the Italian copyist, whose name alone appears upon it—drew very largely upon native information. Still, he has not ventured to disassociate himself altogether from Ptolemy. He has, however, made some use of Marco Polo, though he puts the names taken from him—such as Murfulu, Var and Coilu—in the wrong places. The island in the middle of the Indian ocean—Y. rana—is not one of the Mascarenhas, as might be supposed, but the Illa Iaua of the Catalan map, that is, Java. The legend tells us that "In this island is much benjoim, and silk and porcelain." Still further south there are three islands, representing the Mascarenhas, then known by Malabari names.

A few words remain to be said about the Portuguese maps published in the Strassburg edition of Ptolemy, in 1513. The originals upon which these maps are based were sent to Duke Renée II of Lorraine (died 1508), from Portugal. Uebelin and Essler, the editors of Ptolemy, state that they were drawn by an "admiral" of King Ferdinand. But Lelewel[1] points out that the king meant must be D. Manuel of Portugal. They may have been forwarded together with the French translation of Vespucci's *Four Voyages*, 1504, and Vespucci may even have had something to do with their compilation, even though not the actual compiler. But however this may be, and whatever the date of actual publication, there can be no doubt that they are identical

---

[1] *Geographie du Moyen Age*, ii, p. 143.

in all essentials with Canerio's chart, and must be referred to the same date, that is 1502.[1]

On placing side by side some of the above charts it almost looks as if they were not merely based upon the same original authorities, but had actually been slavishly copied one from the other, or from some common prototype. On a closer examination, however, this opinion is not sustainable, for the latitudes and longitudes assigned by the authors to the leading points will be found to differ very considerably. The following little table show this as regards the latitudes :—

—	True Lat.	Cosa.	Hamy.	Cantino.	Canerio.	Strassburg Ptolemy.
Congo . . .	6° 5′ S.	5° 30′ S.	7° 50′ S.	6° S.	10° S.	10° S.
Cape of Good Hope	34° 22′ S.	29° S.	30° 40′ S.	32° 45′ S.	34° S.	33° 40′ S.
Malindi . .	3° 20° S.	—	3° N.	3° 25′ S.	1° S.	1° N.
Calecut . .	11° 50′ N.	18° N.	13° N.	10° N.	13° 20′ N.	17° 30′ N.
Malacca . .	2° 13′ N.	—	2° 30′ N.	14° S.	12° 30′ N.	8° S.

The latitudes from Dr. Hamy's chart are referred to the Western Equator.

I now append the legends to be found in Canerio's chart, together with a translation. The spelling is that of the original. A few legends from the Cantino chart, not to be found in Canerio's, have been added. The bold Roman Capitals are references to Map vii. The printer is not responsible for the mistakes of the original copyist.

A. Aqui he amina douro emque dia multra abondancia de la mais que em outro.

(Here is the gold mine yielding greater abundance than any other.)

---

[1] In Nordenskiöld's *Atlas* will be found facsimiles of these maps.

B Aqui ha laquar et panos finos de toda sortes et figuos pasados et ubas et ensenso et almizquer et ambre et aljofar que tudo bem de demtro pello a sertam da careto [cidade].

(Here are to be found lac, fine cloth of all kinds, corn, food-stuffs, grapes, incense, perfumes, ambergris and seed-pearls, all of which come to this city from the interior.)

C. Aqui he Caliqut he multo noble cidade descoberta pel el muy escarrado prip. Rey dom Manoel Rey de Portugall aqui ay molto menxas [benjoim] desua naturea [de fina natura] e pimenta et outras muitas mercedarias que vem de multas partes, & canella gengiber cravo emcenso sandalos et tode sortes de especiaria pedras de grande vallor et perlas de grande vallor et aliofar.

(This is Caliqut, the most noble city discovered by the most illustrious prince Dom Manuel, King of Portugal. There is here much fine benzoin, pepper, and many other kinds of merchandise coming from many parts, also cinnamon, ginger, cloves, incense, sandal-wood and all kinds of spices; stones and pearls of great value and seed-pearls.)

D. Aqui ha panos muitos finos de reda et dalgodom et aros e azucar et cera, e outras multas mercedarias.

(There are here very fine silk and cotton stuffs, and rice, sugar, wax, and many other kinds of merchandise.)

E. Aqui a sandalos e menxuim e ruibarbo e aiofa.

(Here are sandal-wood, benzoin, rhubarb and seed-pearls.)

F. Em esta cidade ha todas as mercadarias que bem a Caliqut, cravo e benjoym e lenhaloes e sandalos, estoraque, ruybarbo e marfim e pedras preciosas de muyto valor e perlas ed almizquer e porçelanas finas e outras muytas mercadarias. (From the Cantino Chart.)

(In this city are to be found all kinds of merchandise which go to Caliqut: cloves, benzoin, aloes, sandal-wood, storax, rhubarb, ivory, precious stones of much value, pearls, perfumes, fine porcelain and many other kinds of merchandise.)

G Aqui ha chumbo almizquer e menzoy e sandalos.

(Here are lead [tin], perfumes, benzoin and sandal-wood.)

H. Aqui ha almizquer e sandalos e menioim e estoraque e linolos et chumbo.

(Here are perfumes, sandal-wood, benzoin, storax, aloes and lead [tin]).

I. Esta insulla chamada ataprobana he maior insulla que se en lo mondo et mais richa de todos os cousas s. auro e praia e predas preciosos et perlas et rubis muito grandes et finos et todas sortes de speciaria et sedas et borcados et a gente son idolatres et multo dispostas e tradam com os de fora et achan daqui multas mercedarias per a fora, e trasem outras que [nam] ay em esta insulla.

(This island, called Taprobana, is the largest island in the world, and is very rich in all things, such as gold, silver, pearls, precious stones and rubies of large size and fine quality; all kinds of spices, silks and brocades. The inhabitants are idolators and well disposed, and take much merchandise abroad, bringing back other kinds not to be found in their island.)

K. Aqui naca a canella e muitos sortes de espeçiaria, ed aqui pescam as perlas ed aljofar, sam as gentes de esta ylha idolatres e tratam muito cravo com Caliqut.

(Here grows cinnamon and many kinds of spices, and there they fish pearls and seed-pearls. The people of the island are idolators, and take many cloves to Caliqut.)

L. Em esta ylha ha gente do que comase huum as outras. (Cantino Chart.)

(In this island there are people who eat one another.)

M. Em estas tres ylhas nam ai nada sinam gente nuito pobre a nua (Cantino Chart.)

(In these three islands the people are very poor and naked.)

The following list of place-names includes all names found upon the maps referred to from the Cape of Good Hope to Malindi. Beyond that place the principal names only are given.

In addition to the names to be found on the maps, we have introduced those given in Duarte Pacheco Pereira's *Esmeraldo de Situ Orbis*, written in 1505.

LIST OF PLACE-NAMES.

The authorities are referred to by Arabic numerals thus:—

1. Henricus Martellus Germanus. 2. Juan de la Cosa. 3. Dr. Hamy's Chart. 4. Cantino Chart. 5. Canerio. 6. Strassburg Ptolemy. 7. Duarte Pacheco.

Place-names having an asterisk prefixed to them are mentioned in the *Roteiro*. The small letters in *Italics* refer to the Notes.

The Dates, in the first column, are those of the Saints after whom localities have been named.

In Portuguese.	Names on the Maps.	Modern Names.
***Cabo da boa Esperança**	1, Cavo desperanza; 2, C. de boa esperança; 3, Cabo di bona speranza; 4, Cabo de boa esperança; 5 and 6, Cabo di bona speranza	**Cape of Good Hope**
G. dentro das serras (gulf within the mountain ranges)	1, Golfo dnt[o] delle serre; 3, Praia sabio (pablo?) *a*; 4, abaia	False Bay
Ponta espinhosa *b* (thorny point)	2, Punta espinosa (chrinosa?) . .	Cape Hangklip
As serras . .	4, As seia (a serra?)	
Ponta de S. Brandão, May 16	2, Mastradios (nutrador?); 4, S. biado; 7, Ponta de S. Brandam	Quoin Point
Cabo das Agulhas	2, Punta de gra?; 7, Cabo dos agulhos	**Cape Agulhas** *c*
Golfo das agulhas (Needle Cape or Bay)	4, G. das agullas	Struys Bay
Serras seccas (dry ridges)	2, Sieras secos	Bare sandhills to E. of Struys Point
A bahia	2, Abaia dal es . . . las	Marcus Bay
A praia (shore) .	4, Apraia	
Cabo de Infante (Cape of João Infante)	3, C. de infante; 4, C. do infante; 5, Cabo donfante; 6, C. do infante; 7, Punta de infante	Cape Infanta !
——	4, G. do Coberti	St. Sebastian Bay.
Rio de Nazaret .	2, R. de nazaren; 3, Croa de nazare;	Breede River
Cabo do Salto . .	4, C. de resunancal...; 5, Cabo do lalta; 6, G. de Salco	Cape Barracouta
——	3, Rio de fo...oas	Kaffirkuyl River
Rio dos vaqueiros (herdsman river)	1, Rio della vacche; 3, Rio vachoeros	Gouritz River
Angra das vaccas .	2, Angra das vaccas	Flesh Bay
Cabo das Vaccas (Cow point) or C. delgado (slender or cattle cape)	2, C delgado; 7, Cabo dos vaccas .	Cape Vacca
Ponta da estrella (Star point)	2, Punta destrella	Cape St. Blaise
Terra de S. João, June 24 and Dec. 27	5 and 6, Terra de S. Joham . .	The country west of Mossel Bay
Golfo dos Vaqueiros (herdsmen bay) or **Angra** (aguada) **de São Braz** (bay or watering-place of St. Blasius) Feb. 3	2, G. de baguros; 3, Baia de anguada; 4, G. de Sanbras; 5, G. de Sanbras; 6, G. de Sanbras; 7, Angra or Anguada de S. Braz	Mossel Bay *d*
——	4, Rio de frung	Harten bosch River
Serra de S. Lazaro, Dec. 17	3, Serra de S. Lazaro . . .	W. Outeniqua mountains (Brocks Bosch, 5,000 ft.)
Ponta da Pescaria (Fishery Point)	5 and 6, Ponta da pescaria . .	Gerieke Point

In Portuguese.	Names on the Maps.	Modern Names.
Lago cerrado and Angra da lagôa	4, Alago carrado; 5, Lago cairado; 6, Lago cairado; 7, Angra de lagoa	Zwarte Vlei
Serra da Estrella .	3, M. dastrella; 4 Serra da estrella	Outeniqua mountains
Cabo talhado (steep cape)	1, Cavo dalhado; 2, Punta de canar (astar? astros?); 3, C. ta . . de 4, C. talhado; 5, Cabo talcado; 6, C. calcado	Seal Cape
Bahia das alagoas (Bay of the Lagoons)	4, Abaia das alagoas; 5 and 6, Plaia das alagoas; 7, Angra dos alagoas	Plettenburg Bay *e*
Terra das trovoadas (land of thunderstorms)	2, Montanas; 4, terra dos montes; 3, terra dos trovados	Langekloof
Ponta de Ruy Pirez	4, Punta de Ruyez	Seal corner
Costa da areia (sandy shore)	5 and 6, Costa darea	
Ponta (golfo) das queimadas *f*	3, Pta. da semados; 4, Pũta dasqũmadas; 5 and 6, G. dos quemadas	Cape St. Francis and Krom Bay
Golfo dos vaqueiros (Herdsmen Bay) *g*	1, Golfo de pastori; 3, G, vacheoros; 5, Angra	St. Francis Bay
Cabo do recife (reef cape)	5, P. do reciffe; 4, C. do arreciffe; 5 and 6, Cabo do recisi; 7, C. de recife	Cape Recife
G. da Roca (rock bay)	3, G. do Roca; 4, Baia da Roca; 5, G. do raca; 6, G. daraca	Algoa Bay *h*
Serra branca (white mountains)	3, Serra do blanco	Zuurberg, or Addo Heights
I héo da Cruz (Cross Island)	4, Ilheos da Cruz; 5, Ilheos da Cruz; 6, Insule de Cruz; 7, Penedo dos Fontes or I. da Cruz	St. Croix Island
Ilhéos chãos (low islands)	4, Ilheoos chaos; 5, Ilheos chaaos; 6, Insule chaaos	Bird Islands
Ponta do carrascal *i* (Green-oak Point)	4, Puta do carascal; 5, Porto de charseal; 6, Porto datharson	Woody Cape
Padrão de S. Gregorio, March 12	1, Padrom de S. George; 3, P. de S. Gregorio; 4, Padro de S. Gregorio	Cape Padrone
Rio da lagoa (Lagoon river)	3, Rio de lago; 4, Rio de lagoa .	Kasuga River
Praia das alagôas .	4, Praia das alagoas	
Penedo das fontes *j* (Fountain Rock)	2, Penedos; 4, penedo da	Ship Rock
Furna (cove) . .	4, Furna	Port Arthur
Ilha de Infante .	1, Ilha de Fonte; 2, Y^s de ynfante .	Three Sisters off Riet Point?
***Rio de Infante** .	4, Rio do infante; 5 and 6, Rio de infante	Great Fish river
——	5, Cabo	
Rio S. Thomé, Dec. 21	5, Rio san tome; 7, R. S. thome .	Umtata River
Ilha de S. Christovão, July 25	3, Ilha de San Xpistofa; 5, Ilheos San Cristofe; 6, Insule de S. Chrifero; 7, Ilheos de Sanxpono;	Keiskamma Point *k*

In Portuguese.	Names on the Maps.	Modern Names.
Praia corada ? *l* .	4, Praia ; 5, Praia ; 6, Corrada	
——	5, Gorffo boscho ; *m* 6, G. postho (hostio ?)	
Cabo primeiro (first cape)	3, Cabo primero ; 4, Cabo primeiro	Cape Morgan
Porto de Natal, Dec. 25	5, Gorffo de natal ; 6, G. do natal .	Port Natal
Terra do Natal .	3, Terra de Natall	
Porto da pescaria .	3, Pescarias ; 5 and 6, Porto das pescarias	Durnford Bay
Porto de S. Lucia, Dec. 13	3, Pr. de S. lucia ; 5 and 6, Porto de Sta. lucia	St. Lucia Bay
Terra das mesas (land of table-hills)	5, Tierram das mesas ; 6, Tiram das mesas	Flat hills S. of Cape Vidal
Rio dos medões de Ouro (river of the golden downs)	3, Modosdosoro ; 4, Rio dos medos douro ; 5 and 6, Rio do medos	Kosi River
Serranias (mountain ridges)	5 and 6, Serramas	Sandhills N. of Kosi River
Ponta dos medões (point of downs)	5, Ponta de medons . . .	Cape Colatto, 250 feet.
Terra dos Fumos *n* .	3, Terra dos Fumos ; 5, T. chrimias ; 6, T. thrimias	
Rio da lagoa *o* .	Rio do lagoa ; 4, Rio da lagoa ; 5 and 6, Rio de lago	Umbelasi River, Delagoa Bay
Rio dos reis, Jan. 6	3, Ri do reis ; 5, G. de lom raios De Barros confounds the Rio dos Reis and the Rio do Cobre	Inkomati River
***Rio do Cobre** *p* and ***Terra da boa Gente**	3, Agoa de bona passa ; 5, Rio d'aguada ; 6, Rio dagarda	Zavora River
Barreiras . .	5 and 6, Bariras	
Cabo das correntes (Cape of Currents)	3, C. das correntes ; 4, Cabo das correntes ; 5 and 6, C. das coreateso	Cabo das Correntes
Cabo de S. Maria .	3, C. de Sta Maria	Ponta da Burra
Golfo das Manchas (g. of specks)	5 and 6, Gorffo (b.) das manchas .	Inyamban
G. de meros (g. of whitings)	5 and 6, Gorffo de meros . .	Cove at Burra falsa
Cabo do Pichel (tankard cape)	3, Cabo de picell ; 5 and 6, Cabo de pichel	Shivala Cliff
Cabo de S. Sebastian, Jan. 20	4, Cabo de Sam Sebastiam . .	Cape St. Sebastian
Ilha de S. Domingos, ? Aug. 4	3, Igoa decico texoda ; 5, Ilha de Sam Domingo ; 7, Insule S. Dominico	Bazaruto Islands
Ilha de S. Sebastian, Jan. 20	3, Sanustiam ; 5, Ilha de Sam Sebastiam ; 6, Insule de S. Sebastiam	,, ,,
Çofalla . . .	3, Zafalla, Sofalla ; 4, Cafalla ; 5 and 6, flag shown, but name omitted	Sofala
Rio de S. Vicente, Jan. 22	3, Rio de Sam Vincenso ; 5, Rio de San Vicenso	Pungwe River
***Rio dos bons** *q* **Signaes**	3, Rio de bon signale ; 4, Rio das bons sinaes ; 5, Rio de bono futaes ; 6, Rio de bonsuraes.	Kilimani River

In Portuguese.	Names on the Maps.	Modern Names.
***Padrão de S. Raphael,** Oct. 24	3, Padro de San Rafaell; 5, Porto de Sam Rafaell	
Barreiras . . .	5, Barreiras; 6, bareiras	
	3, "Questo avemo visto" (this we saw) *r*	
***Ilhas primeiras** *s* .	3, Insulas primeras, 4, Ilhas primeras; 5 and 6, Insulla primeras	Ilhas primeiras
Cabo das ilhas . .	5, Cabo dos ilhas; 6, C. insularum	Makalanga Cape
Ilhas de S. Maricha	5, Ilhas de Sta maricha; 6, Insule de S. Maricha	Angoshe Islands
Aguada do Lago .	3, Agea do Lago	Angoshe River
	5, Ilhetos	
	5 and 6, Curaes *t*	
***Moçambique** . .	3, Mõsenbichi; 4, Moçambique; 5 and 6, Moncambiqui	Mozambe
*Ilhéos de S. Jorge, April 23, p. 31	——	Ilhéo de S. Jorge
	3, Monquique (duplication of Moçambique)	
Rio de Fernão Veloso *u*	3, Rio de Fernanesso; 4, Rio de fernam veloso; 5 and 6, Rio do fernam Velloso	Mazazima Bay
Furna (cove) . .	5 and 6, Furna	
***Ilha do açoutado** *v*	3, P. asoutado; 5, Ilha de acutado; 7, Insule de amrado	Kiziwa Island
Ilha das palmas .	5, Ilha das palmas; 6, Insule de palinis	Ibo
Ilhas de S. Lazaro, Dec. 17	4, Ilhas de S. Lazaro . . .	Kerimba Islds.
Ilhas das cabaças (gourd islands)	3, Cabesa seca; 5, Ilhas das cabecas; 6, Insule das Cabeas	Islands S. of Cabo Delgado
Cabo delgado . .	3, Cavo de Sco	Cabo Delgado
Rio de S. Pantaleone July 28	5 and 6, Rio de Sam Pantaleone .	Lindi River
***Quiloa** . . .	3, Quilloa; 4, Quillua; 5, Quiola; 6, Quiloa	Kilwa
Ilhas desertas . .	3, Ilha de sechas; 5, Ilhas desertas; 6, Insule desertas	Islands thence to Mafia
——	3, Ilha de baxo	
——	3, Baxo	
Ponta redonda .	3, Punta redonda	Ras Kimbiji
***Zanzibar** . .	4, Zamzibar	
*Tamugata, pp. 33, 92		Mtamgata
***Baixos de S. Raphael** *w*	3, Baxi dop lochio (*i.e.*, farolhos, shoals); 4, 5, and 6, Baixos de Sam Rafaell	Mtangata Reefs
*Serras de S. Raphael	3, T . . . de Rafael; 5 and 6, Terra de baixos	Usambara Mountains
***Mombaça** *x* . .	3, Mombaça; 4, Mõbaça; 5, Monbacha; 6, Monbacha	Mombasa
——	5, Vutual; 6, butual	
*Benapa, p. 40 . .	——	Mtwapa
*Toça (Tocanugua) p. 40	——	Takaungu

In Portuguese.	Names on the Maps.	Modern Names.
*Nuguoquioniete (Quioniete), p. 40	——	Kioni
***Melinde**	3, Melindi; 4, 5 and 6, Melinde	Malindi
*Pate *y*	4, Pate; 5, Parte	Pata
Bar (Land) Lamu	4, Berrama; 5, Berlama	Lamu
***Magadoxo** *z*	4, Mogodoxo; 5, Magadoxo; 6, Magadozo	Mukhdisho
Obbia	5, Opim	Obbia, 6° 40′ N
——	5, Animalla, caralla, lacurcella, carapui, gargella (gargeia), cabo dangra	Along coast to Cape Guardafui
Socotora	5, Çacotoia	Sokotra
Aden	5, Adam	Aden
Mascate	5, Porto dama lemeniaco	Maskat
Soar	5, Siffar	Sohar
Ormuz	5, Collomoco; 6, Collomoro (Marco Polo's Cormuso)	Hormuz
——	5, Betras; 6, Bertas	Beyt Island, at entrance to Gulf of Cutch
——	5, Dabo	Diu
Cambaia	* Cuambey; 4, Combaya; 5, Cambaia	Cambay
Surat	5, Cuia; 6, Cura	Surat
Baroche	5, paruça; 5, paruca; 6, Parnea	Broach
Damão	5, Dema	Daman
Canara	5, Canarea	Kanara
	5, Ginia; 6, Binia. The Ras boria of the "Mohit"	
	5, Meria. The Ras Meria of the "Mohit"	
Ilhéos queimados (burnt islands)	5, Dobascha; 6, Dobastha. Dandabashi of the "Mohit"	Vengorla Rocks
Goa	5, A flag, name omitted	
Anjediva *aa*	5, Andegiba	Anjediva
Ilhas dos pombos	5, Niture; 6, Nicare	Netrani,
*Ilhas de S. Maria	——	St. Mary's Islands *bb*
Onor	——	Honowar
Mangalor	5, Mãgalor	Mangalore
Cananor *cc*	6, Cananor	Cannanore
*Capua, Capocate *dd*	*Capua (Capucate of Castanheda and Barros)	
*Pandarani *ee*	*5, Pandarani	Pantharini Kollam
***Calecut**	2, Calitcut; 3, Colochuti; 4, Caliqut; 5 and 6, Calliqut	Calicut
Panane	5, Panade; 6, Panane	Ponani
Cranganor	5, Cangalor. *Quorongoliz of the "Roteiro"	Kranganur
Cochijn	5, Cochin: 6, Cothim	Cochin
Coulãoo	5, Collium; 6, Collum. *Coleu of the "Roteiro"	Quilon
Cabo Camorij	4, Comaria; 5, Cano de curiam	Cape Comorin
Cael, *Cael	5, Cail. Qail of the "Mohit"	Kayal, see p. 98

In Portuguese.	Names on the Maps.	Modern Names.
Mutapili . . .	4, Mutapalay	
Masulipatão . .	5, Tessulpata	Masulipatam
Godavari . .	4, 5 and 7, Gudarim	Godavari River
Satigam . . .	4, 5 and 6, Çatiguam, the capital of Bangala. Shadigam of the "Mohit"	Satgaon, on Hugli
Chatigam . .	4, Çatigam	Chittagong
Arracam . .	4, Arecãgni; 5, Arcagna . .	Arakan
Pegú . . .	4, Çatimpegno; 5, Carinpaguo .	Pegu, near the Satam or Sittang
Sadoe . . .	4, Patoo; 5, Facto. Satowahi of the "Mohit"	Sandoway
Martabão . .	4 and 5, Martabane . . .	Martaban
Tavai . . .	4, Taoo; 5, Lioa; 6, Taoo . .	Tavoy
Tenaçarij . .	4 and 5, Danasaguim. *Tenacar of the "Roteiro"	Tenasserim
Cara . . .	4, Carza; 5 Carta	Kra
Tacoa . . .	4, Tacoaa; 5, Tacoa . . .	Takuwa or Takoa
Modobar . .	4, 5 and 6, Modobar . . .	Meduar on Lingga River
Malaca . . .	4, 5 and 6, Malaqua . . .	Malacca
Cingapura . .	4, Bar Singuapura; 5, Bar siniga-pura; 6, Barginigapor	Singapore
Os baixos de Padua	4 and 5, Os baixos de Padua . .	Munyal-par
Ilha malique . .	4, Malaqym; 5, Mallo. Molaki of the "Mohit"	Minicoy
Ceylão . . .	4, Cillam	Ceylon
Triquinamala . .	4, Tragonamalay; 5, Traganollaneos; 6, Tragana	Trincomali
Andemão . .	3, Bonae fortunae (Ptolemy); 4 and 5, Indana and Indrona	Andaman Islands
Nicovade . .	4, Nagolarim; 5, Nagolainu . .	Nicobar Islands
Çumatra . . .	4, Ataporbana; 5, Ataprobana; 6, Taprobann	Sumatra

a. Juan de la Cosa places "a praia s. plo" (pablo) outside the Cape.

b. On the anonymous map published by Dr. Hamy, this Point (punta spinosa) is placed on the *west* coast, and may possibly be Bok Point.

c. The name of Ponta de gran ("scarlet cloth cape") may have been given to the Needle Cape before the supposed fact that the needle in its vicinity pointed due north had been observed.

d. For notes on the identification of this bay, see p. 9, note 4.

e. Bay of lagoons seems a misnomer. Subsequently the bay was dedicated to S. Catherine.

f. "Queimada" means a forest-fire, but there are no "forests", at all events near the coast. The hills, however, are partially covered with bush, which may have been set on fire.

g. This second "golfo dos vaqueiros" may be a duplication.

h. Our present Lagoa Bay seems originally to have been called "Bay of the Rock". Subsequently it became known as Bahia dos lobos (Seal Bay) and Bahia de lagoa (Lagoon Bay), perhaps after the Rio da lagoa (Lagoon River), which figures very prominently on Dr. Hamy's and Cantino's Charts, and almost seems to represent the Rio de Infante in the case of the former.

The Kasuga River, which is closed at its mouth, and forms a lake-like expansion at the back of the dunes, seems to correspond more nearly with the conditions required. Several other rivers, to the east and west of it, present the same feature, and these may have given rise to the designation "Praia das alagôas", *i.e.*, Shore of Lagoons.

For identifications of localities within this bay, see p. 14, *note.*

i. Thus named after the evergreen oak (*Ilex crocea*), known in South Africa as Safraan hout.

j. Along this coast the pent-up water of several rivulets soaks through the coast-ridge, giving rise to springs. This may account for the "Fountain Rock".

k. Keiskamma Point looks like an island when seen from the sea, and this may account for the island of St. Christopher, of the first explorers, developing into a river dedicated to the same Saint when the country became better known.

l. "Praia corada" (Red shore), I am unable to identify, as there are no red cliffs along this part of the coast. Perhaps we ought to read "*cerrada*", with reference to the rocks which fringe the coast.

m. I can make nothing of "Golfo boscho". Bósco is the Italian for "wood, forest", and is the synonym of "bosque" in Portuguese. Woods are plentiful along this coast.

n. For its identification, see p. 17.

o. Delagoa Bay seems to have been known originally as "Golfo dos tres Reis magos" (Gulf of the Three Kings); see p. 18, *note.* The Ri do Ouro is the Limpopo.

p. See p. 19, *note:* The "barreiras" to the east of it may be a reef forming a "barrier" along the coast.

q. See p. 19, note 1, and p. 21.

r. These words prove that the compiler of Dr. Hamy's Chart was able to utilise materials brought home by Vasco da Gama's pilots, for it is just in this locality that he again turned to the land, and discovered his "first islands". See p. 21.

s. See p. 21, note 2.

t. "Coraes" means "corals". "Moçambique Flat" is a great coral bank.

u. This river was named after one of Vasco da Gama's companions. See p. 177.

v. See p. 32.

w. For the baixos de S. Raphael, etc., see pp. 33, 92.

x. For Mombaça and places to the north of it, see p. 40.

y. See p. 58. *z*. See p. 88. *aa*. See p. 80.

bb. See p. 200. *cc*. See p. 79. *dd*. See p. 48.

ee. See p. 48.

APPENDIX H.

THE COAT-OF-ARMS OF VASCO DA GAMA.

HONOURS AND REWARDS BESTOWED UPON VASCO DA GAMA, 1499-1524.[1]

KING MANUEL has not infrequently been charged with a niggardly disposition, but whatever his conduct may have been in other instances there can be no doubt that he dealt most liberally with the navigator who was the first to sail a ship from a European port to India. This liberality had been called forth by the sensation produced by the discovery of an ocean highway to India, and the expectation that great wealth would pour into Portugal as a consequence; it was kept alive by the persistent importunities of the discoverer.

Vasco da Gama certainly did not undervalue the services he had rendered to the King. He considered himself entitled to a high reward, and in the end secured it. His ambition, from the very first, seems to have been to take his place among the territorial nobles of his native land. His father, Estevão da Gama, had at one time been Alcaide-mór of Sines, he himself had been born at that picturesque old fishing town, and his desire to be territorially connected with it was therefore only natural. The King was quite willing that this should be, but Sines belonged

[1] Instead of a full translation of the two documents on this subject, which are printed as an appendix to the original edition of the *Roteiro*, we have given abstracts of all the available documents bearing upon it. Most of these will be found *in extenso* in Texeira de Aragão's *Vasco da Gama e a Vidigueira* (Boletim, Lisbon Geogr. Soc., 1886, pp. 541-702); Luciano Cordeiro's *De come e quando foi feito Conde Vasco da Gama* (Boletim, 1892, pp. 257-303); and Cordeiro's *O Premio da Descoberta*, Lisbon, 1897.

to the Order of S. Thiago, of which D. Jorge, Duke of Coimbra, a natural son of D. João II, was master; and although a papal dispensation had been received in 1501, which empowered the Order to exchange Sines for some other town, the Order refused to part with it (see Document 1). Meanwhile the King, on February 22, 1501, had granted Vasco da Gama not only an annual pension of 1,000 cruzados (£483), but also the territorial title of "Dom" (Documents 2 and 3).[1]

Still further favours were conferred upon Vasco da Gama on January 10, 1502, only one month previous to his second departure for India; and this, we are told, was done "freely", and without these favours having been solicited either by their recipient or by any of his friends (see Document 4). These favours included an annual hereditary pension of 300,000 reis (£362), the title of "Admiral of India", with all the valuable privileges conferred by it;[2] the right of sending annually to India 200 cruzados, to be laid out in merchandise, upon which no import duties were to be levied, excepting the 5 per cent. claimed by the Order of Christ,[3] and confirmation of the hereditary title of "Dom", which was also to be borne by his brother Ayres, and in its feminine form of "Dona" by his sister Theresa.

A few months after Vasco da Gama's return from his second voyage, the King, who was especially pleased with the "tribute" received from the Sultan of Kilwa, bestowed upon him a further hereditary pension of 400,000 reis (1,000 cruzados, or £483). This was done on February 4, 1504 (Document 5).

Meanwhile the negotiations for putting Gama in possession of Sines had made no progress, and the Admiral,

---

[1] The original document bestowing this title is not available, but the King makes use of it in his Order of Nov. 19th, 1501.

[2] Compare Document 18 at end of this Appendix.

[3] See also Documents 10 and 11.

impatient of the delay, took up his residence in that town, began to build himself a manor-house, and generally conducted himself as if the town were his own. The alcaide-mór, D. Luiz de Noronha, did not venture to interfere, but the Order of S. Thiago complained to the King; and the King, justly incensed at the masterful conduct of his vassal, peremptorily ordered his Admiral to quit Sines within thirty days, and not to return to it except by special permission of the Master of S. Thiago. This order was dated March 21, 1507 (see Document 7). We need scarcely say that it was obeyed.

But the Admiral still hankered after the territorial honours which had been promised him. He enjoyed already three royal pensions amounting to 2,750 cruzados (£1,328), and Leonardo Masser,[1] the Venetian Ambassador at Lisbon, estimated the whole of his income at that time at 4,000 ducats, or rather cruzados (£1,930). This was a very large sum indeed. There were at that time only six noblemen, two archbishops, and seven bishops in all Portugal whose income exceeded his.[2]

In November, 1508, the King authorised Luiz d'Arca to cede to Vasco da Gama the alcaideria-mór of Villafranca de Xira (see Document 8), but the negotiations appear to have led to no result. Ten years were allowed to pass, when the Admiral informed the King that, the promised title of "Count" not having been conferred upon him, he desired permission to emigrate with his family. The King,

---

[1] Peragallo, *Carta de El-Rei D. Manuel ao Rei Catholico*, Lisbon, 1892, p. 89. Leonardo Masser describes the Admiral as being ill-tempered and unreasonable, and as exhibiting but little gratitude in return for the favours conferred upon him by the King.

[2] Peragallo, *loc. cit.*, p. 92. The highest incomes were enjoyed by the Duke of Coimbra (16,000 cruz.), the Duke of Bragança (16,000 cruz.), the Bishop of Evora (12,000 cruz.), the Marquis of Villa Real and the Archbishop of Lisbon (10,000 cruz. each).

on August 17, 1518 (see Document 13), granted this permission, on condition that the Admiral should defer his departure until the end of the year. In the meantime he seriously looked about him for the territorial qualification which would enable him to confer upon his importunate Admiral the title of Count. D. Jayme, Duke of Bragança, a nephew of the King, who held Vasco da Gama in high respect, was willing to accommodate his uncle. By an agreement signed on November 4, 1519, he surrendered the towns of Vidigueira and Villa de Frades, in consideration of Vasco da Gama ceding to him an hereditary Royal pension of 400,000 reis (1,000 cruzados), and in addition, paying the sum of 4,000 cruzados in gold. This transaction having been completed at Evora, on November 7, the King, in Document 16, granted to Vasco da Gama, his heirs and successors, the towns of Vidigueira and Villa de Frades, together with all revenues and privileges hitherto enjoyed by the Duke of Bragança; and on December 29 he conferred upon his Admiral the title of "Conde de Vidigueira" (see Documents 14-17).

And thus, when Vasco da Gama, in April, 1524, departed for the last time for India, the great ambition of his life had been realised. He died at Cochin, on Christmas eve of the same year.

Abstracts of Official Documents.

1.—*Lisbon, December* 24, 1499.[1]

By Letters Patent, dated Lisbon, December 24, 1499, the King, in recogition of the merits of Vasco da Gama, and the great services rendered by him in the discovery of India, grants to him, his heirs and successors, the town of Sines, together with all the revenues, privileges, and tithes pertaining thereto, as well as civil and criminal jurisdiction. But inasmuch as this town

[1] Cordeiro, *Boletim*, 1892, p. 285.

belongs to the Order of São Thiago, the formal title-deeds are to be drawn up only after this Order shall have received satisfaction by the grant of another town belonging to the Crown, and dispensation of the Holy Father, sanctioning this exchange, shall have been received.

Satisfaction was, moreover, to be given to D. Luiz de Noronha, the alcaide-mór of the said city. But should D. Luiz refuse to surrender the said alcaideria, then, the dispensation of the Pope having been received, the King promises at once to put Vasco da Gama in possession of the said town, and likewise of the castle, as soon as terms shall have been arranged with D. Luiz de Noronha.

2.—*Lisbon, February* 22, 1501.[1]

D. Manuel orders the Casa da Mina to pay annually to Vasco da Gama the of sum 1,000 cruzados in gold [at that time equal to 390,000 reis], until he shall have been placed in possession of the manor of Sines.

3.—*Lisbon, November* 19, 1501.[2]

The King orders Gonçalo de Sequeira, chief treasurer of the Casa de Ceuta, to deliver to Dom Vasco da Gama 15 moios [43 imperial quarters] of wheat, of the value of 28,000 reis, in part-payment of 70,000 reis due to him this year, the balance of 41,200 reis to be levied upon the Casa da Mina.

The receipt given by Vasco da Gama for this wheat is still extant, and is one of the very few autographs of the Admiral in existence.

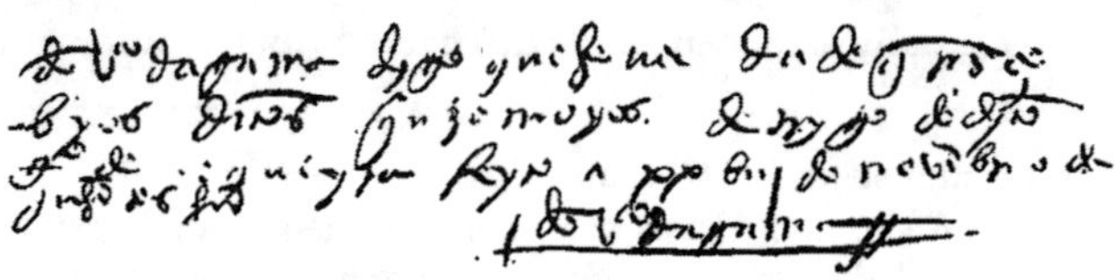

That is to say:

> dõ v^{co} da gama dygo que he verdade que rece
> by os dytos q'nze moyos de trygo do dyto
> g^{o} de sequeyra feito a xxbiij de novẽbro de
> q'nhẽtos hũ. dõ v^{co} da gama.

---

[1] Quoted by Texeira de Aragão, p. 572, from a document in the Torre do Tombo.

[2] Texeira de Aragão, p. 573.

Or, in English:—

Don Vasco da Gama acknowledges to have received said 15 moios of wheat from said g° de Sequeyra. Done on November 28, 1501.

Dom Vasco da Gama.

4.—*Lisbon, January* 10, 1502.[1]

D. Manuel after pointing out, in these letters-patent, that the explorations begun by the Infante D. Henry [the Navigator] in 1433,[2] in the hope of discovering a new highway to India, had been continued by King Alfonso and King John, at an expenditure of many lives and of much treasure, until, in 1482,[3] the Rio do Infante, at a distance of 1,885 leagues, had been reached, continues:

"Being animated by an ardent desire to continue the work initiated by the Infante and our predecessors, and being assured that Vasco da Gama, a gentleman of our household, was well qualified for rendering us this service, and would disregard the perils to his person and the risk of life which he ran in accomplishing the task set him, we sent him to India as captain-major of our fleet, and with him Paulo da Gama, his brother, and Nicolau Coelho, likewise a gentleman of our household. In this voyage he did most excellent service, for whilst only 1885 leagues of coast had been discovered during the many years which had elapsed since the commencement of this enterprise, and by the many captains sent out, he by himself, in this single voyage, discovered 1550 leagues, in addition to a great gold-mine and many wealthy towns and cities, having a great trade, and finally reached and discovered that India, which

[1] This document was first printed as an Appendix to the second edition of the *Roteiro*, and has since been published as an Appendix to Lord Stanley of Alderley's *Vasco da Gama*, and in *Alguns Documentos*, p. 127. Its provisions were confirmed in favour of D. Francisco da Gama by King John III, May 4th, 1526 (Cordeiro, *O Premio da Descoberta*, pp. 48-55.

[2] In 1434 (not 1433) Gil Eanes doubled Cape Bojador.

[3] In 1482 Diogo Cão discovered the Congo. We ought evidently to read 1488, for the Congo is only 1,240 leagues from Lisbon, whilst the 1,885 leagues actually carry us to the Rio do Infante. The name is thus spelt in this document as if the river had been named in honour of Prince Henry, and not after João Infante, the companion of Dias.

all those who have given descriptions of the world rank higher in wealth than any other country, which from all time had been coveted by the Emperors and Kings of the world, and for the sake of which such heavy expenses had been incurred in this kingdom, and so many captains and others forfeited their lives—a country, in fact, which all kings not only desired to possess but even to discover.

"This discovery, begun years ago, he accomplished at a greater sacrifice of life and of treasure, and at greater peril to his own person, than suffered by those who preceded him. Paulo da Gama, his brother, died in the course of the voyage, as also one-half of the people whom we sent out with this *armada*, they having passed through many perils, not only because of the length of this voyage, which exceeded two years, but also because of the desire to furnish trustworthy information on these territories and all connected with them.

"And bearing in mind the great services yielded to ourselves and our kingdoms by this voyage and discovery: the great advantages accruing thence, not only to our kingdoms but to all Christendom: the injury done to the infidels [*i.e.*, Mohammedans] who, up till now, have enjoyed the advantages offered by India: and more especially the hope that all the people of India will rally round Our Lord, seeing that they may easily be led to a knowledge of His holy faith, some of them already being instructed in it: desiring, moreover, to recompense him for his services, as befits a prince when dealing with those who have so greatly and so well served him, and to bestow upon him a grace and favour: with full knowledge, and out of our royal and absolute power, without his having solicited it, nor any other person on his behalf, we grant him, freely and irrevocably, from this day in perpetuity, an annuity of 300,000 reis, to be paid to him and his descendants."

For the payment of this annuity the King assigns the new tithe on fish imposed upon the towns of Sines and Villanova de Milfontes, supposed to yield 60,000 reis annually, which tithe has been surrendered by Martinho de Castelbranco, who held it from the Crown, and has been compensated elsewhere. Any surplus receipts out of this tithe were to be retained by Vasco da Gama, the King, on the other hand, not being obliged to make up any deficiencies. Secondly, the King surrenders 130,000 reis annually out of the excise levied upon Sines, any deficiency in that amount to be made up out of the excise of S. Thiago de Cacem. Thirdly, the King assigns to him 40,000 reis, to be paid out of the excise of S. Thiago. Lastly, the 70,000 reis still wanted to make up the 300,000 reis shall be paid out of the receipts of the timber octroi of the city of Lisbon.

In addition the King appoints him Admiral of India, conferring all honours, franchises and revenues which that rank carries with it, throughout the territories which shall be placed under the rule of the King.

Moreover, he is granted the privilege of sending annually, by the royal vessels, 200 cruzados to India, to be laid out in merchandise, upon the importation of which no duties whatever shall be levied except the 5 per cent. payable to the Order of Christ; this privilege to be transmitted to his descendants.

The King, moreover, confers upon him, his brother Ayres da Gama, and his sister, Tarayja (Theresa) da Gama, the hereditary title of Dom (Dona).

Finally, the King desires that the heirs of Vasco da Gama shall always bear the name of Gama, in memory of the said Vasco da Gama.

5.—*Lisbon, February* 4, 1504.[1]

The King, having pointed out that as Divine justice recompenses, in the other world, those who have firmly adhered to the Catholic faith and practised good works, so should the Kings and Princes of this world recompense those who have rendered them faithful service, directs attention to the signal services rendered by Vasco da Gama during his first voyage, when he discovered India. This discovery has resulted in a great accession of wealth. What the Romans, and Emperors and Kings have vainly attempted, has been accomplished by the said Admiral, and the advantages coveted by all nations have been secured to his kingdoms. These results have been attained at a great loss of life, for more than half the men in this first expedition have succumbed, and among them Paulo da Gama, the brother of the Admiral. On his return honours and other rewards were conferred on the Admiral.

---

[1] Published *in extenso* in the 2nd edition of the *Roteiro*, p. 175.

In the course of a second voyage[1] the services rendered by him have been equally brilliant. The King of Kilwa has been reduced to submission, and compelled to pay an annual tribute of 1,500 mitkals in gold,[2] the first instalment of which has been received. This king is very powerful, and the owner of the gold mines of Sofala, the richest in that part of the world. In all other respects Vasco da Gama has faithfully guarded the royal interests, both in making war upon the Moors of Mecca, and in peaceable negotiations with the kings of those countries. The fleet intrusted to him, owing to the wisdom and judgment exercised, has returned richly laden. On these grounds he is entitled to some recompense. Acting as becomes a King, and considering his merits, he, D. Manuel, therefore grants him, and his male descendants in the direct line, an annuity of 400,000 reis, to commence on the first of January of this year, 1504, and to be secured on the salt tax of the city of Lisbon.

6.—*Lisbon, February* 20, 1504.[3]

The King instructs Fernão Lourenço, factor of the Guinea and India trade, to pay henceforth the annuity of 1,000 cruzados to Vasco da Gama; each caravel coming from the city of S. Jorge da Mina is to contribute 32,050 reis, the payments out of twelve caravels thus making up a total of 390,000 reis.

7.—*Thomar, March* 21, 1507.[4]

In a letter dated Thomar, March 21, 1507, and signed by Antonio Carneiro, the King's chief secretary,[5] Vasco da Gama, the Admiral of India, is informed that within thirty days after date he must withdraw from the town of Sines, with his wife and the whole of his household, and that neither himself, nor his wife, nor his household can be permitted to return to that town,

---

[1] Departure from Lisbon, February 10, 1502; return, September 1, 1503.

[2] About £900. The King had this gold converted into a "custodia", which he presented to the church of Belem.

[3] Cordeiro, *Boletim*, 1892, p. 287.

[4] Texeira de Aragão, p. 675.

[5] Leonardo da Chá Masser calls him "discreet and experienced, although quite illiterate" (see Peragallo, *Carta de El-Rei D. Manuel* Lisbon, 1892, p. 89).

or its precincts, except by permission of the Master [of the Order of São Thiago and Aviz]. In case any of them should enter the town without such permission, they will render themselves liable to a fine of fifty cruzados, beyond which they will incur the punishment deserved by those who refuse obedience to the orders of their King and Lord. In a postcript the King orders, moreover, that the same penalty shall be incurred if Vasco da Gama continue the buildings he has commenced.

(This Royal Edict was presented on June 26, 1507, at the office of the Master of the Order at S. Thiago de Cacem, by one João da Gama,[1] and ordered to be placed in the Archives of the Order).

8.—*Tavira, November* 18, 1508.[2]

The King authorises Luiz d'Arca to surrender his Alcaideria-mór of Villafranca de Xira[3] to the Admiral of India (Vasco da Gama).

9.—*Lisbon, November* 19, 1511.[2]

The King orders the authorities ("judges") of the Order of S. Thiago to afford the receiver appointed by the Admiral every facility for collecting the revenues assigned him in the towns of S. Thiago de Cacem, Sines and Villanova de Milfontes.

10.—*Lisbon, June* 1, 1513.[4]

The King informs all whom it may concern that in consideration of the merits and very great services of Dom Vasco da Gama, it pleases him to order that no freights be charged upon merchandise forwarded to the Admiral from India, whether sent by royal or private ships, the expenses, in the latter case, being charged to the India House. This privilege is not to extend to certain spices reserved for the Crown.

---

[1] This Gama was the third son of the first Vasco, and consequently an uncle of the Admiral. He was Comptroller of the Revenues ("casa da fazenda") of the Order.

[2] Cordeiro, *Boletim*, 1892, p. 287.

[3] A town on the Tejo, 20 miles above Lisbon.

[4] Cordeiro, *Boletim* 1892, p. 288. This *Alvaró* was confirmed by King John, June 17, 1522 (Cordeiro, *O Premio da Descoberta*, p. 45).

11.—*Lisbon, August* 22, 1515.[1]

The King authorises the Admiral to send with each fleet sailing to India a person to attend to his business, this person to draw pay as a man-at-arms.

12.—*Lisbon, August* 29, 1515.[2]

D. Manuel, having quoted *in extenso* the conditions of a pension of 400,000 reis granted on February 4, 1504, orders that one-half this pension shall be paid in future out of the revenues of the town of Niza,[3] and the other out of the salt-tax, as before.

13.—*Lisbon, August* 17, 1518.[4]

The Admiral having reminded the King that the title of "Count" has been promised him, but has not yet been conferred, asks permission to leave the kingdom. The King, in a letter in which he addresses Vasco da Gama as "Almirante amiguo", replies: "We order you to remain in our kingdom up to the end of December of the present year, and we hope by that time you will have seen the error you are about to commit, and desire to serve us as is seeming, and not take the extreme course proposed. But if by that time you are still minded to go, we shall not hinder your departure, with your wife, your sons, and all your moveable property. Done at Lisbon by the Secretary [Antonio Carneiro], August 17, 1518. . . . The King."

14.—*Evora, October* 24, 1519.[5]

The King authorises Vasco da Gama to surrender his pension of 400,000 reis [see No. 5], to D. Jayme, Duke of Bragança, and the latter to give in exchange the towns of Vidigueira and Villa de Frades.

---

[1] Cordeiro, *O Premio da Descoberta*, p. 46.

[2] *Roteiro*, Appendice, p. 175.

[3] Niza, a town in the district of Portalegre, about 100 miles to the N.E. of Lisbon. When the 5th Count da Gama was raised to the dignity of a "Marquis" in 1648, he took his title from this town.

[4] Cordeiro, *Boletim*, 1892, p. 289.

[5] Cordeiro, *Boletim*, 1892, p. 292.

15.—*Villa Viçosa, November* 4, 1519.[1]

D. Jayme, Duke of Bragança and Guimaraes, authorises his "ouvidor" (bailiff), João Alves, to surrender the towns of Vidigueira and Villa de Frades, with all their revenues, etc., to D. Vasco da Gama, on condition of the latter ceding to him an hereditary pension of 400,000 reis, which he has from the King, and of paying, in addition, a sum of 4,000 cruzados in gold.

[This transaction was completed at Evora, where Vasco da Gama resided, on November 7, the 4,000 cruzados being paid in Portugueses of 10 cruzados each. As the eldest sons of the contracting parties, D. Theodesio of Bragança and D. Francisco da Gama, were still minors, it was agreed that the King should be asked to "overlook this deficiency of age", so that they, too, should be bound by this agreement.[2]]

16.—*Evora, December* 17, 1519.[3]

The King, having sanctioned the arrangement between the Duke of Bragança and Vasco da Gama, and having dwelt once more upon the good services rendered by the latter not only to the Crown, but also to the inhabitants of the kingdom, and to all Christendom, grants to him and his heirs, irrevocably and for all time, the towns of Vidigueira and Villa de Frades, together with all privileges, including civil and criminal jurisdiction and church patronage, which had been enjoyed by the Dukes of Bragança. [These privileges, it should be understood, exceeded those usually enjoyed by a mere Count.]

17.—*Evora, December* 29, 1519.[4]

D. Manoel, after a glowing eulogy of the services rendered by his Admiral of India, confers upon him the title of Count of Vidigueira, together with all prerogatives, rights, graces, privileges, liberties and franchises enjoyed by the Counts of the Kingdom by usage and ancient custom.

---

[1] Cordeiro, *Boletim*, 1892, pp. 278, 291.

[2] Cordeiro, pp. 274, 295.

[3] Cordeiro, *Boletim*, p. 295.

[4] Cordeiro, p. 289.

18.—*Lisbon, March* 30, 1522.[1]

D. João III confirms Vasco da Gama's claim, as Admiral, to the anchorage dues paid at Malacca, Goa and Ormuz, and authorises him to appoint receivers.

19.—*Evora, February* 5, 1524.[2]

The Admiral, being about to proceed to India for a third time, the King, D. João III, is pleased to order that in case of his death his son and heir shall forthwith assume the title of Count of Vidigueira, and enter upon the enjoyment of all privileges, etc., to which this rank entitles him.

---

[1] Cordeiro, *O Premio da Descoberta*, p. 46.
[2] *Cordeiro*, p. 302.

Church and Monastery of Our Lady of the Relics at Vidigueira.

(From a woodcut in Texeira de Aragão's Paper.)

INDEX AND GLOSSARY.

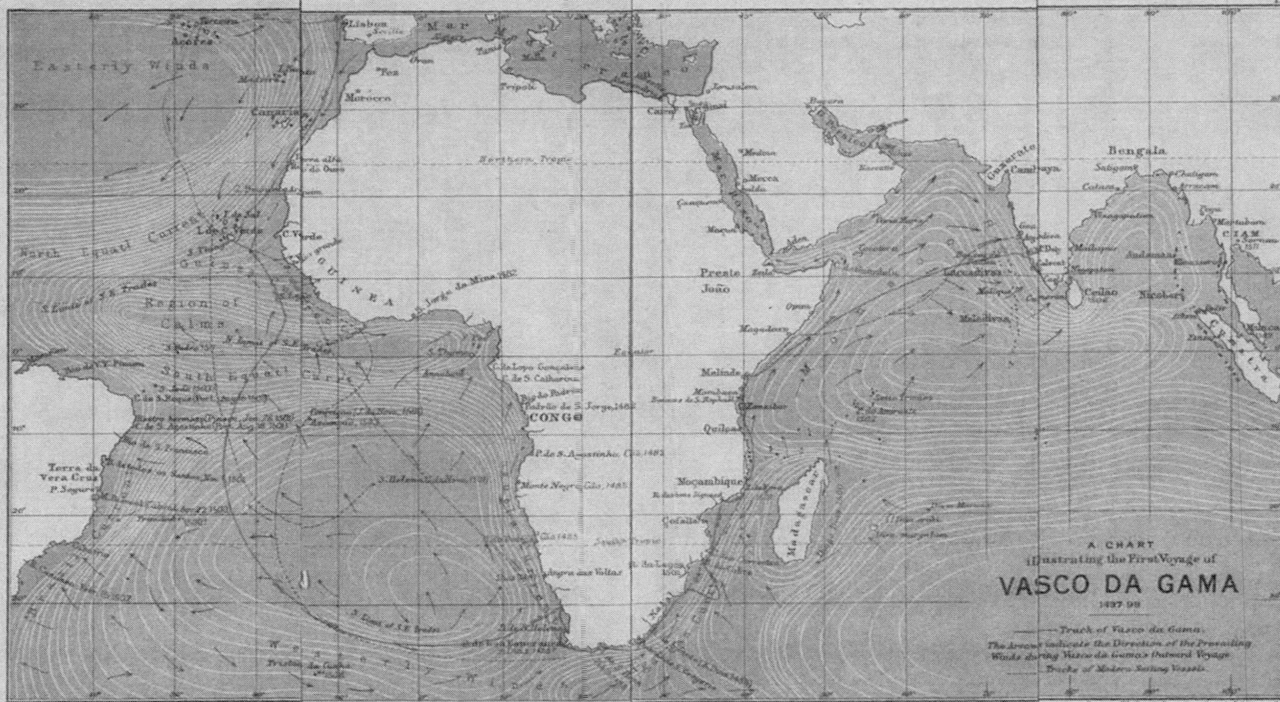
A CHART
Illustrating the First Voyage of
VASCO DA GAMA
1497-99
Track of Vasco da Gama.
The Arrows indicate the Direction of the Prevailing Winds during Vasco da Gama's Outward Voyage
Tracks of Modern Sailing Vessels.
Easterly Winds
North Equatl Current
Region of Calms
South Equatl Curr.
GUINEA
CONGO
Lisbon
Morocco
Tripoli
Jerusalem
Cairo
Mecca
Preste João
Melinde
Quiloa
Moçambique
Madagascar
Lacadives
Maldivas
Cambayn
Bengala
Ceilão
Nicobar
CIAM
Çamatra
Terra da Vera Cruz
P. Seguro
Equator
Northern Tropic
Southern Tropic
George Philip & Son, London & Liverpool.

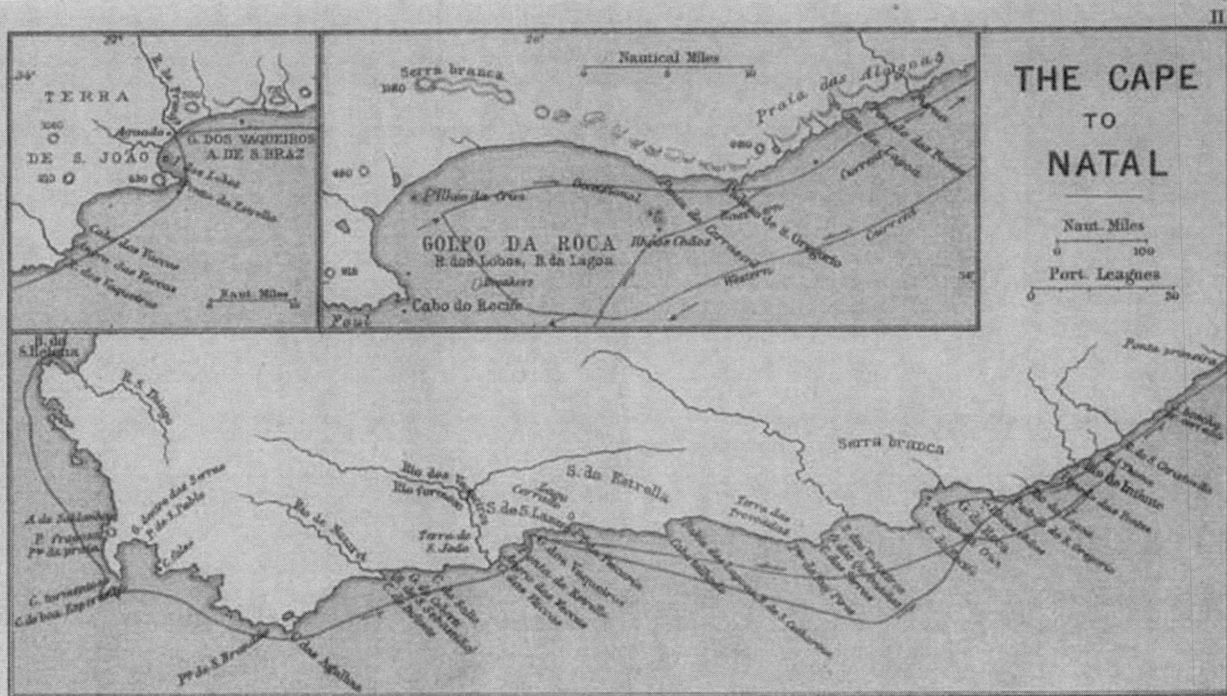
II
THE CAPE
TO
NATAL
Naut. Miles
Port. Leagues
Nautical Miles
Serra branca
TERRA
DE S. JOÃO
G. DOS VAQUEIROS
A. DE S. BRAZ
Aguada
Nant. Miles
Praia das Alagoas
GOLFO DA ROCA
B. dos Lobos, B. da Lagoa
Cabo do Recife
Breakers
Western
Serra branca
S. da Estrella
Rio de Nazaré
R. S. Thiago
Terra de S. João
das Agulhas
C. da boa Esperança
Ponta primeira
George Philip & Son

III.

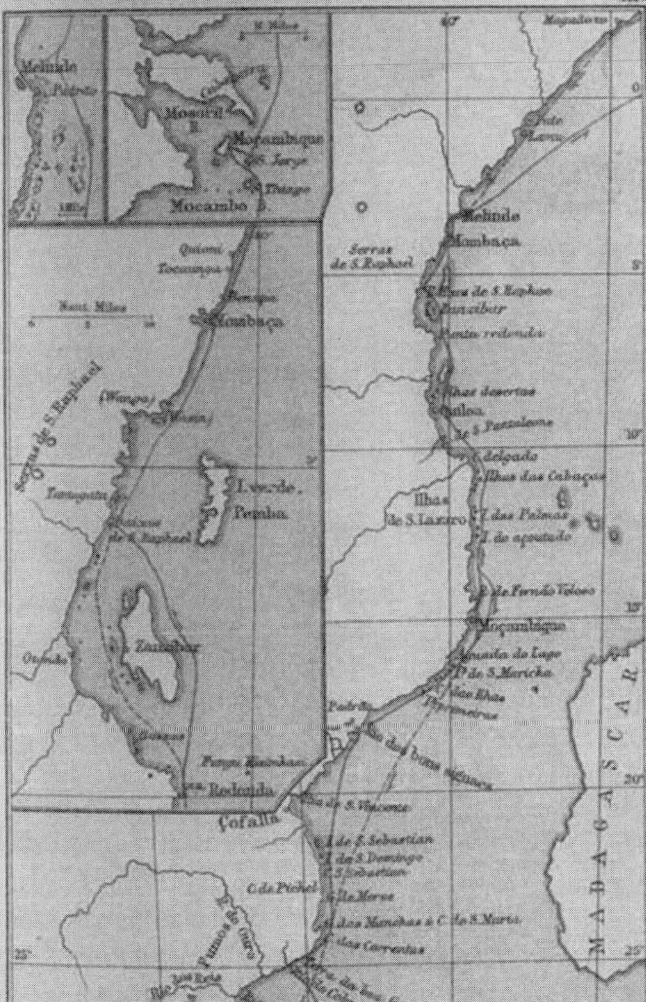
NATAL
TO
MAGADOXO
Nautical Miles
0
200
400
Magadoxo
Melinde
Mombaça
Serras de S. Raphael
Zanzibar
Ilhas desertas
Quiloa
Ilhas das Cabaças
Ilhas de S. Lazaro
I. das Palmas
Moçambique
MADAGASCAR
Çofalla
Ilha de S. Vicente
I. de S. Sebastian
C. da Pichel
Terra das Fumos
Terra das meas
Terra do Natal
Porto do Natal
Mocambo
Mosuril
Pemba
Redonda

IV

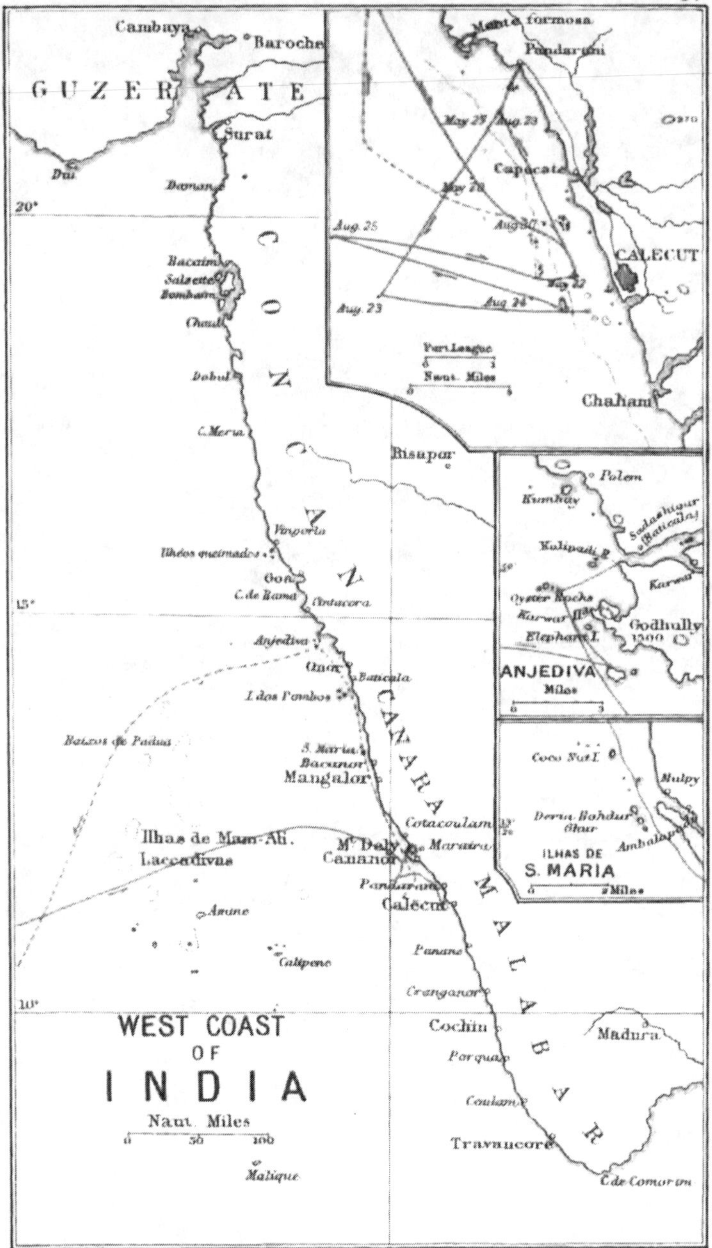

E.G.R.

Geo. Philip & Son

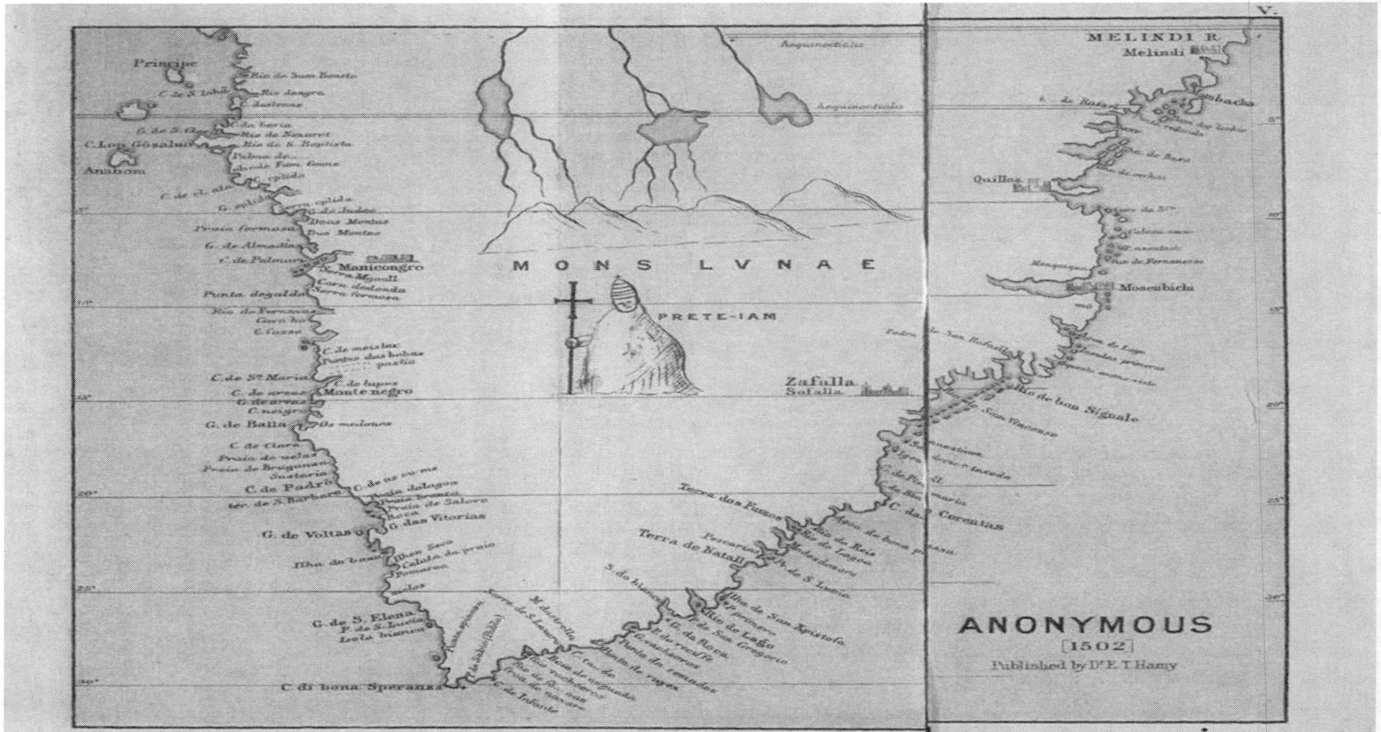
V.
MELINDI R.
Melindi
Quilloa
Mocenbiche
Rio de bon Signale
C. das Corentas
MONS LVNAE
PRETE-IAM
Zafalla
Sofalla
Principe
Anabom
C. Lop Gôsalues
Manicongro
Montenegro
Punta degalda
G. de Balla
C. de Padrô
G. de Voltas
G. de S. Elena
C. di bona Speranza
Terra dos Fumos
Terra de Natall
ANONYMOUS
[1502]
Published by Dr E. T. Hamy

VI.

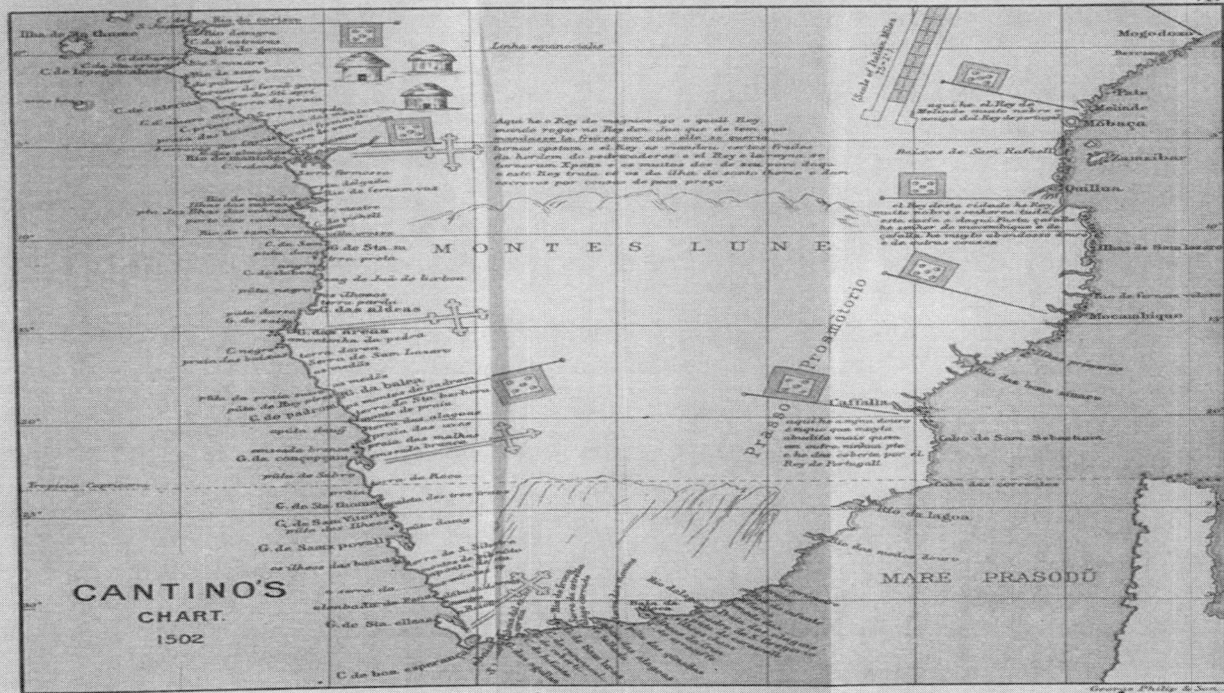
CANTINO'S
CHART.
1502
MONTES LUNE
MARE PRASODŪ
Prasso Prosmotorio
Linha equinocialis
Tropicus Capricorni
Mogodoxo
Pate
Melinde
Môbaça
Zanzibar
Quilloa
Mocambique
Caffalla
Cabo de Sam Sebastian
Cabo das correntes
Ilha de Sã thomé
C. de lopo gonçalues
C. das aldeas
G. de Sam Vicente
G. de Sam povall
G. de Sta. ellena
C. de bon esperança
George Philip & Son.

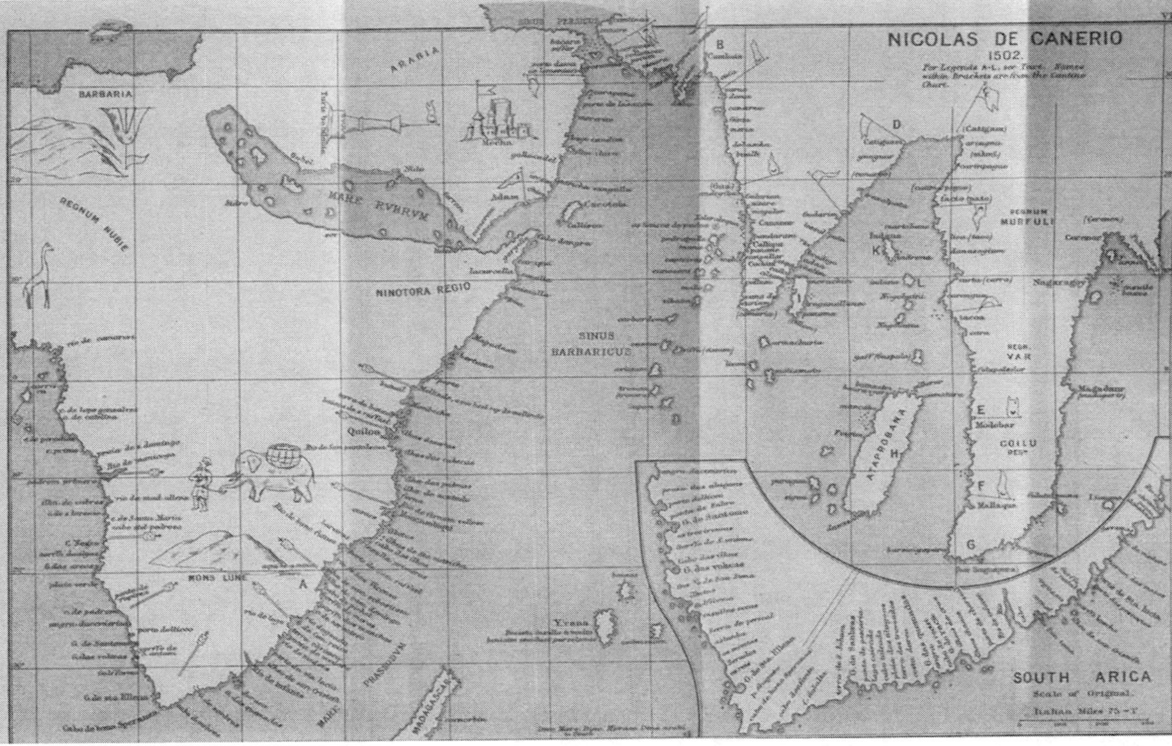
VII.
NICOLAS DE CANERIO
1502.
For Legends A–L, see Text. Names within Brackets are from the Cantino Chart.
BARBARIA
ARABIA
REGNUM NUBIE
MARE RUBRUM
NINOTORA REGIO
SINUS BARBARICUS
REGNUM MURFULI
REGN. VAR
COILU
ATAPROBANA
MONS LUNE
PRASSODUM
MADAGASCAR
Quiloa
Yrana
SOUTH ARICA
Scale of Original.
Italian Miles 75 = 1°